CAPITALISM OR WORKER CONTROL?

CAPITALISM OR WORKER CONTROL?

An Ethical and Economic Appraisal

David Schweickart

PRAEGER

PRAEGER SPECIAL STUDIES • PRAEGER SCIENTIFIC

Library of Congress Cataloging in Publication Data

Schweickart, David.
      Capitalism or worker control?

      Bibliography: p.
      Includes index.
      1. Comparative economics. 2. Capitalism.
3. Socialism. I. Title.
HB90.S38   338.6   80-15655
ISBN 0-03-056724-6

Published in 1980 by Praeger Publishers
CBS Educational and Professional Publishing
A Division of CBS, Inc.
521 Fifth Avenue, New York, New York 10017 U.S.A.

© 1980 by Praeger Publishers

23456789 145   98765432

Printed in the United States of America

57,037

CAPITALISM OR WORKER CONTROL?

An Ethical and Economic Appraisal

David Schweickart

PRAEGER

PRAEGER SPECIAL STUDIES • PRAEGER SCIENTIFIC

Library of Congress Cataloging in Publication Data

Schweickart, David.
    Capitalism or worker control?

    Bibliography: p.
    Includes index.
    1. Comparative economics. 2. Capitalism.
3. Socialism. I. Title.
HB90.S38   338.6   80-15655
ISBN 0-03-056724-6

Published in 1980 by Praeger Publishers
CBS Educational and Professional Publishing
A Division of CBS, Inc.
521 Fifth Avenue, New York, New York 10017 U.S.A.

© 1980 by Praeger Publishers

23456789 145   98765432

Printed in the United States of America

57,037

CAPITALISM OR WORKER CONTROL?

An Ethical and Economic Appraisal

David Schweickart

PRAEGER

PRAEGER SPECIAL STUDIES • PRAEGER SCIENTIFIC

Library of Congress Cataloging in Publication Data

Schweickart, David.
       Capitalism or worker control?

       Bibliography: p.
       Includes index.
       1. Comparative economics.   2.   Capitalism.
3. Socialism.   I.   Title.
HB90.S38   338.6   80-15655
ISBN   0-03-056724-6

Published in 1980 by Praeger Publishers
CBS Educational and Professional Publishing
A Division of CBS, Inc.
521 Fifth Avenue, New York, New York 10017 U.S.A.

23456789 145   98765432

Printed in the United States of America

57,037

CAPITALISM OR WORKER CONTROL?

An Ethical and Economic Appraisal

David Schweickart

PRAEGER

PRAEGER SPECIAL STUDIES • PRAEGER SCIENTIFIC

Library of Congress Cataloging in Publication Data

Schweickart, David.
       Capitalism or worker control?

       Bibliography: p.
       Includes index.
       1. Comparative economics. 2. Capitalism.
3. Socialism.   I. Title.
HB90.S38   338.6   80-15655
ISBN 0-03-056724-6

Published in 1980 by Praeger Publishers
CBS Educational and Professional Publishing
A Division of CBS, Inc.
521 Fifth Avenue, New York, New York 10017 U.S.A.

© 1980 by Praeger Publishers

23456789 145   98765432

Printed in the United States of America

57,037

For
Charles and Dorothy,
Tomas and Caridad

PREFACE

The young Alfred Marshall, a mathematician and a philosopher, but not yet the economist he was destined to become, was troubled by a social conscience.

> From Metaphysics I went to Ethics, and thought that the justification of the existing condition of society was not easy. A friend, who had read a great deal of what are called the Moral Sciences, constantly said: 'Aha! if you understood Political Economy you would not say that.'[1]

A similar experience has prompted this book. A decade ago I was a mathematician, with a fresh Ph.D., a teaching position, and a growing suspicion that my profession was irrelevant to important things. I escaped to philosophy. From the philosophy of mathematics I went through existentialism and ethics, arriving at social philosophy— and Marshall's uneasiness concerning the justification of the existing conditions of society. Then I encountered professors of economics. We argued heatedly. On the whole I found them complacent, conde- scending, infuriating—but also unnerving. They knew things I didn't know. The reverse was also true, but no matter—economics was a "science" and philosophy merely a "humanity." The contest was not among equals.

I resolved to get to the truth of the matter. I knew what I wanted to ask: could the existing order be justified? I even knew the answer: no! What was lacking was the proof.

I had an answer, but I soon discovered that the question was wrong.

I discovered that I needed to prove a different proposition from the one I had set out to validate. I learned that nobody who thinks seriously about such matters (an important qualification) is content with the existing order. Contemporary life is too squalid, and the trends too foreboding. All serious thinkers agree that change is nec- essary. The disagreement concerns the kind of change. Of course everyone wants a society less squalid, less violent, less dehuman- ized—but how can that be brought about? What structural changes are in order, what changes in the basic institutions of society?

More specifically still, what changes, if any, should be made in our economic institutions? This is the question I eventually settled upon. It was (and is) such a basic question, so controversial—and I had accounts to settle with those economics professors. Is it true, as they maintained, that capitalism itself is sound, that reform in accordance with this or that ideal is needed, but the roots are firm? Or is a radical restructuring, i.e., a restructuring of the roots themselves, in order?

Notice, the issue is fundamentally normative. To speak of conscious change is to speak of transforming what is into what ought to be. Such discourse is within the province of philosophy. At the same time, since ought implies can, the changes suggested by a normative ideal must be viable, a consideration that lands us in economics. So our inquiry must of necessity be interdisciplinary. A philosophical perspective must be maintained, so as to keep the ethical parameters in view, but we must not hesitate to range into the thicket of contemporary economics. This intrusion will be resented by some economists. It is commonplace to decry the fragmentation of the disciplines, but the territorial imperative remains strong in academia. (I know my own reaction when an outsider dares "philosophize.") The reaction is especially fierce when the intruder lacks respect, and I must confess, I'm in that category. I have learned much from economists, but frankly, I'm not much taken by the current state of the art. (I'm none too happy about contemporary philosophy either.) In particular, I think the reigning neoclassical paradigm—which has come under heavy attack in recent years from an important minority within the discipline—is a construction of (pardon the pun) marginal utility. It is of little use in comprehending a modern economy and even less in making sense of the normative issues with which we shall be concerned.

I will offer some evidence in support of this claim as we proceed, but the main purpose of this work is not to refute neoclassicism. My concern is with the justification of capitalism. My response to the inadequacies of neoclassicism is to keep my analysis free from the problematic assumptions that underlie that paradigm. I have also attempted to keep my economic (and philosophical) argumentation as free as possible of technical jargon—in order to make it accessible to a broader range of readers, but even more, because I am convinced that the issues crucial to the basic question are more fruitfully approached without the technical apparatus. Sometimes this involves belaboring an argument that can be readily expressed in technical terms, but on the whole I think the technical terminology obscures more than it reveals.

If an answer to the question "What kind of change?" requires an appropriate interaction of philosophy and economics, it requires more than that. When an economist is asked to justify the system he has devoted his life to investigating, the standard reply is that justification goes beyond the discipline. When pressed, he usually responds in platitudes, for it is not something he has thought much about. (One professor to whom I put the question remarked that the question of justifying capitalism had never occurred to him.) I find this appalling—but it is also appalling that the tradition that most often raises the justification question and pushes most ardently for an answer, namely the socialist tradition, has a platitude problem of its own. "What is your alternative?" the antisocialist thunders, and the rejoinder, for all its passion, is rarely reassuring. Some blurt out hopeless utopias or edifying abstractions; the more sophisticated adroitly dodge. I'm inclined to call it a scandal, the inability of socialists to say concretely what they (we) want.

This work will not dodge. My overall strategy can now be stated. I raise the normative question, what socioeconomic structure best accords with current capabilities and a certain set of widely shared values? I offer a concrete socialist model, and compare it, not so much with current reality (it's unfair to compare "a model with a muddle"[2]), but with the ideal models that inspire conservative and liberal reform proposals. (No one, I've already noted, defends the muddle, so there's no point in battling straw.) My conclusion: justification of capitalism is indeed difficult. Marshall, the philosopher, was right. In fact, justification is impossible. Marshall, the economist, is wrong. Political economy can no longer save the day.

Some acknowledgements are in order. There are two intellectual influences at work in what follows more pronounced than a count of footnotes would indicate. Some years ago I crawled between the covers of Capital, and the world has never looked the same since. Still, this is not exactly a Marxist work. The structure is wrong: the moral dimension is too prominent, and there is a lack of dialectical exposition. Is that good or bad? Perhaps it's a strength and a weakness. A decision had to be made. I think the structure I've adopted accomplishes my purpose.

Shortly after my encounter with Marx, while I was struggling to come to terms with contemporary economics, I discovered the writings of Joan Robinson. A light pierced the fog. Her lucidity, elan, and remarkable intelligence greatly influenced my perception of the economic problem. My debt to her is enormous.

I should also thank the many persons—colleagues, students, referees and friends—who have responded to earlier versions of this project. Special thanks extend to James Scanlan for countless long and fruitful discussions; to Patsy Schweickart for criticisms, insights and incalculable support; to Bernard Rosen, Michael Piecuch, and Mary Anne Connelly. My thanks also to Loyola University of Chicago for a summer research grant to accomplish a final revision of this work.

NOTES

1. Quoted by Joan Robinson, <u>Collected Works</u>, vol. 4 (New York: Humanities Press, 1973), p. 242.
2. The phrase is from Alec Nove, <u>The Soviet Economic System</u> (London: George Allen and Unwin, 1977), p. 9. Nove employs this apt expression for the equally illicit comparison of contemporary socialist societies with "perfectly-competitive" capitalism.

CONTENTS

		Page
PREFACE		vi

Chapter

1	CONTRIBUTION, SACRIFICE, ENTITLEMENT	1

Capitalist Contribution as the Marginal
   Product of Capital   5
Capitalist Contribution as Entrepreneurial
   Activity   14
Interest as a Reward for Waiting   20
Capitalism Is Just Because It Is Just   27
Notes   32

2	ALTERNATIVE MODELS	36

Capitalism: the Laissez-Faire Ideal   43
Worker-Control Socialism   48
Notes   55

3	CAPITALISM OR SOCIALISM: EFFICIENCY	58

The Efficiency Strengths of Laissez-Faire   64
How Efficient Is Worker Control?   70
A Comparison: Unemployment   74
More Trouble: the Sales Effort   81
The Distribution of Income   90
Notes   98

4	CAPITALISM OR SOCIALISM: GROWTH	103

What Kind of Growth?   106
How Fast to Grow?   114
Instability   124
Notes   133

Chapter   Page

5   CAPITALISM OR SOCIALISM: LIBERTY AND AUTONOMY   137

     Liberty   142
     Democracy   150
     Capitalism and Work   158
     Notes   171

6   MODERN LIBERALISM   176

     John Rawls and the Keynesian-Liberal Ideal   182
     The Post-Keynesian Vision of John Kenneth
        Galbraith   192
     Notes   206

7   CONCLUDING REMARKS: HOW, WHICH, AND
     THEN WHAT?   210

     The Transition to Socialism   210
     Varieties of Socialism   213
     The Transition to Communism   219
     Notes   220

BIBLIOGRAPHY   222

INDEX   243

ABOUT THE AUTHOR   251

CAPITALISM OR WORKER CONTROL?

1

CONTRIBUTION, SACRIFICE, ENTITLEMENT

    Capitalism—how can it be justified? How has it been justified? As capitalism struggled to establish itself, the concept of self-interest moved center-stage. Proponents of the rising order were divided as to the intrinsic morality of this "fundamental human passion," but all agreed that it could be immensely useful to society when suitably harnessed to a free market.[1]

    These arguments, or in any event capitalism, carried the day. But soon trouble was brewing in another pot. Using the economic categories of Adam Smith and David Ricardo—specifically the labor theory of value—Karl Marx argued that capitalism is inherently exploitative. Even without monopolies (Smith's bane) or landowners (Ricardo's), free, competitive capitalism exploited the working class—for workers are the source of all value, and yet they are excluded from the economic surplus. Capital, said Marx, is not a thing, possessing mysterious productive power, but a social relationship among human beings, a power relationship. The free market masks the fact that capitalist society is formally homologous to a slave or feudal society with a ruling class controlling the means of production and an exploited class doing the work.

    This chapter is reprinted with permission from The Philosophical Forum, Vol. X, nos. 2-3-4, Philosophical Forum: Boston, 1980.

The Marxian challenge, particularly when backed by an increasingly militant working class, placed capitalism on the defensive. But the Marxian argument had a crucial vulnerability—the labor theory of value. Soon, throughout Europe and America, a new economics came into being. Jevons in England, Walrus in Switzerland, Menger, Bohm-Bewerk and Wieser in Austria, J. B. Clark in the United States proclaimed the obsolescence of the labor theory of value. "Classical" analysis gave way to "marginalist" analysis. Neoclassical economics was born.

The intellectual victory of neoclassical economics did not prevent the Russian Revolution. Socialism descended from the ideal to the real. For a decade or so certain neoclassical economists tried to prove the economic impossibility of socialism,* but soon the profession took a different turn. The fact-value distinction was invoked, and economists declared themselves independent (qua economists) of ethical concerns.[2] Henceforth, justification of capitalism would be left to philosophers, politicians and economists-qua-citizens.

Economic arguments, of course, remained important—that capitalism is more efficient than socialism or more conducive to economic growth. Human nature arguments asserting the natural link between innate egoism and free enterprise were still invoked, though with decreasing frequency as socialism spread throughout the world. But another argument became increasingly prominent. With the Russian Revolution deteriorating into Stalinism, the causal connection between capitalism and freedom was vigorously reaffirmed. Or rather since fascist and other authoritarian capitalist regimes undercut that link, the connection was affirmed between socialism and totalitarianism. "Socialism," Friedrich von Hayek proclaimed, "is the road to serfdom."[3]

How do things stand today? Not altogether settled. Among economists the neoclassical paradigm still reigns. It was disrupted for awhile by Keynes, but the pieces were reassembled with much Keynesian economics incorporated. (Joan Robinson calls the contemporary version "neo-neoclassicism" or more bluntly "bastard Keynesianism.")[4] This revised neoclassicism, however, has come

---

*Ludwig von Mises was the most prominent figure. We will consider his argument in Chapter 2.

under fierce and increasing attack from a variety of quarters. Marxists and neo-Marxists, neo-Ricardians, institutionalists, neo-Keynesians all reject the neoclassical model, all are suspicious of marginalist categories.* Many (though not all) are critical of capitalism itself.

On the other hand, political philosophy has come to the aid of capitalism. Two of the most widely discussed works of recent years provide ethical defenses. John Rawls argues that certain forms of (liberal) capitalism can be just (he allows that certain forms of socialism can also be).[5] Robert Nozick, critical of Rawls's liberal, redistributive ethic and of all concessions to socialism, defends a more conservative, "libertarian" version of capitalism.[6] Not all political philosophers are so sympathetic to capitalism. As in all academic disciplines today, there is a radical contingent, but, as in all, it remains a minority.†

The purpose of this work is not to count hands but to examine arguments. If we look at the arguments that have been advanced in defense of capitalism, we see that they fall into two categories, comparative and noncomparative. By "comparative" I mean an "in light of the viable alternatives, capitalism is best" argument. The utilitarian argument belongs in this category, as do many liberty-based arguments. Noncomparative arguments, by contrast, claim capitalism to be just because it satisfies a particular standard of justice. Those who advance such arguments often also claim that socialism fails the standard, but such a claim is not essential. The form of the noncomparative argument is "X satisfies standard J," whereas the form of a comparative argument is "X better satisfies standard J than Y" or "X is more likely to satisfy J than Y."

---

*Many of these tendencies, particularly the less radical, are coalescing into a rival "post-Keynesian" paradigm. This will be discussed more fully in Chapters 2 and 6.

†I am speaking here of Anglo-American academia. This work is addressed to an Anglo-American audience and is situated in that milieu. Political philosophy on the Continent, to say nothing of the rest of the world, is a different game.

It is my view that the comparative arguments for capitalism are by far the more important. Thus they will occupy the greater part of this work. However, certain noncomparative arguments are also significant, both historically and because they are still frequently invoked, though more often obliquely than directly. They deserve careful attention, not so much because they are difficult to refute (they aren't), but because the conceptual frameworks within which they are articulated are often sources of serious misconceptions, misconceptions that haunt the more sophisticated comparative analyses.

In this chapter we will analyze several noncomparative arguments. All are "entitlement" arguments. To the Marxian charge that profit is derived from unpaid labor, all reply that the charge is false, that the capitalist is entitled to that profit. On what grounds? "Productive contribution," say many. "Sacrifice," say a few. "Liberty," says Nozick. We will examine these responses.

But first a word about the key term. What is this "capitalism" about which our discussion will pivot? I shall understand capitalism to be a socioeconomic system characterized by three sets of institutions. First, the means of production are for the most part privately owned—by individuals directly or through the mediation of corporations. Secondly, the bulk of the economic activity is directed toward the production of goods and services for sale on a free market. Prices are determined largely without governmental interference by producer-consumer interaction. Third, labor-power is a commodity. That is, a large percentage of the workforce sell their capacity to labor to those who can provide them with tools, raw materials, and a place to work.

To be capitalist, a society must feature all three sets of institutions: private property,* a market, and wage-labor. Many societies have existed, and do exist, which exhibit one or two of these characteristics, but not all three. For example, a feudal society consisting of self-sufficient estates worked by serfs has private property, but neither a market nor wage-labor. A society of small farmers and artisans—Colonial New England, say—is not capitalist, for despite private property and a market, there is little wage-labor. On the other

---

*I shall adopt the Marxian terminology, which distinguishes between private property—factories, farmland, productive machinery—and personal property—consumer goods purchased for their own sake, not for the sake of making money.

hand, all noncommunist industrial nations today are capitalist. The presence of an elaborate welfare apparatus, a number of nationalized industries, and/or a ruling party self-labelled socialist does not render a society noncapitalist. So long as the bulk of the enterprises are privately owned, worked by hired labor, and produce goods for sale on the market, a society is capitalist.

With this characterization in mind, let us now consider how such societies might be justified.

CAPITALIST CONTRIBUTION AS THE
MARGINAL PRODUCT OF CAPITAL

John Bates Clark was an early exponent of the claim that capitalist distribution accords with the ethical standard of productive contribution, that capitalism is just because it returns to each individual the value he produces. "The indictment that hangs over society," he writes, "is that of 'exploited labor'." But the charge, he avows, is false, for it can be shown that "the natural effect of competition is . . . to give to each producer the amount of wealth that he specifically brings into existence."[7] Friedrich von Hayek agrees. He sees the fundamental issue to be "whether it is desirable that people should enjoy advantages in proportion to the benefits which their fellows derive from their activity or whether the distribution of advantages should be based on other men's views of their merit." The first alternative, he insists, is that of a free (capitalist) society.[8] Nozick takes exception to Hayek, citing "inheritance, gifts for arbitrary reasons and charity" as countervailing considerations, but he concurs that "distribution according to benefit is a major patterned strand in a free capitalist society."[9]

But is it? That is what we will investigate in this and the next section of this chapter. Specifically, we wish to inquire whether property income—income derived from the ownership of means of production—can be legitimized by the canon that "justice consists in the treatment of people according to their actual productive contribution to their group."[10]

According to Milton Friedman and virtually all other neoclassical economists, the essential principle of capitalist distribution is "to each according to what he and the instruments he owns produces."[11] Since it is characteristic of capitalism that those who own means of production are often distinct from those who operate them, this claim presupposes that one can quantitatively distinguish the contribution of the instrument from that of the operator. Marx provided one answer. The value of the instrument is simply passed on to the final product, while new value is created by living labor. If a $100 machine produces 1000 items during its normal lifetime, it contributes ten cents to the value of each item. And since the machine itself is the product of labor, even that ten cents is ultimately traceable to labor. This answer is unacceptable to the neoclassical tradition, which much prefers Clark's alternative.

The modern, textbook version of Clark's solution begins with a concept, adds a couple of definitions, and then adroitly invokes a mathematical theorem (a simple theorem, but perhaps the most ideologically significant in history). The basic concept is that of a <u>production function</u>, a technical function that specifies for a given technology the maximum productive output for each and every combination of relevant technical inputs. Suppose, for example, that corn is the joint product of labor and land, each unit of everything being homogeneous in quality.* The production function can be represented as $z = P(x, y)$, where z is the maximum number of bushels of corn that can be produced by x laborers working y acres of land using the prevailing technology. Now the question is, what are the distinct contributions of labor and land?

The key to the answer is the notion of <u>marginal product.</u> The marginal product of a particular technical input is defined to be the extra output resulting from the addition of <u>one extra unit</u> of that input while holding all other inputs constant. For example, the marginal product of labor, given ten laborers and five acres of land, is the difference between what eleven and ten laborers would produce on those five acres, i.e., $P(11, 5) - P(10, 5)$. The marginal product of land in the same case is $P(10, 6) - P(10, 5)$. Now, when the quantities involved are large, the marginal product of a technical input is closely approximated by the partial derivative of the production function with

---

*For the sake of simplicity we will carry through our analysis in terms of a two-variable function instead of the more traditional three-variable function (land, labor, and capital). We will ignore the "Cambridge Controversy" surrounding the neoclassical treatment of capital as a factor of production on par with land and labor, and simply identify capital with land. The Cambridge (England) critique of the neoclassical argument is independent of the one given here. (For details of the Cambridge critique, see G. C. Harcourt, <u>Some Cambridge Controversies in the Theory of Capital</u> [Cambridge: At the University Press, 1972] and his update, "The Cambridge Controversies: Old Ways and New Horizons or—Dead-End?" <u>Oxford Economic Papers</u> 28 [March 1976]: 25-65).

respect to that input. It is a standard result of elementary calculus that $P(x+1, y) - P(x, y)$ is approximately $P_x(x, y)$ (the partial derivative of P with respect to x), and $P(x, y+1) - P(x, y)$ is approximately $P_y(x, y)$ (the partial derivative of P with respect to y), when x and y are both large. ($P_x(x, y)$ and $P_y(x, y)$ are both functions of x and y derived from $P(x, y)$ by standard mathematical procedures.)

So far nothing has been proved. We have merely defined some terms. But now consider a curious mathematical result first demonstrated by the great eighteenth-century mathematician Leonard Euler. If $P(x, y)$ is a "well-behaved" function,* then $P(x, y) = (P_x(x, y))x + (P_y(x, y))y$. That is, the output of x laborers working y acres of land is equal to the sum of two quantities, the first being the marginal product of labor multiplied by the number of laborers, the second being the marginal product of land multiplied by the number of acres. That is what Euler's Theorem says, when given an economic interpretation. Thus if we define the contribution of each laborer to be the marginal product of labor (i.e., $P_x(x, y)$), and the contribution of each acre to be the marginal product of land (i.e., $P_y(x, y)$), then the total contribution of labor, $(P_x(x, y))x$, plus the total contribution of land, $(P_y(x, y))y$ is precisely equal to the total output, $P(x, y)$. We thus have a "natural" division of the total output into the contribution of labor and the contribution of land, computed from purely technical information. No reference has been made to private property, wage-labor, or the market.

Equipped with a systems-neutral definition of contribution, the neoclassical economist can now ask whether or not capitalism distributes its total output accordingly. The answer is a reassuring "not always." Adam Smith's distrust of monopoly is vindicated: monopolies distort distribution. However, in a state of "perfect competition," where uniform goods and services command uniform prices, and where no monopolistic collusions exist, the distribution resulting

-----

*It is sufficient that $P(x, y)$ be smooth and homogeneous of order one. This latter condition, in mathematical terms that $P(ax, ay) = aP(x, y)$ for all a, translates into the economic condition that there be constant returns to scale. Increasing all the production factors by 'a' percent results in an 'a' percent increase in the total output. The former condition requires that a smooth variation in input factors produce a smooth variation in output.

from each individual striving to maximize her own well-being will be precisely that proposed by Euler's Theorem.* In a society of x equally skilled laborers and y acres of uniformly fertile land, the wage rate (per worker) will be $P_x(x, y)$ and the ground rent (per acre) will be $P_y(x, y)$. With sufficient assumptions, this can be rigorously demonstrated.[12]

These results are nontrivial—but what exactly has been proved? Has it been established that perfectly competitive capitalism distributes in accordance with the canon of contribution? Is it true that each person receives in proportion to what he produces? Clark himself has no doubts:

> If each productive factor is paid according to the amount of its product, then each man gets what he himself produces. If he works, he gets what he creates by working; if he also provides capital, he gets what his capital produces, and if further, he renders services by coordinating labor and capital, he gets the product that can be traced separately to that function. Only in one of these three ways can a man produce anything. If he receives all that he brings into existence through any of these three functions, he receives all that he creates at all.[13]

For Clark this conclusion has enormous ethical and political import:

> The welfare of the laboring class depends on whether they get much or little; but their attitude toward other classes—and therefore the stability of society—depends chiefly on the question whether the amount they get, be it large or small, is what they produce. If they create a small amount of wealth and get the whole of it, they may not seek to revolutionize society; but if it were to appear that they produce an ample amount and get only a part of it, many of them would become revolutionists and all would have the right to do so.[14]

---

*As a small step toward eliminating the identification of "human" with "male," I will alternate the masculine and feminine pronouns when the generic is intended. (It is interesting how different certain expressions sound when the feminine generic is used.)

In fact Clark has not shown that perfectly competitive capitalism distributes according to contribution, not if "contribution" is to be taken to mean what it means in the ethical canon. Clark has shown that there exists a partition of the total product which can be defined independently of the market mechanism, and that "well-behaved" capitalism distributes according to this partition. That is no mean accomplishment—but it remains to be argued that this notion of contribution is ethically appropriate.

To decide this question, let us consider Clark's analysis more closely. Why is a laborer said to receive exactly what he has produced? The neoclassical answer: if he ceases to work, the total product will decline by precisely the value of his wage. ($P_x(x,y)$ also approximates $P(x,y) - P(x-1,y)$.) Does it follow that if two workers quit together, the total output will decline by the sum of their wages? Not at all—the total product will decline by more than that. The wage each worker receives under conditions of perfect competition is the marginal product of the last laborer. Moreover, the neoclassical argument presumes a declining marginal productivity; that is, the marginal product of the tenth laborer is less than that of the ninth, that of the ninth less than that of the eighth, etc. This decline is not due to declining skills, since all laborers are presumed equally skilled, but to a diminishing-returns assumption. It is presumed that $x + 1$ laborers on a fixed piece of land (for x sufficiently large) will produce more than x laborers, but that the average production of each will be slightly less.

Perhaps a picture will add some clarity. (See Figure 1.)

If we plot the marginal product of the first laborer, the second, etc., the function declines (at least eventually). The area beneath the step-curve represents the total product; the shaded area is the "contribution" of labor. Because of declining marginal productivity, the total contribution of labor is less than the total product; the difference is precisely the contribution of the land—and hence of the landowner.

What exactly is this latter contribution? Mathematically, it is the marginal product of the y'th acre of land multiplied by the number of acres. But what is its physical significance? It is not the quantity of corn that would have been produced on the land without any laborers, nor is it the amount that could have been produced had the landlords themselves tilled the soil. Nor does it bear any relation to that portion of the social product that must be saved for seed, or plowed back in to replenish fertility. In physical terms, the marginal product of the land is simply the amount by which production would decline if one acre were taken out of cultivation. It does not reflect any productive activity whatsoever on the part of the landowner. It does not, therefore, reflect her productive contribution.

FIGURE 1

<u>Marginalist</u>
Calculation of Labor Contribution

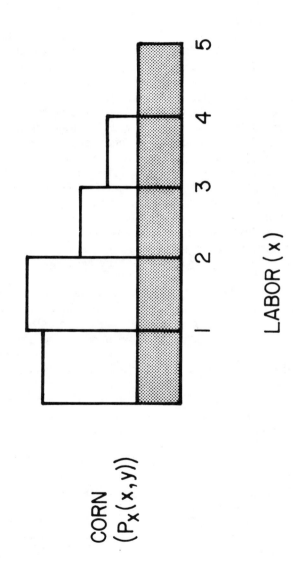

Let me repeat this argument in a slightly different form, to highlight how the neoclassical terminology obscures the important issue. Clark claims that a person can create wealth in one of three ways: by working, by providing capital, and by coordinating labor and capital. If we regard "coordinating labor and capital" as a managerial activity directly related to the productive process,* then both working and coordinating labor and capital are productive activities in a perfectly straightforward sense: should laborers and managers cease their mental and physical work, the production of wealth would likewise cease. The economy would grind to a halt.

"Providing capital," however, is something quite different. In Clark's perfectly competitive world, technology is fixed and risks are nonexistent. "Providing capital" means nothing more than "allowing it to be used." But the act of granting permission can scarcely be considered a productive activity. If laborers ceased to labor, production would cease in any society. But if owners ceased to grant permission, production would cease only if their ownership claims were enforced. If they ceased to grant permission because their authority over the means of production was no longer recognized, then production need not be affected at all. (If the government nationalized the means of production and charged workers a use-tax, we wouldn't say, would we, that the government was being rewarded for productive activity?) But is providing capital is not a productive activity (at least not within a static neoclassical model), then income derived from this function can hardly be justified as being proportional to one's productive contribution to the group.

(The peculiarity of this notion of "providing capital" becomes even more apparent if we try to apply it to other forms of society to ascertain who creates what, and whether distribution in that society accords with "contribution." A feudal lord, for example, who owns far more land than his peasants can till, creates, in "providing land," no wealth at all, because the marginal product of his last acre is zero. But as his peasant population increases, and with it the marginal product of that last acre, his "contribution" also increases. The tribute once unjustly extracted becomes fair, even philanthropic, as the share of the wealth "he creates" expands.)

---

*This is not quite how Clark conceives of it. For Clark this coordination is meant to characterize the entrepreneur, the person who borrows money from the capitalist to hire laborers. But since this activity is tied definitionally to capitalism, I will reinterpret "coordinating labor and capital" to make it less problematic as a universal wealth-creating activity.

In fairness to contemporary neoclassical economists, it should be noted that not many who think seriously about such things accept the ethical dimension of Clark's analysis. H. G. Johnson is typical in this respect:

> The positive theory that factors derive their incomes
> from their contributions to the productive process should
> be sharply distinguished from the question of whether the
> owners of the factors are ethically entitled to own them,
> or whether their returns would be different if ownership
> or preferences were different.[15]

Johnson thus distances himself from Clark's ethical claim—but not, it should be noted, for reasons I have put forth. To the contrary, Johnson's remark implicitly rejects my argument; it is not so neutral as it might appear. It well represents, in fact, the tendency of neo-classical analysis to mislead ethical thought.

Johnson states, contrary to my assertion, that providing capital is a productive activity. He doesn't say that exactly; what he does say is incoherent: "Factors derive their incomes from their contributions." But "factors," e.g., land, labor and capital, do not receive income; owners of factors do. So the statement must mean "owners of factors derive their incomes from their contributions to the productive process." The ethical issue, therefore, must be (for Johnson) whether owners are entitled to their productive contributions. In other words, the neoclassical formulation, "factors derive income from productive contributions," shifts one's ethical attention to the ethical canon itself—should one receive according to contribution?—and away from an examination of the nature of that peculiar "productive activity" of providing capital.

This is an unfortunate shift, one with consequences for political philosophy. It is not surprising that when philosophers consider the contribution canon, they find it wanting as an exclusive and exhaustive general principle of distributive justice. But often it strikes them as partly right (which, arguably, it is). But if it is partly right, what part of the distribution of income does it justify? Well, Nicholas Rescher's approach is not unusual. Distributive justice, he argues, should be based on a "canon of claims" that embraces a variety of canons—one of which (but only one) is the canon of productive contribution. And it is precisely this canon that justifies property income. How? Rescher's "argument" is a vague reference to "claim bases . . . traditionally considered in economics."[16]

At the risk of repetition, let me summarize my discontent with neoclassicism. The problem in justifying capitalist distribution is not the suitability or nonsuitability of the ethical canon of contribution, a problem economists are content to leave to philosophers and politicians. The problem with a contribution defense is the notion that providing capital is a productive activity. It is this issue that the neoclassical model obscures. For in conceiving of output as the joint product of "productive factors," and in defining the respective "contributions" of each in such a way as to yield a "natural" division of the product into these respective contributions, what could seem more natural than to call the contribution of the factor the contribution of the owner—particularly when it is precisely that "contribution" which the free market returns to each owner? And if each owner "contributes" to the final product, what could seem more natural than to regard her as engaging in productive activity? What could be more natural?— and yet a sleight-of-hand (no doubt unwittingly) has been performed. For when the "contribution" of the factor is shifted to the owner, a technically-defined, ethically-neutral concept suddenly takes on an ethical dimension, since "contribution" when applied to human beings normally has such a dimension. If I contribute to a collective project, don't I deserve a share of the reward? If I engage in a productive activity, don't I deserve a share of the product? If words were being used in their ordinary sense, we would say yes to both these questions. Only when we look closely at the neoclassical definition of contribution do we realize that when this sense is employed, the answer to the first question is "Not necessarily" and to the second—when asked by a landowner or capitalist—"But you haven't!"

The marginal product definition of contribution is thus not only inadequate to the task of showing that capitalist distribution accords with the ethical canon of contribution; it is highly misleading in any ethical context. It provides a criterion for judging the assertion, "'X' percent of the product was the contribution of labor; 'Y' percent, of capital, and so on," but it does so at the cost of severing the "contribution" of a factor owner from anything but a legal relation to the factor itself. In a technologically-fixed, perfectly-competitive world capitalists qua capitalists take no risks, do not innovate, do not sacrifice, do not engage in anything that could be called a productive activity. The abstraction from individual activity that allows one to define the contribution of a factor in a precise mathematical manner also removes from consideration any reason one might give for claiming that the "contribution" of the factor is, in any ethically relevant sense, the contribution of the owner. If one is to defend capitalism, one must either redefine "capitalist contribution" or abandon the contribution canon as its justification. However mathematically elegant marginal product theory may be, it fails as the basis for an ethical argument.

CAPITALIST CONTRIBUTION AS ENTREPRENEURIAL ACTIVITY

The marginalist definition of contribution fails to agree with ordinary ethical usage because it abstracts completely from all characteristic activities of property owners. An alternative definition is suggested by Joseph Schumpeter's well-known critique of the neoclassical, static-equilibrium model we have just considered:

> The essential point to grasp is that in dealing with capitalism we are dealing with an evolutionary process. It may seem strange that anyone can fail to see so obvious a fact which moreover was long ago emphasized by Karl Marx. Yet that fragmentary analysis which yields the bulk of our propositions about the functioning of modern capitalism persistently neglects it. . . .
> The fundamental impulse that sets and keeps the capitalist engine in motion comes from new consumer goods, the new markets, the new forms of industrial organization that capitalist enterprise creates.[17]

If it is true as Schumpeter and Marx propose, that the fundamental feature of capitalism is its dynamism, then it would seem more appropriate in determining the respective contribution of laborers and capitalists to compare society at different points in time than to assume a given production function (with a fixed technology) at a given point in time. Insofar as a particular increase in output over time can be attributed to the activities of a capitalist, perhaps we can define his contribution to be that increase. A simple model illustrates this definition. Suppose a capitalist-landowner employs ten people to grow corn. Working in the usual fashion these workers could produce, let us say, 1500 bushels of corn. But suppose our capitalist-landowner reorganizes production, innovates, with the result that his workers can now produce 2000 bushels. The extra 500 bushels, by our new definition, is the capitalist's contribution.

This definition appears promising, but a difficulty surfaces at once. It will not serve an appeal to the canon of contribution, because the capitalist will receive more than 500 bushels at the end of the year. Unless he were paying his workers the full 1500 bushels before—an unlikely gesture for a self-interested capitalist—he will receive 500 bushels plus the "reward" he usually receives. Thus he receives more than his contribution justifies.

Perhaps we can avoid this difficulty by considering a newly arrived capitalist. When we look at a representative capitalist, it appears that a portion of his income derives solely from his ownership of means of production. But appearances, it might be argued, are misleading, for what appears to be a reward for ownership is in fact a reward for <u>prior</u> activity. To consider this case, let us modify our model. Suppose that land is plentiful and free, and that a worker, working in the usual fashion, produces 150 bushels of corn a year. Suppose an entrepreneur appears. Eating little and thinking a lot, he has accumulated 1500 bushels of corn <u>and</u> a new idea: an innovative concept for a new kind of plow. He hires ten workers with his "capital" and sets them to work, first building the plow and then using it. If the result is a 2000 bushel harvest, then we can surely call 500 <u>his</u> contribution.

This concept of contribution seems both unambiguous and straightforwardly ethical. The contribution of the capitalist is linked to a specific productive activity, namely, innovation. But a complication arises if we continue our analysis into the second year. The process just described can now repeat itself with one important difference: no <u>new</u> innovation is necessary for a two thousand bushel harvest. The blueprint for the plow, the reorganization scheme, in short, the technology, is now in existence. Suppose the laborers work the second year as they did in the first, and another two thousand bushel harvest is recorded. <u>Who</u>, we must ask, contributed this two thousand bushels? In a sense the capitalist has contributed five hundred, since the increase, measured from the original basepoint, is five hundred and is due to his innovation. But if we take the basepoint to be the preceding year, then there has been no increase, a conclusion consistent with our assumption that the capitalist introduced no <u>new</u> innovation. Which sense of capitalist contribution do we intend when we define it to be the increase in production which can be attributed to his activities?

The second sense surely cannot be intended, for it depends on a completely arbitrary specification of a time interval. To measure the increase from the preceding year might seem natural in the case of corn, which has an annual growing season, but it seems hardly so natural in the case of steel production or shoe-making. We might just as well specify two years or ten, or six months or six weeks. There is no "natural" time interval beyond which the contribution ceases to be that of the capitalist and becomes that of his workers. (The lifetime of the innovator might seem tempting, particularly to advocates of confiscatory inheritance taxes, but that won't do. It would violate our language to define the quantitative contribution of an innovation in terms of the longevity of the innovator. If Edison had lived ten years longer in an advanced state of senility, we cannot say, can we, that his contribution would have been greater?)

On the other hand, if we do not specify a limit, we have a definition of contribution which entails that certain contributions are perpetual while others are only transitory. The capitalist and his laborers both expend mental and physical energy during the first year, and each makes a "contribution." However, the contribution of the capitalist continues into the next year and into the next. If he innovates anew, he will be entitled (by the canon of contribution) to the increase brought on by his new innovation as well, but his original contribution never ceases. The contribution of a laborer, by contrast, ends with his labor.

The reader has perhaps become uneasy with the direction this argument has taken. My model is vastly oversimplified as a version of capitalist reality; there is no competition, no risk, no obsolescence of technology. Do we really need the concept of "perpetual contribution" to justify capitalism? Have not our simplifications led us astray? We can approach these questions by looking at the problem from another perspective, from the opposite end, so to speak. To justify capitalism in terms of the contribution canon, one needs first of all a definition of contribution, then a demonstration of its ethical significance, and finally an argument that capitalism does in fact reward according to that definition. We have defined contribution as increase effected over time, and then, using a simplified model, we have uncovered "perpetual contribution," a rather disturbing concept. Let us look up from our simple model and consider capitalist reality in all its complexity. (Any example will do; pick your favorite.) To see whether we need the concept "perpetual contribution," we need to see whether there are "perpetual rewards" under capitalism.

As a matter of fact there are. In all capitalist societies there are institutions that reward an individual irrespective of her present activity. An accumulation of money, however acquired, may be invested as an individual sees fit. She may put it in a savings account, or buy government or corporate bonds, and collect interest indefinitely. He may purchase stocks and receive annual dividends. Such income is quite independent of any original innovation (if there was any) to which the original accumulation is traceable. Of course the reward is not eternal as a matter of logical necessity; we live after all in a contingent world. But the reward is not tied either legally or in practice to the continued performance of any productive activity. As John Kenneth Galbraith observes:

> No grant of feudal privilege has ever equalled, for effortless return, that of the grandparent who bought and endowed his descendants with a thousand shares of General Motors or General Electric. The beneficiaries of this foresight have become and remain rich by no exercise or intelligence beyond the decision to do nothing, embracing as it did the decision not to sell. [18]

It should be conceded that our model is not irrelevant to reality. Capitalism does reward some individuals perpetually. Thus, if it is to be justified by the canon of contribution, one must defend the claim that some contributions are indeed perpetual. Perhaps this can be done. Certain innovations, even when superceded, have served as the basis for new technologies. (Didn't Einstein stand on Newton's shoulders?) Surely there is nothing objectionable ethically about rewarding lasting contributions lastingly.

Perhaps not—but this line of argument will not justify capitalism. To see why, let us return to our entrepreneur and his innovative plow. What exactly was the nature of his "contribution" that qualified it as perpetual? The seemingly obvious answer that he created a new kind of productive instrument and reorganized production in a more efficient manner will not do, for he need not have done these things himself to receive a perpetual reward. He could have hired an engineer to design his plow and a management consultant to reorganize his enterprise. Such people are regularly employed for wages under capitalism. Nor will it do to say that the idea to construct the plow was his and hence justifies his reward, for the idea itself could have originated with his research and development division. Ideas and their execution frequently originate in such places. A perpetual reward may follow from an idea, but it does not necessarily go to its originator.

It is tempting to say that the capitalist supplies the money; she provides the capital. This is certainly her distinctive "service" qua capitalist. But we are back to the problem encountered in the neoclassical argument. And our conclusion is the same. Providing capital is no more a productive activity in a dynamic setting than in a static one. Let us dwell on this point, for it is as significant to our culture as it is counterintuitive. Objections scream to be heard. Isn't capital vital to growth? Isn't supplying it a productive endeavor nonpareil? Do not all countries, especially underdeveloped ones, strain mightily to acquire capital? Do they not offer investment incentives and tax credits to attract it? Such policies are not irrational, are they?

In fact such policies may well be irrational. Such is the contention of many (usually radical) development economists.[19] We need not join the development controversy, but we do need to look carefully at "providing capital." Its analysis is as important to the ethical issue we are concerned with as it is to that controversy. At the heart of the matter is the concept of capital itself. What is "capital"? Marx says it is a social relation, but few contemporary economists think in such terms. Capital, for most, is one of two things—or rather both at once: physical things (equipment and material) and money for investment.[20] Now of course capital, as existing material means of production, is crucial to production. Without means of production, nothing can be produced. But "providing" this sort of capital—an existing material thing—is simply "allowing it to be used, " the non-productive activity analyzed in the last section.

Capital as investment funds would seem to be another matter. Investment funds generate growth, do they not? Isn't that an axiom of economic theory? Let us think for a moment. Consider a person with a chest full of cash, eager to invest. How he acquired it need not concern us. We want to understand how his disposal of it will increase production. To produce something there must be brought together equipment, raw materials and laborers. Let our investor loan his money to an entrepreneur who purchases these necessaries. The laborers are set to work with the machinery on the raw materials, and soon goods are produced. It is all quite simple.

But notice, this case is also a matter of granting permission. The workers, raw material, and machinery already exist. The workers might have begun production themselves (perhaps at the instigation of an enterprising comrade)—except that property rights intervened. "Providing capital" is simply a means by which certain property rights are transferred from one set of owners to another, the latter then granting permission that things be used.

But what if the machinery were not already in existence? Suppose our entrepreneur used her borrowed capital to place an order. Wouldn't that bring a machine into being? Yes—but she (or the workers) could have placed that order without borrowing money. In either case human beings exist who could produce the desired machine. Would they do so? With borrowed money the entrepreneur can pay them in advance, or on delivery. But if the machinist to whom our entrepreneur advances a sum can buy food with it, then that food already exists. So the farmer, say, could advance that food. And the things the farmer would buy already exist, so they could be advanced. The farmers, machinists, and laborers (including entrepreneurial laborers) are all necessary for production and for growth—but not people to "provide capital. " (We are not concerned here with questions of motivation and incentive. How best to motivate people to interact in socially desirable ways is a matter for comparative analysis; that will come later. Here I am simply arguing that a class of people who "provide capital" are not necessary for production.

Two arguments are sometimes better than one. Let us look at the matter from another angle. Suppose, instead of relying on our friend with the chest full of money, the government simply rolled its presses to produce the same quantity of crisp bills, and gave them to our entrepreneur. Exactly the same production would result. But would we want to call the printing of money a productive activity? That might be very dangerous usage, tempting officials to believe that rolling the presses longer and longer would miraculously generate wealth. It is equally dangerous—at least to clear thinking about the ethical issues—to speak of providing capital as a productive activity.

To bolster our arguments with an appeal to authority, we could do worse than look to Keynes:

> It is much preferable to speak of capital as having a yield over the course of its life in excess of its original cost, than as being productive. For the only reason why an asset offers a prospect of yielding during its life services having an aggregate value greater than its initial supply price is because it is scarce. . . . If capital becomes less scarce, the excess yield will diminish, without its having become less productive—at least not in the physical sense.
>
> I sympathize, therefore, with the pre-classical doctrine that everything is produced by labour, aided by what used to be called art and is now called technique, by natural resources . . . and by the results of past labour, embodied in assets, which also command a price according to their scarcity or abundance. It is preferable to regard labour, including, of course, the personal services of the entrepreneur and his assistants, as the sole factor of production, operating in a given environment of technique, natural resources, capital equipment and effective demand.[21]

Let us be clear about the above arguments. I have not (yet) argued that the government ought to take control of investments, much less that they should be financed by printing money. I have made no claims as to the relative efficiency or innovativeness of alternative structures. These are crucial issues, but they belong to a comparative analysis of capitalism and socialism. Questions concerning efficiency, innovativeness or risk are totally irrelevant to our present concern, namely, whether capitalism can be ethically justified on the grounds that individuals receive in proportion to their productive contribution to society. Such a justification requires that we identify a productive activity engaged in exclusively by capitalists that merits not merely a reward but a perpetual reward. This we have not been able to do. Innovative activity seemed the best candidate, but this "entrepreneurial" definition has not survived analysis. The only distinctive activity of a capitalist is providing capital, and that, I have argued, is not productive at all.*

---

*Nor is "saving" a productive activity. This is discussed shortly.

The neoclassical definition of contribution considered in the first section fails for lack of ethical content; the entrepreneurial definition of this section fails not for that reason but because the class of entrepreneurs is not at all coextensive with the class of capitalists. Such a coexistence might once have been (roughly) the case, but it is not so today. Nor is there anything in the structure of capitalism to keep the classes from diverging. Indeed, the capitalist entrepreneur as Schumpeter himself observes, declines in functional importance as capitalism develops:

> To act with confidence beyond the range of familiar beacons and to overcome that resistance to change requires aptitudes that are present in only a small fraction of the population, and that define the entrepreneurial type as well as the entrepreneurial function. . . .
> This social function is already losing importance and is bound to lose it at an accelerating rate in the future even if the economic process itself of which entrepreneurship was the prime mover went on unabated. For, on the one hand, it is much easier now than it has been in the past to do things that lie outside the familiar routine—innovation itself is being reduced to routine. Technological progress is increasingly becoming the business of trained specialists who turn out what is required of them and make it work in predictable ways. . . .
> On the other hand, personality and will power must count for less in environments which have become accustomed to change—best instanced by an incessant stream of new consumers' and producers' goods—and which instead of resisting accepts it as a matter of course. The resistance which comes from interests threatened by innovations in the productive process is not likely to die out as long as the capitalist order persists. . . . But every other kind of resistance—the resistance in particular of consumers and producers to a kind of thing because it is new—has well-nigh vanished already. [22]

INTEREST AS A REWARD FOR WAITING

The basic problem in trying to justify capitalism by an appeal to contribution is the impossibility of identifying an activity (or set of activities) engaged in by all and only capitalists which can be called (preserving the ethical connotations of the word) "contribution." It is true that some capitalists innovate, reorganize, manage, but it is also true that many do not. This fact (if not its ethical implications) is readily acknowledged by most economists; it is reflected, for example, in their distinction between interest and profit. Interest (in the neoclassical camp) is the return to capital, the reward for owning a productive asset. Profit is the residual accruing to the entrepreneur after wage, rental, and interest bills have been paid; it is his reward for risk and innovative achievement. Samuelson's definition exemplifies this distinction:

> The market rate of interest is that percentage of return per year which has to be paid on any safe loan of money, which has to be yielded on any safe bond or other security, and which has to be earned on the value of any capital asset (such as a machine, a hotel building, a patent right) in any competitive market where there are no risks or where all the risk factors have already been taken care of by special premium payments to protect against any risks.[23]

The basic problem in justifying capitalism is precisely this element: interest, a return that requires neither risk nor entrepreneurial activity on the part of the recipient. If interest cannot be justified by productive contribution, what can be its justification? Alfred Marshall, the enormously influential British pre-Keynesian, responds with an alternative neoclassical answer: interest is the reward for waiting. Like Clark, Marshall confronts the Marxian critique:

> It is not true that the spinning of yarn in a factory, after allowance has been made for the wear and tear of the machinery, is the product of the labor of the operatives. It is the product of their labor, together with that of the employer and subordinate managers, and of the capital employed; and that capital itself is the product of labor and waiting. If we admit it is the product of labor alone, and not of labor and waiting, we can no doubt be compelled by an inexorable logic to admit that there is no justification of interest, the reward of waiting; for the conclusion is implied in the premises. . . .
> To put the same thing in other words, if it be true that the postponement of gratification involves in general a sacrifice on the part of him who postpones, just as additional effort does on the part of him who labors, and if it be true that this postponement enables man to use methods of production of which the first cost is great but by which the aggregate of enjoyment is

increased, as certainly as it would be by an increase
of labor, then it cannot be true that the value of the
thing depends simply on the amount of labor spent on
it. Every attempt to establish this premise has necessarily assumed implicitly that the service performed by
capital is a 'free good,' rendered without sacrifice, and
therefore needing no interest as a reward for its continuance.[24]

We notice at once that Marshall, in true neoclassical fashion,
conflates production factors with their owners. This is striking in the
last sentence. The premise Marshall is bent on destroying—that the
service performed by <u>capital</u> is a free good rendered without sacrifice
and therefore needing no reward for its continuance—is surely true. A
<u>field</u> does not sacrifice in growing corn; a <u>spinning wheel</u> needs no re-
ward for turning cotton into yarn. Their owners are another matter.

What about these owners? Marshall has introduced a new element into the neoclassical story; his appeal is not to productive contribution, but to <u>sacrifice</u>. A different ethical canon has been invoked.

Now sacrifice arguments have always appeared ludicrous to
critics of capitalism. (Does the owner of a mine really sacrifice more
than a miner? A major stockholder in General Motors more than an
autoworker?) Marshall himself is not unaware of this objection; hence
his stress on the "in general" qualification.[25] But as we shall see,
this qualification cannot save what really is at bottom an impossible
ethical argument. The argument is worth analyzing, however, because
some not-so-obvious misconceptions underlie it that often persist
even when the ethical argument itself is rejected.

Any demonstration that capitalist distribution accords with the
ethical canon of sacrifice must involve three steps: first, a specification of the nature of each person's sacrifice; second, an identification of some standard for quantitative interpersonal comparisons;
third, a demonstration that capitalism (in general) distributes according to the sacrifice so defined. (A complete argument would also require a justification of the canon itself and a proof that the defined
sacrifice is appropriate to the canon, but these steps will not concern
us. The argument fails before it gets that far.)

The first step seems straightforward enough, at least in the
case of workers. All sacrifice their leisure; many also undergo mental and physical discomfort. As for capitalists, Marshall answers that
they <u>wait</u>, i.e., they postpone gratification; when a person has to
choose between consuming at once and deferring consumption, she
normally finds it painful to postpone gratification, and this pain is not
fully compensated by later consumption of an equal amount.

The second step of the argument involves comparison. Marshall asserts that the sacrifice of deferred consumption leads to an increase in the aggregate enjoyment, an increase which could have also been effected by additional labor. Now of course we cannot <u>define</u> the quantity of postponement-sacrifice to be the quantity of increase, for that would reduce a seeming appeal to sacrifice to a disguised (and confused) appeal to contribution. On the other hand, if it could be shown to be an <u>empirical fact</u> that (in general) the pain and discomfort of deferred gratification is proportional to the increase effected by that sacrifice, then the argument would be in much better shape. We would have, in fact, an ethically relevant link (such as we were unable to discover in the appeals to contribution) between the owner of a productive asset and the asset's effect on production.

It is precisely this link that Marshall attempts to forge. His method is to bring the neoclassical categories to bear on <u>interest rates</u>. These rates, according to Marshall, are determined by the "money market," which brings entrepreneurs in search of capital face to face with households tempted to save. The market is in equilibrium when interest rates are such as to call forth exactly as much savings as entrepreneurs are desirous of borrowing. If the market is in equilibrium at 6 percent say, this indicates that savers require a 6 percent premium as a reward for deferred gratification, while at the same time entrepreneurs expect to be able to increase productivity enough with the money they borrow to pay this premium and still have sufficient excess to reward themselves for risk and entrepreneurial skills. Thus the connection between pain and productivity.

Common sense suggests that something is amiss here. Analysis reveals some difficulties. Even if we assume the general validity of the neoclassical account of interest-rate formation, the argument does not show that capitalism rewards in accordance with sacrifice. In fact the neoclassical account <u>demonstrates</u> that it does not. The 6 percent premium is not what the average saver or savers "in general" require as an inducement to save; it is what the <u>most reluctant</u> saver requires, the saver at the margin. It is the premium required to entice the last few dollars from the last few households to bring total savings into line with total investments. Unless it were the case that nobody would save without a 6 percent compensation (scarcely a plausible assumption nor one compatible with the neoclassical worldview), some people would have saved at 4 percent though presumably fewer, some at 2 percent, etc. These people, according to the neoclassical tale, have evaluated their pain of deferred gratification at less than 6 percent, and so are being <u>over</u>-compensated by the market. Indeed, for some it is extremely convenient that there are social institutions that will pay for the use of accumulated wealth. Beyond a certain point personal consumption might prove difficult and alternative arrangements expensive (storage facilities and guards would need to be employed). One's "pain of abstinence" in such cases might well be negative; one would pay not to consume. One's "pain," that is, is pleasure. Now plainly a system which rewards pleasure—or which rewards generally in excess of a saver's pain—cannot be justified by the canon of sacrifice.

An alternative, more straightforward critique of Marshall's argument is to deny that his paradigm applies to reality. The plausibility of Marshall's analysis, with its "in general" clause, rests on the assumption that the typical saving unit is a small or medium income household; for such a household "waiting" might plausibly involve pain comparable to a laborer's discomfort. But in contemporary capitalist societies such households are not the typical savers; the bulk of the interest payments do not go to them. As Simon Kuznets has noted, "according to all recent studies, only the upper income groups save; the total savings of groups below the top decile are fairly close to zero."[26]

But if the significant savers are not the small or medium income households but the wealthy, then the plausibility of comparing the "sacrifice" of postponement with the sacrifice of labor evaporates. Marx makes the obvious point:

> The more, therefore, capital increases by successive
> accumulations, the more does the sum of value increase
> which is divided into consumption-fund and accumulation-
> fund. The capitalist can, therefore, live a more jolly
> life and at the same time practice more 'abstinence.'[27]

Marshall's analysis, as an ethical argument appealing to the canon of sacrifice, is plainly fallacious. This we have just seen. But there remains a facet of Marshall's case that deserves further attention. We have not yet addressed his basic assertion that capital is the product of labor and waiting. Is it? Is "waiting" identifiable with "saving"? Does production require saving? Political philosophers often take the neoclassical assumptions for granted. Nozick, for example, repeats the standard litany: "The total product is produced by individuals laboring, using means of production others have saved to bring into existence, by people organizing production or creating means to produce new things or things in a new way."[28]

I will argue that all of the above questions should be answered in the negative: capital is not the product of waiting; waiting is not identifiable with saving; neither waiting nor saving is necessary for production. Savers do not, as Nozick thinks, bring means of production into being.

To be sure, there is an economic truth underlying Marshall's thought, but his formulation of that truth is inaccurate and unfortunate. There is a sense in which "waiting" is a condition for capital accumulation—though not for capital itself. Consider a society producing its maximally feasible output of consumer goods consistent with its own reproduction. In this society some workers are engaged in producing capital goods to replace those used up in the production process. Since there is maximal production of consumer goods, the workforce in this sector is as large as possible; the workforce in the capital-goods sector produces just enough for replacements. In such a society (which may or may not be capitalist) new means of production are constantly being produced (as replacements), but in such a society there is nothing resembling Marshall's notion of "waiting": a "postponement [which] enables man to use methods of production of which the first cost is great but by which the aggregate enjoyment is increased." Capital goods here are not the product of waiting.*

Of course, if this society wishes to increase its stock of capital goods, it may have to postpone some gratification. If we assume full employment of people and resources (which we must, since we are assuming maximal production),† then a capital-goods increase requires a shifting of a part of the workforce (and/or machinery and raw materials) from the consumer-goods sector to the capital-goods sector. This shift will allow the "aggregate enjoyment" to be increased at a later date, as the increased output of capital goods makes its way to the consumer-goods sector, but in the meantime actual

---

*This example derives from regarding an economy as a mechanism that reproduces itself. The conceptualization is post-Keynesian (and Marxian), not neoclassical. This kind of example would not have occurred to Marshall, or if it had, it would not have seemed significant. (More will be said about post-Keynesianism in Chapters 2 and 6. For a brief comparison of neoclassicism and post-Keynesianism germane to the example at hand, see J. A. Kregel, "Post-Keynesian Theory: Income Distribution," Challenge 21 [September-October 1978]: 37-43.

†Notice that the full-employment assumption is necessary for there to be any correlation between capital and waiting. If unemployed people are set to work on idle resources to produce material means of production, then the capital stock of society is increased without any deferred consumption.

consumption must be cut back from what is technically possible. Society must "wait," but its waiting will pay a social dividend. This is the valid core of Marshall's doctrine.

It is significant—and surprising—to notice that this concept of waiting has nothing whatsoever to do with saving—not if by "saving" we mean the setting aside a portion of the total output. Many societies (and individuals) save in this sense. Grain reserves are maintained; cans of tomatoes are stored in the basement. Saving, too, is deferred consumption, but in a sense quite different from above: what is deferred in this case is a portion of the realized output; what is deferred in the other is potential output. Saving in this sense has no connection with bringing means of production into being—or rather, it has a negative effect: the more the workforce must produce emergency reserves, the less it can produce means of production or goods for current consumption.

Now of course in some societies a different sort of saving occurs. Not things are saved but money. And the money is not stashed in a mattress but put in a bank—which then loans it out again. It is this sort of saving Nozick and the neoclassicals have in mind when they see "saving" as "bringing means of production into being." Again, the formulation is unfortunate, for it suggests that the act of saving (or is it the non-act of not consuming?) is some sort of universal, wealth-creating, productive activity. It is not. I have already argued that "providing capital" is not a productive activity. The act of saving— which is an act distinct from the act of investing, as Keynes keeps reminding us—is better thought of as one element in a rather complex decision-making procedure. When an individual (in a market society) saves his money rather than spends it, his "act" of deferment reduces aggregate demand. A signal is sent (in the form of unsold consumer goods) for the market to contract. He "votes" for less production. If that money is placed in a bank, and if an investor then borrows it, and if she then spends it, a countersignal is given. Since the investor's expenditures are likely to be (at least in part) for capital goods, the net effect of the two signals is to shift workers from the consumer-goods sector of the economy to the capital-goods sector. Thus a societal decision to "wait" is registered.

There are various complications that could be added to the above scenario, but we will not pursue them here.* The important point to

---

*One is perhaps worth noting. If the act of saving is not offset by investment, then that private act, far from bringing means of production into existence, can have the opposite effect. It's the well-known (Keynesian) story: saving reduces aggregate demand; this reduction, in turn, forces workers from their jobs and idles factories. It is a curious system, is it not, which rewards such antisocial acts?

be made is that the institutional arrangements which allow investment funds to be generated by private monetary savings are better regarded as part of the global decision-making apparatus of society than as part of its productive apparatus. The act of saving is no more an act of production than purchasing a commodity or voting to increase govern- mental spending.* The complex institutional arrangements covered by the concept "saving" are but one set among many for arriving at decisions regarding deferment of social consumption and a rechannel- ing of workers. Workers can be ordered or enticed, by investors, voters, or authoritarian figures, from one sector of the economy to another. Investment funds can be generated by private savings, by taxation, or by printing presses. Which of these (or other) methods is optimal is a matter we will consider in detail later. Utilitarian and libertarian considerations will have to be brought to bear. But in such analyses we must keep in mind that societal "waiting" and private saving are quite distinct notions, complexly related. We must avoid simplistic assumptions about the causal links between saving, societal deferment of consumption, and the production of capital goods.

CAPITALISM IS JUST BECAUSE IT IS JUST

An important recent defense of capitalism has been advanced by Robert Nozick. It is a noncomparative defense, purporting to show that a certain form of capitalism fits the correct conception of justice. He also argues that socialism cannot be just, but that is a separate matter which does not concern us now. (Nozick's antisocialist argu- ments will be dealt with later.)

In the preceding sections I have defended the thesis that capi- talism cannot be justified by appealing to the ethical principles of contribution or sacrifice. Nozick agrees—though his reasoning is quite different from mine. These are patterned principles of justice, he says, and liberty upsets all patterns. A patterned principle of jus- tice specifies that a distribution is to vary according to some natural dimension (e.g., contribution or sacrifice or labor) or some combi- nation of natural dimensions. All are unacceptable because none "can

---

*Implicit here is yet another argument against justifying interest (and hence capitalism) by appealing to the canon of contribution. The "reward" of voting is one's vote—the influence one exerts; the reward of purchasing a commodity is that commodity. Similarly, the reward of saving is not interest but one's savings—the ability to consume at a later date.

be continuously realized without continuous interference with people's lives."[29] The same charge is leveled against utilitarian and Rawlsian conceptions of justice.

The appropriate theory of justice, according to Nozick, is his entitlement theory. Its cornerstone is a procedural principle: whatever arises from a just situation by just steps is just. Thus, if original holdings are justly acquired, and if all subsequent transfers are just, then the resulting distribution is just whatever it may be. It need not correlate with contribution, sacrifice, the greatest happiness of the greatest number, or anything else. For Nozick a just transfer is a voluntary exchange; a just original acquisition is one which satisfies the "Lockean proviso" that it not materially worsen the position of others no longer at liberty to acquire that particular holding.[30]

Such a theory of justice might seem wholly inapplicable to modern capitalist reality. In the United States a native population was nearly exterminated, and millions more human beings were stolen from their homelands and enslaved. In Britain enclosure movements altered peasant rights and forced great numbers from their villages. Justice was not a prominent feature of nascent capitalism.[31]

Nozick is not unaware of this difficulty. He supplements his procedural principle and his two principles of just holdings (transfer and original acquisition) with a principle of rectification. Though he admits, "I know of no thorough or theoretically sophisticated treatment of such issues,"[32] the basic conception is simple: if injustices have occurred, then transfers are justifiable in order to bring the present distribution into line with what would have been the case had injustices not occurred. How present societies might be altered by such a rectification cannot be said, though Nozick is confident that "socialism as the punishment for our sins would be to go too far."[33]

Nozick has taken aim at both socialists and liberals. Not any form of capitalism is just, only a free-enterprise system with a minimal state to maintain law and order. Nor is any redistribution of wealth justifiable, apart from rectification. All taxation is theft, unless to compensate for the protective services rendered by the minimal state or to redress past injustices. Not surprisingly Anarchy, State and Utopia has drawn heavy return fire. Much of it, in my view, has been accurate and deadly.[34] Nonetheless, entitlement theory should not be dismissed too quickly, for at least parts of it have intuitive appeal. Certain elements remain alive even when the theory as a whole is rejected. These elements must be confronted.

Consider for example the rectification principle. Admittedly it is impractical. How could one conceivably calculate the effects on the present of past injustices? How could one specify with any precision what redistribution would make things right? And how could one persuade a society to make the appropriate restitution, to give up benefits traceable to the injustices of ancestors and transfer wealth, not necessarily to the poor, but to all whose ancestors were more victims than victimizers? (Notice, the neighborhood grocer with a ruthless ancestor in his past might be required to contribute to the local self-made millionaire. Such bizarre possibilities may be multiplied.)

It is easy to dismiss entitlement theory on account of this principle, but to do so, for us at any rate, would not be appropriate. For Nozick has a point to make. I am bent on showing that capitalism is unjust. Not merely U.S. capitalism or British capitalism, but capitalism as such. The import of Nozick's argument, therefore, is this: what if a radical rectification of wealth were effected in our society? Ignore the practical problems mentioned above; a theoretical point is being made. If holdings were rectified, then wouldn't capitalism be just? If so, then my objection cannot be to capitalism as such, but to a particular form of capitalism. My general thesis collapses.

To respond to Nozick, we must abandon this world. We must assume that a rectification has been made. Better—let us go to the beginning of the story, to Nozick's "state of nature," to see if and how a just capitalism might arise. Whether or not a just capitalism did arise is not our concern. We want to see if one could arise. Recall, by capitalism we mean a commodity-producing society in which the majority of the population gain access to the means of production by selling their labor-power to those who own the means of production. If capitalism is to be justified by entitlement theory, a plausible account must be given as to how this state of affairs might have come about without violating anybody's rights. There is, of course, the classic tale so ridiculed by Marx:

> In times long gone by there were two sorts of people;
> one the diligent, intelligent and above all frugal elite;
> the other, lazy rascals, spending their substance, and
> more, in riotous living. . . . Thus it came to pass that
> the former sort accumulated wealth, and the latter sort
> had at last nothing to sell except their skins. And from
> this original sin dates the poverty of the great major-
> ity that, despite all its labor, has up to now nothing to
> sell but itself, and the wealth of the few that increases
> constantly although they have long ceased to work.[35]

Nozick himself seems to have some such picture in mind. He attacks the Marxian claim that workers are forced to deal with capitalists, by asking rhetorically, "Where did the means of production come from? Who earlier forwent current consumption then in order to gain or produce them? Who now forgoes current consumption in paying wage and factor prices. . . . ? Whose entrepreneurial alertness operated throughout?"[36] For Marx, this is the "insipid childishness . . . everyday preached at us in defense of property."[37] It is certainly a one-sided account of the actual development of capitalism. But as I have pointed out, Nozick need not refer to the actual genesis of capitalism, only to its possible genesis.

Now I cannot deny that it is logically possible for a capitalist society to emerge as in the classic fable. But it is important to note that this account and the brutal reality of original acquisition are not the only possible scenarios. A quite different account can be given, one less sanguine than Nozick's apparent vision, but fully in accordance with his principles of justice. Nozick advocates an unregulated free-market system. In such a system an alert entrepreneur might well increase production: many have. Who benefits? The entrepreneur, of course; also the consumers. But not her competitors. They may go to the wall.

This observation is so obvious that its significance is often overlooked. The impact of productivity changes operating through a free market can be and have been momentous. Millions of native weavers starved when British textiles poured into India. The societal structures of the United States and Western Europe were shaken to their foundations as agricultural mechanization drove small farmers and peasants from the land. No force was used (or at least need not have been). The free market, unregulated and coupled with private ownership, is indeed an invisible hand, one that can quite effectively strip the means of production from individuals and send them in search of employers. There is no force, no fraud, no infringement on liberty. There is no "injustice."

I am not suggesting that the market mechanism is totally pernicious. I will argue, in fact, that it has an important role to play in a well-ordered socialist society. There are significant advantages to be had in utilizing the market. But there are also significant disadvantages—especially when the market is accompanied by private property and wage-labor. Any serious discussion of the capitalism-socialism controversy must confront these issues. An unregulated capitalist market can, as the above examples show, produce enormous social dislocation, enormous pain and suffering. Now it might be the case that the advantages of such a system are sufficient to counterbalance the risk and reality of such pain—but that is scarcely self-evident.

It is precisely this question which cannot be discussed within the framework of entitlement theory. The advantages of capitalism can be elaborated. Nozick appeals to the "familiar social considerations favoring private property" to support his claim that the Lockean proviso regarding original acquisition is not violated by capitalism.[38] But not the disadvantages. (What a clever theory!) The disadvantages cannot be discussed, for, as inspection reveals, the legitimacy of private property, the market and wage-labor are <u>presumed</u> throughout. To put the point more precisely: if one accepts Nozick's procedural principle that whatever emerges from a just situation by just steps is just, his principle concerning the justice of voluntary transfers, and the legitimacy of the original acquisition of property, then one must grant the legitimacy of the capitalism—whatever its disadvantages.

For consider: if a private individual can legitimately claim ownership to the natural resources of the earth and to the products of his labor, then private ownership of the means of production is legitimate. If it is legitimate to make whatever property transfers one wants, so long as personal coercion is avoided, then the free market is legitimate. And since "voluntary transfers" embrace one's own labor power, then wage labor is legitimate.

The legitimacy of the basic institutions of capitalism follow at once from Nozick's principles. There is no space within which to insert an objection. Moreover, it is not implausible that something rather like existing capitalism could evolve by "just steps" from some "just" original position. Even if the original holdings are equal, some persons, through intelligence, luck or plain hard work, are likely to increase productivity. If the market is well-developed and unregulated, then this increase can drive competitors into bankruptcy—thus "freeing" them to sell their labor-power. And so the stage is set for the perpetual reward of some, for the making of money with money and the magic of compound interest, for business cycles, unemployment, and all the rest—and not a single protest can be raised.

Of course, if the ethical principles themselves are solidly grounded, then one must accept their implications. But are they? Consider the most crucial principle: all voluntary transfers are just. Is this self-evident? Well, consider what is to count as "voluntary":

> Other people's actions place limits on one's available opportunities. Whether this makes one's resulting action nonvoluntary depends upon whether these others had the right to act as they did. . . .
> Z is faced with working [for an owner of capital] or starving; the choices and actions of all other persons do not add up to providing Z with some other option. . . . Does Z choose to work voluntarily? . . . Z does choose voluntarily if the other individuals A through Y each acted voluntarily and within their rights.[39]

I submit that if "voluntary" need not imply choice, then the voluntary transfer principle is—to put it mildly—problematic. So too is the procedural principle. It is far from evident that one should accept as just a socially disastrous outcome of seemingly innocuous decisions. And of course socialists scarcely find it self-evident that a private appropriation of natural resources and means of production—with or without a Lockean proviso—is morally legitimate.

In summary, my criticism of Nozick is this. Entitlement theory does indeed justify capitalism. The justice of the basic capitalistic institutions follows immediately from the theory's barely-defended premises. The market mechanism is taken as the paradigm of voluntary exchange; private property is presumed just and since "voluntary" need not imply a choice, wage labor is nonproblematical. Hence the fundamental issues that have traditionally exercised socialist (and liberal) critics of laissez-faire capitalism—the destructive social consequences of an untrammelled free market—are simply excluded from the ethical debate. Capitalism is just, whatever the social consequences, because . . . well, because it is just.

NOTES

1. Cf. A. O. Hirschman, The Passions and the Interests: Political Arguments for Capitalism before its Triumph (Princeton: Princeton University Press, 1977).

2. Cf. Lionel Robbins, An Essay on the Nature and Significance of Economic Science (New York: Macmillan, 1932) for a famous statement of this position. The separation actually began toward the end of the nineteenth century with the realization, by Pareto, that marginalist analysis did not require the assumption that utility be of cardinal magnitude. By 1947, when Paul Samuelson published his classic Foundations of Economic Analysis, the split was complete: "Today it is customary to make a distinction between the pure analysis [of an economist] qua economist and his propaganda, condemnations, recommendations qua citizen. In practice, if pushed to extremes, this somewhat schizophrenic rule becomes difficult to adhere to and leads to rather tedious circumlocutions. But in essence, Robbins is undoubtedly correct. Wishful thinking is a powerful deterrent to good analysis and description, and ethical conclusions cannot be determined in the same way that scientific hypotheses are inferred or verified." Paul Samuelson, Foundations of Economic Analysis (New York: Antheneum, 1965), p. 219.

3. Friedrich A. Hayek, The Road to Serfdom (Chicago: University of Chicago Press, 1944).

4. Joan Robinson, "The Age of Growth," Challenge 13 (May-June 1976): 5.

5. John Rawls, A Theory of Justice (Cambridge, Mass.: The Belknap Press of Harvard University Press, 1971). The primary intent

of this work is to articulate a theory of justice, and not to defend capitalism, but a model of "fair capitalism" is presented as an illustration of the theory. We shall examine this model (and its problematic relationship to Rawls's ethical commitments) in Chapter 6.

6. Robert Nozick, Anarchy, State and Utopia (New York: Basic Books, 1974).

7. John Bates Clark, The Distribution of Wealth (New York: Kelley and Millman, 1956), pp. 4-5. (This work was originally published in 1899).

8. Friedrich A. Hayek, The Constitution of Liberty (London: Routledge and Kegan Paul, 1960), p. 94.

9. Nozick, Anarchy, State and Utopia, p. 158.

10. Nicholas Rescher, Distributive Justice (Indianapolis: Bobbs-Merrill, 1966), p. 78. This canon is called variously the canon of "productivity," "social contribution," "productive contribution," or simply "contribution."

11. Milton Friedman, Capitalism and Freedom (Chicago: University of Chicago Press, 1962), p. 161. This is the essential principle. Contemporary neoclassical distribution theory has added many refinements that need not concern us here.

12. Cf. Jan Pen, Income Distribution: Facts, Theories, Policies (New York: Praeger, 1971), pp. 76-87. Essentially the argument is this: wages will be at least as high as the margianl product of the last laborer, for if they were lower, each landowner would try to entice laborers away from his neighbors; wages will not be any higher than that, for that would involve paying the last person more than he yields.

13. Clark, Distribution of Wealth, p. 7.

14. Ibid., p. 4.

15. Harry G. Johnson, The Theory of Income Distribution (London: Gray-Mills, 1973), p. 37.

16. Rescher, Distributive Justice, p. 78.

17. Joseph Schumpeter, Capitalism, Socialism and Democracy (New York: Harper Torchbooks, 1962), p. 83. Schumpeter himself does not advance the ethical argument we are about to consider. Like so many of his colleagues, he eschews ethics for "science." He is, however, the foremost exponent of the view that the entrepreneur is the cornerstone of capitalism, the view associated with the ehtical argument of this section.

18. John Kenneth Galbraith, The New Industrial State (Boston: Houghton Mifflin, 1967), p. 394.

19. Cf., for example, Samir Amin, Unequal Development (New York: Monthly Review Press, 1976), especially Chapter Four. For an influential (though simpleminded) statement of the conventional view, see. W. W. Rostow, The Stages of Economic Growth. A Non-

Communist Manifesto (Cambridge: At the University Press, 1960).

20. Joan Robinson never tires of arguing that these two aspects of capital are hopelessly confused and logically irreconcilable within the framework of neoclassical theory. Cf. her "Capital Theory Up to Date," Canadian Journal of Economics 3 (May, 1970): 307-17, for details. I think she is right, but that issue, which concerns the viability of the neoclassical paradigm, is not our interest here.

21. John Maynard Keynes, The General Theory of Employment, Interest and Money (New York: Harcourt, Brace and World, 1936), pp. 213-14. Keynes's proposal, notice, is more stringent than mine. He does not even want to call capital productive, whereas I have drawn the line at calling providing capital a productive activity. He is probably right. The slope from capital as productive to providing it as a productive activity is slippery indeed.

22. Schumpeter, Capitalism, Socialism and Democracy, p. 83.

23. Paul Samuelson, Economics, 9th ed. (New York: McGraw-Hill, 1973), p. 599.

24. Alfred Marshall, Principles of Economics, 8th ed. (New York: Macmillan, 1948), p. 587.

25. Ibid., p. 233.

26. Simon Kuznets, Economic Growth and Structure (New York: W. W. Norton, 1965), p. 263.

27. Karl Marx, Capital (New York: The Modern Library, 1906), p. 667.

28. Nozick, Anarchy, State and Utopia, p. 172. My emphasis.

29. Ibid., p. 165.

30. Ibid., pp. 151, 178 ff.

31. For a vivid, well-documented account of the British experience, see Maurice Dobb, Studies in the Development of Capitalism (London: Routledge and Kegan Paul, 1963), Chapter Six. The U.S. experience is, of course, well-known.

32. Nozick, Anarchy, State and Utopia, p. 152.

33. Ibid., p. 231.

34. For two decent liberal critiques, see Thomas Scanlon, "Nozick on Rights, Liberty and Property," Philosophy and Public Affairs 6 (Fall 1976): 3-23, and Thomas Nagel, "Libertarianism Without Foundations," Yale Law Journal 85 (November 1975): 136-49. For views from further Left, Cheyney Ryan's "Yours, Mine and Ours: Property Rights and Individual Liberty," Ethics 87 (January 1977): 126-41, and G. A. Cohen's "Robert Nozick and Wilt Chamberlain: How Patterns Preserve Liberty," Erkentniss 11 (May 1977): 5-23, are good.

35. Marx, Capital, p. 785.

36. Nozick, Anarchy, State and Utopia, p. 254. Notice how the neoclassical categories dominate Nozick's thinking.

37. Marx, Capital, p. 785.
38. Nozick, p. 177.
39. Nozick, Anarchy, State and Utopia, pp. 262-63.

2

ALTERNATIVE MODELS

We have disposed of the main noncomparative arguments purporting to legitimize capitalism. Capitalism cannot be justified by appealing to contribution, because providing capital is not a productive activity. Capitalism cannot be justified by appealing to sacrifice, because many who profit do not sacrifice. A justification can be concocted (immediately) from Nozick's entitlement theory, but that theory begs so many crucial questions that neither the theory nor the justification that flows from it can be accepted.

The noncomparative arguments are out of the way, but the game is far from over. The arguments we have considered all suffer from an overly restrictive ethical base. Each, having grounded its case on one specific ethical value, can be refuted by showing that capitalism does not adhere to that value, or that the value itself is inappropriate or insufficient to the issue at hand. That is precisely what I have done—but it was almost too easy. We can imagine an impatient Clark objecting, "But to distribute at variance with marginalist contribution would lead to disaster!" Or a Schumpeterean proclaiming, "Without capitalist incentives, a dynamic entrepreneurial class will not develop." Or Marshall, "Without interest, insufficient saving will be undertaken to finance needed investment." Or Nozick, "The advantages of socialism do not compensate for our loss of liberty."

These objections, notice, cannot be made within the ethical framework of the last chapter. They are irrelevant to the claim that capitalism satisfies the ethical standard J, where J is a specific value (contribution, sacrifice, or liberty). Each appeals (implicitly) to an ethical theory that permits the weighing of advantages and disadvantages (alternative values) and the comparison of alternative institutional structures. They are <u>comparative</u> claims.

Such claims cannot be forestalled indefinitely. They are basic to the defense of capitalism. The essential claim, which subsumes the above (and much more), is this: given the strengths and weaknesses of various economic systems, capitalism yields the greatest balance of good over evil. Or—a variation of this claim—of all the alternatives capitalism is most likely to yield the greatest balance.

Such claims are formidable. They are difficult to establish, to be sure, but they are also difficult to refute. It is not so hard to pick holes in arguments purporting to demonstrate that capitalism is the best of all possible worlds, to raise doubts about that conclusion. But it is quite another matter to prove it false. To do that, it is not sufficient—though of course it is necessary—to identify specific weaknesses in capitalism. One must also make explicit one's values, to reveal the exact nature of the "good" and "evil" being balanced, and, above all, one must provide a concrete alternative that does not suffer those weaknesses, or other more serious ones. This latter move is the difficult one.

It is a move many critics of capitalism have been reluctant to make. Marx himself ridiculed "utopian" speculation. The construction of alternative models is often viewed as that. I don't think it is—or if the specification of an alternative is utopian, then I think the time has come to take the step to "nowhere."*

There are important reasons for this. First of all, too many socialist experiments have turned out badly. It is a sobering, even chilling, fact that not a single country that has abolished private ownership of the means of production has retained or instituted genuinely democratic elections, not one has retained or instituted civil liberties as extensive as those found in many Western capitalist countries. Certainly there are historical factors to be taken into account, and it is certainly true that capitalist "democracy" is something other than what the high school civics texts describe. Nonetheless the historical record of this century is bound to give pause to anyone who examines it carefully. One can no longer believe that the abolition of private property automatically ushers in a just society.

There is a second important reason for discussion alternatives. We know more now than Marx or Engels did when they polemicized against "utopian socialism." This century has witnessed unprecedented social experimentation. We can see more clearly now what works and

---

*Not all Marxists are opposed to "utopian" speculation. Herbert Marcuse, for one, often called for an end to that injunction. (Cf. An Essay on Liberation [Boston: Beacon Press, 1969], pp. 3-6.)

what does not; we can understand better why certain projects succeed and others fail. There is much we do not know, of course, but we can speak with greater confidence now than would have been warranted a century ago. We have fewer excuses for reticence; we have more to talk about.

But before talking about socialism, I need to say more about capitalism. I have defined capitalism as a commodity-producing society in which the bulk of the means of production are privately owned, and the majority of the population are engaged in wage-labor. This definition is adequate for marking off capitalist from noncapitalist societies, but it does not capture the <u>ideal</u> defended by proponents of capitalism. We must become clearer about this ideal. Many, perhaps most, proponents of capitalism are unhappy about the present system; many, perhaps most, would like reform. To avoid what would appear to be an unfair procedure—comparing an idealized socialism with a very mundane capitalist reality—we must address an idealized capitalism as well.

In fact we must consider several ideals, for the advocates of capitalism are by no means unanimous. We cannot consider all possible variations, but we can do justice to the situation by examining certain key models. Most proponents of capitalism think of themselves as either conservative or liberal. (We'll ignore that peculiar, incoherent creature, the "moderate.") To the conservative position belongs a certain idealized vision of capitalism, internally consistent (more or less), but much at variance with the liberal ideal. Or rather, at variance with the liberal ideals—for modern liberalism is presently rent by two conflicting conceptualizations of capitalism, each suggesting a distinct model as its goal.

Before going any deeper into these woods, I need to clarify some terminology. I've used the terms "conservative" and "liberal," but both are problematic. "Liberalism" is especially ambiguous. The term sometimes designates the intellectual and political tradition that emphasizes liberty and laissez-faire, two key ingredients of contemporary conservatism; sometimes it designates the nonsocialist welfare-oriented tradition opposed to precisely this conservatism; at yet other times it refers to the features common to both these traditions. "Conservative" is also controversial. Many "conservative" theorists advocate change—indeed more drastic change than many of their "liberal" opponents, and so they disavow the "conservative" label. Their legitimate title, they say, has been usurped by their opposition, for they are the true heirs of Locke, Adam Smith, Tocqueville, and other great "liberals" of the past.[1]

Let us acknowledge these "conservative" arguments, for they have merit, and drop the word "conservative" from our analysis.

Henceforth, we will call "classical liberal"* what is more commonly called "conservative," and we will call its nonsocialist opposition "modern liberal." Modern liberalism itself, however, must be further subdivided if we are to do justice to the question of economic ideals. Within modern liberalism a struggle is being waged concerning the neoclassical heritage of modern economics. Classical liberals embrace this heritage without reservation. A large number of modern liberals do also—or rather they embrace a neoclassicism which features certain Keynesian addenda. This segment of modern liberalism we shall call "Keynesian liberalism." The opposition segment, which is fierce in its rejection of neoclassicism, we shall label "post-Keynesian liberalism." With this terminology set, let us now look more closely at the positions themselves, since all three will figure prominently in this work.

The contemporary classical liberals are indeed the heirs of Adam Smith. Their fundamental commitment is to a capitalist economy as free as possible from governmental interference, as close as possible to Adam Smith's laissez-faire ideal. Classical liberals today tend to be critical of governmental welfare programs, labor unions and Keynesian deficit spending. The basic problems of contemporary capitalism are held to be rooted in excessive governmental regulation of the economy. If the role of government were drastically curtailed, the free market, they maintain, would generate liberty and prosperity for all. (This is an oversimplification, but I am painting here with a broad brush.)[2]

The economists in the classical liberal camp are all indissolubly wedded to the neoclassical paradigm. Two of them, Friedrich Hayek and Milton Friedman, are Nobel laureates, each representing a school of economics associated with classical liberalism. Hayek derives from the "Austrian School," which goes back through Ludwig

---

*"Neoconservative" might also be appropriate, since the intellectual movement calling itself that, which has emerged recently, places the "classical liberal" theorists we will be considering in their pantheon. But since it is not yet clear whether neoconservatism is a genuine movement of merely a fad, we will stick with the other terminology. (For a critical exposition of neoconservatism, see Peter Steinfels, The Neoconservatives: The Men Who Are Changing America [New York: Simon and Schuster, 1979].)

von Mises to the nineteenth-century marginalists Böhm-Bawerk, von Wieser and Menger. Friedman represents the "Chicago School," a group of economists centered at the University of Chicago, whose characteristic tenor was set during the inter-war years by Henry Simons and especially Frank Knight. (Hayek in fact is associated with both schools; he left his native Austria prior to the outbreak of World War II; he joined the faculty at the University of Chicago in 1950 where he remained for 12 years.) Hayek and Friedman will be recurring objects of our attention.

Among contemporary philosophers linked to the classical liberal tradition, Robert Nozick is the most prominent. The values stressed in his work are those of classical liberalism: a strong commitment to liberty and individualism, a suspicion of equality, an aversion to governmental control, whether democratic or not. The opening sentences of Nozick's major work exemplify the classical liberal ethos: "Individuals have rights, and there are things no person or group may do to them (without violating their rights). So strong and far-reaching are these rights that they raise the question of what, if anything, the state and its officials may do."[3]

From the time of the Great Depression until the early 1970s, classical liberalism gave ground to Keynesian liberalism. By the 1960s Keynesian liberalism commanded the heights of the economics profession. Enclaves of classical liberalism persisted (most notably at the University of Chicago), and a few Left dissidents fired a shot now and then, but the "new economics" ruled with an untroubled conscience. Those were the happy days. In the 1970s rebellion broke out again, and the heights have been assaulted by both Left and Right. Keynesian liberalism remains a force—probably the dominant force—but its hegemony has been much weakened.

Keynesian liberalism, like classical liberalism, adheres to the neoclassical tradition, though the Keynesians have been freer with supplements. They support a free-market economy, but one in which the government plays an active role in mitigating the harsher effects of laissez-faire.* Historically, the dominant concern of the Keynesians has been unemployment (Keynes's major work, his General Theory, appeared in 1936, during the depths of the Great Depression), but they have also been supportive of labor unions, government regulatory agencies and public welfare programs. In general, Keynesian

---

*"Keynesian" liberalism, in this sense, antedated Keynes himself, but Keynes's theory provided the theoretical justification for governmental intervention into many areas ruled out of bounds by pre-Keynesian neoclassicism.

liberals back a host of measures which are anathema to classical liberalism. Consider the questions Paul Samuelson, a Keynesian-liberal Nobel laureate, puts to Friedman:

> Can a man today seriously be against social security?
> Against flood relief? Fair housing? Pure food and drug
> regulation? Compulsory licensing and qualifying of doc-
> tors? and of auto drivers? Be against foreign aid? Pub-
> lic utility and SEC regulation? Against the post office
> monopoly? Minimum wages? The draft? Price and wage
> controls? Anti-cyclical fiscal and monetary policies?
> Auto-safety standards? Compulsory and free schooling?
> Prohibition of heroin sales? Stricter federal and state
> housing standards for migrant workers? Maximum in-
> terest rate ceilings on usurious lenders? Truth-in-lend-
> ing laws? Government planning? Can a man of good will
> oppose Pope Paul VI's encyclical naming central econo-
> mic planning as they key to development?[4]

If we look from economists to philosophers, we find the Keynes-isn-post-Keynesian distinction more difficult to draw. Most philosophers who work in the areas of social and political philosophy are modern as opposed to classical liberals. They do not subscribe to the laissez-faire ideal, and they are suspicious of the classical-liberal absolute priority (or perhaps more correctly, the classical-liberal concept) of liberty.[5] Modern liberals value liberty, but they also give significant weight to equality. In stark contrast to classical liberals, they regard as legitimate many governmental measures that effect some redictribution of wealth from top to bottom. Unlike socialists, however, they do not regard as necessary the radical restructuring of the basic institutions of private property, the market and wage labor.

One contemporary philosopher who is clearly Keynesian liberal is John Rawls. Unlike most philosophers, he ventures frequently into the terrain of economics, and when he does so, his analysis leans heavily on the neoclassical paradigm. We will pay particular attention to Rawls later on in this work, for his model of "fair capitalism" may be taken as a representative example of the Keynesian-liberal ideal.

Post-Keynesianism is a reaction to the Keynesian-neoclassical theoretical synthesis. Post-Keynesians are sympathetic to much of Keynes's own work, but they disagree strongly with his suggestion that neoclassical theory comes into its own again, once the government acts to secure full employment.[6] In post-Keynesian analysis, the large corporations play a preeminent role. These institutions, and the corresponding institutions of organized labor and big government, remove the reality of modern capitalism so far from the neoclassical "perfect competition" parable that, in their view, the neoclassical categories are useless. They are worse than useless; they are positively detrimental to a clear comprehension of contemporary economic and social problems.

Post-Keynesianism has only recently emerged as a self-conscious movement,* though various iconoclastic economists have long fit our characterization. John Kenneth Galbraith is the best known. He is, in many ways, the representative post-Keynesian liberal.

Now Galbraith—and other post-Keynesians—might object to being called "liberal." And not without reason. They do pose a classification problem. Notice, post-Keynesianism, insofar as it criticizes neoclassicism and proposes an alternative paradigm for understanding contemporary capitalism, is not necessarily incompatible with a socialist vision. On the other hand, the new paradigm also suggests certain reforms of capitalism, and many post-Keynesians, Galbraith among them, advocate these reforms. The question is, do these reforms constitute a "preserving" of capitalism by modifying its excesses—a characteristic of modern liberalism—or do they constitute a new social system, perhaps even a transition to socialism?

It is also a characteristic of modern liberalism to be impatient with such questions, to shrug them off as pointless ideological speculation. That's a mistake, for a serious question is being asked. A socialist wants to know whether these reforms are compatible with the socialist ideal, and hence worthy of support—or whether a counterideal is embedded in the reforms. Reforms are not "ideal-neutral." One wants to know what concept of a just society lies behind the concrete proposals.

In my judgment the reforms proposed by those post-Keynesians inclined to offer reform proposals reveal an essentially modern-liberal

---

*The first major statement of the new movement was J. A. Kregel and Alfred Eichner, "An Essay on Post-Keynesian Theory: A New Paradigm in Economics," Journal of Economic Literature 13 (December 1975): 1293-1314. The Journal of Post-Keynesian Economics appeared in 1978 under the editorship of Paul Davidson and Sidney Weintraub. It should be noted that "post-Keynesianism" is still somewhat ambiguous, though usage is becoming standardized. What I call "post-Keynesian" is sometimes referred to in the literature as neo-Keynesianism; what I have labelled Keynesian (the neoclassical-Keynesian synthesis) is sometimes called post-Keynesian.

vision: a society not so different from existing capitalism, but modified to reduce certain inequities. These proposals will be considered in more detail in Chapter 6, at which time it will be noted that the proposals most at variance with neoclassical "wisdom" are aimed at reducing inequality, correcting certain social imbalances, but above all with stabilizing the system. These proposals make heavy inroads on one key institution of capitalism—the market—but they leave relatively untouched the other two: private property and wage-labor. But it is precisely these two institutions, and not the market, that lie at the heart of the socialist critique of capitalism. It is these two institutions, much more than the market, that will stand altered in the socialist alternative I will defend.

Keynesian liberalism and post-Keynesian liberalism will be analyzed in detail later. Rawls and Galbraith will serve respectively as representatives. But the major portion of this work will involve a comparison of worker-control socialism with classical liberalism's laissez-faire ideal. Laissez-faire is the purest form of capitalism, the one which most clearly exhibits capitalism's underlying structure. It is also the form out of which, by way of reaction, the other ideals have emerged. It is essential to understand this form, its structure and dynamic, its strengths and weaknesses, in order to comprehend adequately the other forms of capitalism—or, for that matter, certain features of worker control. We will return to alternative conceptions of capitalism later, but it is this basic form that we must now analyze.

CAPITALISM: THE LAISSEZ-FAIRE IDEAL

Except for a few libertarian anarchists, no classical liberal theorist advocates complete laissez-faire. All recognize that the government has a certain role to play in society, from defining property rights and enforcing contracts to checking monopolistic power. Nevertheless, laissez-faire lies close to the heart of classical liberalism. However much its advocates may disagree on secondary matters, they are united on this basic point: as much as possible, the economy should run itself.

But how can an economy run itself? How can millions of individuals produce, distribute and consume millions upon millions of products unless guided by some central authority or rigid tradition? The answer of course was enunciated two centuries ago by Adam Smith:

> As every individual, therefore, endeavors as much as he
> can both to employ his capital in the support of domestic
> industry and so to direct that industry that its produce
> may be of the greatest value, every individual necessarily

labours to render the grand revenue of the society as
great as he can. He generally, indeed, neither intends
to promote the public interest, nor knows how much he
is promoting it. . . . He intends his own gain, and he is
in this, as in many other cases, led by an invisible hand
to promote an end which is no part of his intention. . . .
By pursuing his own interest he frequently promotes that
of society more effectually than when he really intends to
promote it. [7]

The essential elements of this mysterious process are now well
known. Individual greed is held in check by competition. The "invisible
hand" directs via that mighty law, Supply and Demand. If society wants
more boots than are being supplied and fewer sandals, then bootmakers
will raise their prices to choke demand, and sandalmakers will lower
theirs to stimulate it. With bootmaking now more profitable, people
and resources will shift from sandalmaking to the boot business. Thus
the supply of boots increases and that of sandals declines—in accordance
with society's desires, but without any central command. (If the reader
objects that modern capitalism doesn't behave this way—that prices
seem to go up even when demand declines—let me reiterate that we are
describing an ideal. Why our present economy deviates from this ideal,
and what reforms might bring it back into line will be discussed later.
For now we want to understand the ideal itself.)

This simple supply-demand paradigm is extremely important, for
in an ideal laissez-faire economy it governs not only the movement of
boots and sandals but a vast array of other economic phenomena: all
consumer goods and services, capital goods, land usage, the labor
market, saving and investment, the stock market, foreign exchange
rates, international trade; the list goes on and on. In view of its importance it is appropriate to ask: how well does it work? What are the
strengths and weaknesses of an economy based on competition, the
pursuit of self-interest, and the law of supply and demand?

Classical liberalism and laissez-faire have long been associated
with liberty. Classical liberalism rose to prominence in the seven-
teenth and nineteenth centuries as a philosophy opposed to aristocratic
privilege, to the unlimited authority of monarchs, to all forms of
governmental tyranny, including "tyranny of the majority." Government, to the classical liberal, is by its very nature coercive, and
coercion is opposed to liberty. "That government is best which governs
least." Hence, a society which organizes its economic activity without
governmental intervention is most desirable.

Laissez-faire is alleged to have other strengths. It not only promotes liberty, but it turns out goods and services efficiently. Adam
Smith laid the basis for this argument, but the neoclassicals have

refined it enormously. They have carefully defined the concept of efficiency; they've specified the requisite conditions; they've proved theorems.

Let us consider a basic result, for it sheds additional light on the neoclassical ideal. The actors begin to stand forth, and the complex dynamic of the system becomes more comprehensible. Self-interest, competition and supply and demand remain the fundamental elements, but they are more finely elaborated.

According to the neoclassical version of laissez-faire, the consumer is king. Consumers express their preferences by purchasing goods and services on the market, and this sets the economy into motion. The consumer is king in this ideal world, and the entrepreneur is prime minister. Consumers express their desires, and entrepreneurs hasten to satisfy them. Consumers, faced with an array of goods, express their wishes by buying. These actions, in accordance with supply and demand, determine prices. Entrepreneurs now respond. Those goods that are seen to be most profitable are produced in greater numbers, those less profitable are cut back. To produce, the entrepreneur must employ factors of production (land, labor, and capital), and must organize them (if she is to be successful) as efficiently as possible.

Individuals under laissez-faire are not merely consumers. They wear two hats. They are also owners, owners of factors of production. Thus, the entrepreneur, to produce, must pay rent to the owners of land, interest to the owners of capital, and wages to the owners of labor, all rates determined by ubiquitous Supply and Demand. The money received by these owners may now be spent on consumer goods again—or, and here the individual dons a third hat—a portion of it may be saved. This saving may be loaned out to an entrepreneur, at a rate again determined by Supply and Demand, this time operating in the money market.

The actors, we see, are now in place for another round. Goods have been produced, individuals have been supplied with funds with which to express their preferences, and a fresh store of capital has been set aside. The process may continue—by itself, automatically, with no need for governmental intervention.

We have described how laissez-faire is seen to operate, but we have not demonstrated its efficiency. Here enters the neoclassical analysis. The first thing needed is a precise notion of efficiency. Economists once thought in terms of utilitarian optimality—the greatest happiness for the greatest number—but that concept was discarded long ago as "unscientific." What is settled on instead is Pareto-optimality. A state of affairs is Pareto-optimal if and only if every alternative state which would make some people better off would also render others worse off. No change is possible, that is, which could make everyone at least as well off as before and someone better off. [8] (Cutting a cake with a reasonably sharp knife results in a Pareto-optimal distribution, no matter how equal or unequal the slices, so long as the entire cake is consumed. Bludgeoning it apart with a baseball bat is not Pareto-optimal.)

Armed with this concept of efficiency, the neoclassical theorist can now proceed to his theorem. But first some assumptions are necessary—for laissez-faire is not always efficient. The most important assumption concerns monopoly. There must not be any. Competition must be "perfect." This means that no individual or collection of individuals can take into account the effect on price levels of their own decisions to buy or sell. Everyone is a "price-taker." There are no "price-makers," neither firms nor labor unions. No one can drive up prices by withholding supplies, nor drive them down by refusing to buy.

Additional assumptions are necessary, which need not concern us here. (They will be noted later.) What we wish to do now is understand the conclusion: given the appropriate restrictions, a perfectly-competitive laissez-faire economy, when all markets are in equilibrium, is in a state of Pareto-optimality. That is, given the structure of preferences, no output that is unambiguously more satisfying could be produced from the given input. No one could be made happier without making someone else unhappier. There is no dead-weight inefficiency in the system that would allow production to expand in some area without contracting in another.

This result is nontrivial. It cannot be established if the system contains a monopolist. One might object that changing a monopolistic system would surely make the monopolist unhappy, but that is to misconstrue the sense of Pareto-optimality operating here. If the monopolist were to produce as much as she would under conditions of perfect competition, then there would be sufficient excess created to make her as well off as before, and some people even better off. This is not to suggest that if she behaved as a perfect competitor, this condition would prevail. Not at all. Her actions are not stupid; it pays to be a monopolist. The situation is not Pareto-optimal because if she had acted as a perfect competitor and if some redistribution were effected, then others could have been made better off without making her worse off. Or, to give an alternative formulation, if the system had begun with a somewhat different initial distribution of existing resources, it would have been possible to reach a perfectly-competitive equilibrium in which everyone—including the ex-monopolist—received as much as before, and some people more.

An example might clarify this point. Suppose an initial distribution of resources of 5 each to A and B would yield, under perfect competition, a resultant distribution of 10 to A and 10 to B. If A behaves as a monopolist, however, he might be able to secure 12 for himself, though B's return might fall to 6. The second situation is not Pareto-optimal because in the first case 2 could have been redistributed from B to A to make A as happy as he is in the second case, and B happier. Or, by the second formulation, some other initial distribution, say 6 to A and 4 to B, would have produced a perfectly competitive equilibrium giving 12 to A and 8 to B. A's monopolizing, in effect, not only steals a slice of B's cake, but bludgeons a portion of it to useless crumbs.

The conclusion that perfectly-competitive laissez-faire will, under suitable conditions, reach a Pareto-optimal equilibrium is a nontrivial result. Its proof is by no means obvious.[9] The significance of the result, however, is a matter of debate, some elements of which we will review later. For now we are content to understand the claim, and the essential structure of the system about which the claim is made.

So far we have noted two basic claims in support of laissez-faire. It is said to be the system most in accordance with liberty. It is said to be an optimally efficient system. A third claim is also often made. Laissez-faire is said to give maximal range to human initiative, and thus to best promote optimal growth. The lure of great reward stimulates talented individuals to take the risks so essential to path-breaking innovation. The relentless pressure of competition spurs the more reluctant to follow suit.

Few thinkers have ever denied the dynamic nature of capitalism. Not even Marx doubted this aspect. Indeed, an extract from the Communist Manifesto reads like a paean:

> The bourgeoisie, during its rule of scarce one hundred
> years, has created more massive and more colossal
> productive forces than have all preceding generations
> together. Subjection of nature's forces to man, machin-
> ery, application of chemistry to industry and agriculture,
> steam-navigation, railways, electric telegraphs, clear-
> ing of whole continents for cultivation, canalization of
> rivers, whole populations conjured out of the ground—
> what earlier century had even a presentiment that such
> productive forces slumbered in the lap of social labor.[10]

It is true that when neoclassicism called the labor theory of value into question, growth arguments gave ground to efficiency arguments as the focus of academic attention. Mainstream theory did not really return to growth questions until after the Second World War.[11] Historical factors no doubt played a role. Soviet productivity surged ahead during the inter-war years, while capitalism floundered in the Great Depression. With the post-war boom, however, growth arguments again gained prominence, in academia and in popular consciousness. The race with the Russians was on, and we seemed to be winning. The general fascination with growth has only recently begun to ebb.

The outline of the grand comparative argument for capitalism is now in view. The argument consists of subarguments purporting to establish three propositions: (1) capitalism is more compatible with liberty than socialism; (2) capitalism is more efficient in the allocation of existing resources than socialism; (3) capitalism is more innovative and dynamic than socialism.

Each of these claims is of fundamental importance; each must be analyzed in detail. But before doing so, we need the comparative term— a vision of socialism to set beside the capitalist ideals.

WORKER-CONTROL SOCIALISM

In the early 1950s a small Eastern European country, a country with "two alphabets, three religions, four languages, five nations, six federal states called republics, seven neighbors and eight national banks,"[12] embarked on a remarkable experiment. In 1948 Stalin accused Yugoslavia of antisovietism. By 1949 all trade between Yugoslavia and other Communist countries had been halted, and an economic boycott imposed. Pressed by events, Yugoslavia began a highly original construction—a decentralized socialist economy featuring worker self-management of factories. The system has undergone many modifications during the succeeding three decades, but the basic structure of worker self-management has persisted and has been combined with ever greater reliance on the market. The experiment has encountered difficulties, but it has been by no means unsuccessful. Between 1952 and 1960, Yugoslavia recorded the highest growth rate of any country in the world.[13] And though the pendulum has swung back and forth between liberalization and repression, Yugoslavia has been without doubt the freest (by Western standards) of any Communist country.

The socialist model we will examine resembles Yugoslavian socialism in many respects, though it is not a stylized abstraction from that reality. Our model differs from the Yugoslavian model in several crucial respects, which will be noted as we proceed. Yugoslavian successes and failures, however, constitute empirical evidence highly relevant to our analysis. The fact that worker self-management <u>works</u> is immensely important. The problems that have surfaced in the Yugoslavian economy bear on the structural differences between their model and the one I propose.

Before sketching the particular model I will defend, let me make some terminological specifications, since usage is by no means standard in this area. I will call "socialist" any economic system that does not feature private ownership of the means of production. This usage is not wholly rigorous (since a primitive hunter-gatherer society is not really "socialist"), and it is certainly controversial (since some would reserve "socialist" for those societies embodying certain ideals, others for the transition stage between capitalism and communism), but it will suffice for our purposes. The particular socialist model that I will defend shall be designated "worker-control socialism" or simply "worker control." "Worker control," as I will use the term, means something more than general control of an economy by workers. It also means something different from that feature of the Yugoslavian economy wherein workers of a given firm democratically control the operation of that firm. This latter feature, which will be an element of worker control, I will designate "worker self-management." Thus, worker control is a form of socialism featuring (among other things) worker self-management.

Like Yugoslavian socialism, worker control is a worker self-managed market socialism. Unlike the Yugoslavian variety, it is a democratic socialism. I will not attempt to detail the political particulars, but I will assume a constitutional government that guarantees civil liberties to all; I will assume a representative government, with democratically elected bodies at the community, regional and national level. Of course it has been argued that such a structure is incompatible with socialism, and that argument cannot be neglected. (It will be taken up in Chapter 5.) But for now I will assume that political democracy is not contradictory to the economic structure I propose. (If this assumption is correct—and I will argue that it is—then our model will be more democratic than either Yugoslavian socialism or Western capitalism. Yugoslavian society is democratic at the workplace, but has an authoritarian government; Western capitalism operates under democratic governments,* but is authoritarian at the workplace. Our model will be democratic in both spheres.)

The economic structure of the model I propose has three basic features: (1) each productive enterprise is managed democratically by its workers; (2) the economy is essentially a market economy: raw materials and consumer goods are bought and sold at prices determined by the forces of supply and demand; (3) the government controls

----

*I will later challenge the claim that Western capitalism (any capitalism) is compatible with political democracy, but that will involve construing democracy more in accord with its etymological meaning than is usually done. For now we will stick with contemporary usage.

all new investment: it generates its investment fund by taxation, and dispenses it according to plan.[14] Let me elaborate on each of these elements.

Each productive enterprise is managed by those who work there. Workers are responsible for the day-to-day operation of the facility: organization of the workplace, factory discipline, techniques of production, what and how much to produce, how the net proceeds are to be distributed. Decisions concerning these matters are made democratically, one person, one vote. Of course, in a firm of significant size some delegation of authority will no doubt be necessary. A workers' council or general manager (or both) will be empowered to make certain kinds of decisions. But these officials are elected by the workers. They are not appointed by the State, nor elected by the community at large.

Though workers manage the workplace, they do not own the means of production. These are the collective property of the society. Societal ownership manifests itself in an insistence (backed by law) that the capital stock of a firm be kept intact. Depreciation reserves must be maintained; workers are not permitted to allow the assets in their trust to deteriorate in value or to sell them off for personal gain. If an enterprise finds itself in economic difficulty, workers are free to reorganize the facility, or to leave and seek work elsewhere. They are not free, however, to sell off their capital stocks without replacing them with others of equal value—not, at any rate, without explicit governmental authorization. If a firm is unable to generate even the minimum per-capita income, then it must declare bankruptcy. Movable capital will be sold off to pay creditors; any excess, as well as the fixed capital, returns to the government investment fund. Workers must seek employment elsewhere. (The unemployment problem and other efficiency concerns will be discussed in the next chapter.)

Worker self-management is the first basic feature of our model; the market is the second. Our socialist economy is a market economy, at least insofar as the allocation of existing consumer and movable productive goods are concerned. The alternative to market allocation is central planning, and central planning, the historical record shows, is both inefficient and conducive to an authoritarian concentration of power. (The contentions embedded in this last sentence are ferociously controversial among socialists, and will be discussed in more detail in a later chapter. But consider only one small example, of a type familiar to students of the Soviet system. Consider what is involved in drawing up, and then getting executed, a plan for the production of nails:

> If the target is merely for "tons of nails shorter than two inches," the factory will try to produce all 1 9/10" nails

because this is the easiest. If it is for "number of nails,"
the factory will try to produce all 1/2" nails. But if the
plan is set in terms of 1/2", 1", 1 1/2" and 1 9/10" nails,
there will be overcentralization. If the target is set in
terms of gross value of output, the factory will maximize
its use of raw materials and semi-fabs and minimize the
net value it adds to each product. [15]

Notice, the problem is not (necessarily) one of ill-will or selfishness. Without a price mechanism regulated by supply and demand,
it is extremely difficult for a producer or planner to know what and
how much and what variety to produce; it is extremely difficult to know
which means are the most efficient. The market, as we have seen, re-
solves these problems in a nonauthoritarian, nonbureaucratic fashion.
That is no mean achievement.

Our socialist economy is a market economy. Firms buy raw materials and machinery from other firms, and sell their products to
other enterprises or consumers. Prices are largely unregulated, except by supply and demand. In some cases, however, selective price
controls might be in order, especially in those industries which exhibit monopolistic concentrations. Our socialist society has no overriding commitment to laissez-faire; like modern liberalism it is willing
to permit governmental intervention when the market malfunctions. The
market is not viewed as good-in-itself, a paradigm of free human interaction (á la Nozick), but as a useful instrument for accomplishing certain societal goals. It has inherent defects—but so do all alternatives.

Since enterprises in our economy buy and sell on the market,
they strive to make a "profit." "Profit" here, however, is not the
same as capitalist profit. Firms strive to maximize the difference
between total sales and total nonlabor costs. Unlike a capitalist enterprise, labor is not another "factor of production" technically on par
with land and capital. Labor is not a commodity at all, for when a
worker joins a firm, she becomes a voting member, and entitled to a
specific share of the net revenue.

Now these shares (percentages of net revenue, not absolute
quantities) need not be equal for all members. The workers themselves
must decide how to distribute the revenue. They may opt for equality,
but they may also decide to remunerate the more difficult tasks more
highly; they may find it in their interest to offer special premiums
for scarce skills, to attract and hold the talent they need. Such decisions are made democratically. (The government might want to set
a minimum "wage" or minimum share; it might couple this with job-
security provisions which prohibit an individual's being dismissed

without cause when there is sufficient revenue available to pay the minimum share.* Such provisions would interfere somewhat with allocational efficiency—when a business declines and these egalitarian constraints come into force, skilled people who might be able to revive declining fortunes could not be readily attracted, and skilled people in the firm might be tempted to leave. On the other hand, such "institutionalized solidarity" would prevent those better off from making those worse off bear the brunt of an economic downturn. These—and many other details—will not be fully treated in this work; my aim here is to highlight the essential structure, to show its soundness, and to compare it with other similarly drawn models. I don't think anything vital has been omitted. Details like land usage, personal saving and borrowing, public services will be left—to employ the language of the economics texts—as "exercises for the reader."

The third fundamental feature of our worker-control socialism is a feature not found at all in the Yugoslavian system—governmental control of investment.[16] It is a crucial feature. Worker self-management is aimed at breaking the commodity character of labor-power and the attendant alienation. The market is a check to overcentralization and bureaucracy. Government control of new investment is the counterfoil to the market, designed to alleviate the "anarchy" of the market. Under capitalism the market serves to allocate existing goods and resources, and to determine the course and rate of future development. In our model these two conceptually distinct features are radically separated. There is no "money market" bringing together savers and investors who interact to determine the interest rate. (Yugoslavia's failure to recognize this distinction, its over-reliance on the market, accounts, in my judgment, for a great portion of its current difficulties. Why this is so will become clearer when we compare our model with laissez-faire.)

In our model, investment funds are generated and dispensed by the government. They are generated, not by offering the enticement of interest to savers, but by taxing capital assets. These taxes serve two important functions. They encourage the efficient usage of scarce capital goods (since enterprises must pay taxes on their capital assets, they will want to economize on their use). The taxes also generate the

---

*This provision would, of course, force incomes toward equality in a declining business. A weaker provision, which would allow some incentives to remain, would set limits on the degree of inequality permitted in a declining firm—say, top shares cannot be greater than twice bottom shares.

funds for new investment. This "capital tax" is the surrogate of interest" in a capitalist economy, which serves the same double function.
(In fact, since taxation is the source of investment funds, there is no
reason at all to pay individuals interest on their personal savings- nor,
for that matter, is there a need to charge interest on personal loans.
The medieval proscription on "usury" returns under worker-control
socialism.)*

Investment funds are generated by taxation. How are they to be
dispensed? Though our society is democratic, it would not be at all
wise to attempt a popular vote on each investment project. The sheer
number of projects would render such a proposal unworkable; moreover, such a procedure would negate a major benefit of socialized investment: the conscious adoption of a coordinated, coherent investment
plan.

To dispense investment funds, investment boards and investment
banks are needed. Investment boards draw up the general plans; investment banks evaluate incoming proposals and dispense allocated
funds. A national investment board—a governmental body appointed by
the elected administration—begins by drawing up a general plan for the
distribution of the investment funds. It indicates general priorities:
"A" percent of the fund should go to developing new energy sources,
"B" percent to new housing, "C" percent to expanding the production of
consumer goods. It also decides that "X" percent of the total fund should
be given to community investment banks, "Y" percent to regional investment banks, and "Z" percent reserved for the national investment bank,
for projects of national scope. The general plan is then submitted to
the legislative body. Hearings are held. Individuals or groups who
oppose certain projects or priorities are provided a forum to state
their cases. The legislature then accepts the plan or sends it back
for revision. (Notice—this is not a plan for the whole economy; it is
a plan for the new investments to be undertaken. Individual firms

---

*For the medievals "usury" was synonymous with charging inter-
est (not just exorbitant interest). The proscription goes back at least
to Aristotle: "The most hated sort of wealth getting and with greatest
reason, is usury, which makes a gain out of money itself and not from
the natural object of it. For money was intended to be used in exchange,
but not to increase at interest." (Politics 1258 b 2-5.) Worker-control
socialism would agree. Banks may keep an individual's savings safe—
for a service charge perhaps—and may make personal loans, but with
saving separated from investment, there is no need for interest.
(Again there are details here that I must pass over.)

already operating are unaffected by the plan unless they want to make changes in their operations that cannot be financed from their depreciation funds.* Though a substantial amount of funds is involved, it constitutes but a fraction of the total economic activity of the nation. In 1977, for example, net investment in the United States was $102.6 billion out of a Gross National Product of $1887.2 billion. That is less than 6 percent. Total government expenditures during 1977 were $689.2 billion; total depreciation was $195.2 billion.)[17]

Once a national plan is adopted, regions and communities draw up their own plans (consistent with the national plan), which set the priorities for the investment banks under their jurisdiction. These plans are constructed by the regional and local planning boards, and each must be approved by an elected assembly. The procedure is the same as for the national plan.

People now come forward– individuals, collectives, representatives of existing firms– who want a share of the funds. They present specific proposals (as they would if applying to a capitalist financial institution) in which they argue for the economic feasibility of their projects, and explain the function of their projects in the overall plan. The investment banks evaluate these proposals and distribute funds to those that are most promising. No interest is charged on the grant, though the recipients must pay taxes on the social capital now under their control. (Economically, this is a distinction without a difference, but the sociopsychological associations are not the same.) Individuals are under no obligation to repay the grant, though they may not, as noted earlier, squander the funds on personal consumption. In addition to this initiative from the "private" sector, governmental agencies also request funds to initiate projects mandated by (or simply in accord with) the investment plan for the region. They may undertake to have construction firms build new factories, and to recruit management teams and workforces to run them. (All such facilities, of course, are turned over to their workers when they become operational.)

---

*In this model I have distinguished depreciation funds, which are controlled by the enterprises, from new investment, which is controlled by the government. This feature is a somewhat arbitrary way of giving firms some autonomous control over their investment policy. It may in fact be too much control. Vanek, for one, urges that all depreciation funds be incorporated into the investment fund. Though this makes sense from the point of view of Pareto-optimality, I'm inclined to favor more enterprise autonomy than that requirement would permit. (Cf. Vanek, The Labor-Managed Economy, p. 60.)

Thus our society provides for, and indeed requires, a number of "socialist entrepreneurs," individuals or collectives willing to innovate, to take risks, in hopes of providing new goods or services or old ones in new ways. Their role, however, differs from that of their capitalist counterparts in significant ways. The risks, for example, are quite different. A capitalist entrepreneur risks a portion of the social surplus when he undertakes a new venture, as does the socialist entrepreneur, but the former, unlike the latter, loses a portion of his personal wealth if the project fails. On the other hand, the socialist entrepreneur risks her prestige, self-esteem, her job (if she is employed by the government), her anticipated income and the incomes of the others who have joined in the venture (if she is not). Failure, for either a capitalist or socialist entrepreneur, would make future financing difficult to obtain.

Why would a socialist undertake entrepreneurial risks at all? Unlike her capitalist counterpart, she has no chance of reaping truly spectacular gains; if the project is successful, all who participate will share in the benefits. Her motivations are likely to be various: the appeal of seeing her "great idea" materialize, of providing a desirable good or service now nonexistent or in short supply. If she is a "private" entrepreneur, she may hope for better employment for herself and her comrades; if she is a "governmental entrepreneur," her reward lies in a promotion or bonus and in her satisfaction with a job well done. Society can make additional provisions to stimulate entrepreneurial activity is stimulation seems necessary. Special schools or university programs can be set up to develop the necessary skills; prizes for successful ventures can be awarded by the community. What cannot be permitted, however, is to allow the entrepreneur to acquire a share in a company that would reward her permanently, quite apart from her employment there. There can be no "perpetual rewards" under socialism.

We now have before us the bare bones of the worker-control model. We are in position to consider the dynamics of the system, and to compare it with a different, also simplified model, that of competitive laissez-faire. A system which features private property, a totally free market and labor as a commodity will be compared with a system based on worker control, a somewhat restricted market and socialized investment. Now the argument begins in earnest.

NOTES

1. Cf., for example, F. A. Hayek's postscript to The Constitution of Liberty (London: Routledge and Kegan Paul, 1960) or Milton Friedman's introduction to Capitalism and Freedom (Chicago: Univer-

sity of Chicago Press, 1962).

2. Cf. Friedrich Hayek, The Road to Serfdom (Chicago: University of Chicago Press, 1944), pp. 36-39, for a discussion by a classical liberal of his distance from "dogmatic" laissez-faire.

3. Robert Nozick, Anarchy, State and Utopia (New York: Basic Books, 1974), p. ix.

4. Paul Samuelson, Economics, 9th ed. (New York: McGraw-Hill, 1973), p. 848. Given the context of the quote, one should not infer that Samuelson and other Keynesian liberals support all of the mentioned issues, though they do support most of them. Nor should one presume that all classical liberals share all of Friedman's views.

5. Cf. Ronald Dworkin, "Liberalism," in Public and Private Morality, ed. Stuart Hampshire (Cambridge: Cambridge University Press, 1978), pp. 113-43.

6. See John Maynard Keynes, The General Theory of Employment, Interest and Money (New York: Harcourt, Brace and World, 1936), p. 378.

7. Adam Smith, An Inquiry into the Nature and Causes of the Wealth of Nations (New York: Modern Library, 1937), p. 423.

8. Cf. Amartya K. Sen, On Economic Inequality (Oxford: Clarendon Press, 1973), pp. 1-23, for a good discussion of Pareto-optimality and its relation to utilitarianism and to welfare economics.

9. For a highly sophisticated mathematical treatment, see Gerald Debreau, Theory of Value: An Axiomatic Analysis of Economic Equilibrium (New Haven: Yale University Press, 1959). A more familiar version of the standard neoclassical argument can be found in Abba Lerner, The Economics of Control (New York: Macmillian, 1944), Chapters Two, Five and Six.

10. Karl Marx and Frederick Engels, Communist Manifesto (New York: International Publishers, 1948), pp. 13-14. Marx and Engels criticize bourgeois society, not for its lack of productivity, but for its being based on structures "too narrow to comprise the wealth created . . ." Ibid., p. 34.

11. Roy Harrod's "An Essay in Dynamic Theory," Economic Journal, 49 (1939): 14-33 provided the initial stimulus, though growth theory did not really revive until after the war. See the editor's introduction to Growth Economics, ed. Amartya K. Sen (Baltimore: Penguin Education, 1970) for a lucid sketch of modern developments.

12. Branko Horvat, The Yugoslav Economic System: The First Labor-Managed Economy in the Making (White Plains, N.Y.: International Arts and Sciences Press, 1976), p. 3.

13. Ibid., p. 12. Needless to say, growth statistics are not unproblematic. Still, no one denies that Yugoslavia grew rapidly.

14. Theoretical models of worker-control have not been widely discussed in the economic literature. The first formal model was

Benjamin Ward's, presented in his 1958 article, "Market Syndicalism," American Economic Review, 48: 566-89. This model, slightly revised and greatly expanded, is one of three basic models discussed in Benjamin Ward, The Socialist Economy: A Study of Organizational Alternatives (New York: Random House, 1967). The second important paper on the subject was Evesy Domar, "The Soviet Collective Farm as a Producer Cooperative," American Economic Review, 56 (1966): 734-57. Today Jaroslav Vanek reigns as the chief American theoretician of worker-control socialism. His General Theory of Labor-Managed Market Economies (Ithaca: Cornell University Press, 1970) is an extensive technical analysis of a worker-control model in terms of the standard neoclassical categories. A less technical treatment can be found in his companion piece, The Participatory Economy (Ithaca: Cornell University Press, 1971). Vanek has also edited a useful reader, Self-Management: Economic Liberation of Man (Baltimore: Penguin Education, 1975), and has compiled a collection of his recent articles, The Labor-Managed Economy (Ithaca: Cornell University Press, 1977).

My treatment of worker-control will be less technical than that of the economists. I will avoid the neoclassical categories, and give a straightforward analysis. I will make fewer simplifications than Vanek, Domar and Ward, for I am not aiming at mathematical theorems.

15. R. W. Davies, "Planning a Mature Economy in the U.S.S.R.," Economics of Planning, 6 (1966): 147. Cited by Charles Lindblom, Politics and Markets (New York: Basic Books, 1978), p. 71.

16. See Horvat, Yugoslav Economic System, pp. 218 ff., for an account of the various investment policies attempted in Yugoslavia over the years. In the early phase of its transition to a full market economy, the Yugoslavian government did control investments, but this policy was abandoned, along with other forms of governmental control, in a climate of general opposition to all forms of governmental interference. Now, "in many important respects . . . Yugoslavia bears more resemblance to the type of liberal market economy envisaged by Adam Smith than is the case in any country in western Europe." David Granick, Enterprise Guidance in Eastern Europe, (Princeton: Princeton University Press, 1975), p. 25.

17. U.S. Department of Commerce, Survey of Current Business (January 1979): 14-15.

3

CAPITALISM OR SOCIALISM: EFFICIENCY

In a sense, the efficiency question is the first question for all societies. Unless a society is reasonably efficient in marshalling its resources, it cannot expect a blossoming of innovative growth. And of course liberty is a hollow concept to a starving population. As Brecht would have it, "Grub first, and then morality."[1]

Economists are inclined to treat economic efficiency as an ethically neutral concept, but of course it is not. Economic efficiency is as much a value as liberty or equality. To be sure, the word "efficiency" can be taken in a strictly instrumental sense to mean "productive of a desired effect." But economic efficiency means more than that. In ordinary usage, the effect is presumed to be material goods and services, and its accomplishment is presumed to be with minimal expenditure of labor and resources. Thus embedded in a commitment to economic efficiency are numerous value judgments: that material "goods" are indeed good, that scarce resources ought not be wasted (and implicit in this, that the future ought not be sacrificed to the present), that leisure is a good, and that it is better to labor less than more. Each of these judgments would have to be qualified to be non-problematic- e.g., not all material goods are good, some labor is intrinsically satisfying, etc. Nor would any of them likely be regarded as absolute, no more than the economic efficiency itself. Nonetheless, a commitment to economic efficiency is a commitment to certain values; it is by no means ethically neutral.

Mainstream economists might well object that the notion of efficiency sanctioned by the profession is not that of ordinary usage. Their notion, we have already noted, is that of Pareto-optimality: a state of affairs is economically efficient if no movement from that state is possible which would make some people better off and no one worse off. But even this notion of efficiency embodies a major value judgment, namely, that the welfare of each individual is significant. If one were unconcerned about the welfare of a certain segment of the population, one would have little interest in the society's being Pareto-optimal. So what if some are made worse off, so long as those who count are made better off?

This technical notion of efficiency, as commonly employed, embodies an additional value judgment. When one attempts to apply the Pareto principle, the question immediately arises concerning the criteria for individual welfare. Who determines when an individual is better off than before? The profession is nearly unanimous: the individual himself. A situation is Pareto-optimal when no one can be made better off in terms of his own preferences without making another worse off. Thus the judgment is made—if one is committed to Pareto-optimality—that individuals ought to decide their own welfare. This, of course, is a highly significant value judgment.

Before we proceed further some remarks are in order about values in general, and also about the basic ethical framework which will undergird my analysis. The arguments soon to be considered are essentially moral arguments. To choose between capitalism and socialism is to make a moral choice. This is not to say that considerations of practicality, economic efficiency and the like are irrelevant. Far from it. But any argument at whatever level of concreteness or abstractness which purports to demonstrate that one set of institutions is better than another appeals implicitly or explicitly to values. It aims to influence feelings or behavior by appealing to something presumed to be good, be it liberty, equality, economic efficiency or whatever. Thus it situates itself, consciously or not, within a moral framework.

Fortunately, there is no need to specify a full-blown ethical theory before debating moral questions. There is no one theory currently hegemonic in Western culture, and so to do so would be restrictive in view of the fact there is widespread agreement concerning the basic values that an acceptable theory must explain. Philosophers disagree as to the nature of moral utterances, the source of moral values, and the structure of value hierarchies, but few would countenance torture, despotism or grinding poverty as good. Virtually all would assign a positive value to material well-being, to liberty, to democracy, to happiness.

Though many values are relatively non-controversial, it is useful in a work such as this to lay out clearly the specific values to which our arguments will appeal. For one thing, though there is much agreement concerning the values we will specify, agreement is not universal. (Equality, in particular, is problematic, as we shall see below.) More importantly, I wish to make it clear that the case for worker control does not rest on esoteric values alien to our culture. What I intend to show is that anyone who shares a certain set of rather noncontroversial values ought to prefer worker-control socialism to any capitalist alternative.

One further clarification, to head off misunderstandings. When I specify a particular value as good, say material well-being, I am not claiming it to be an absolute value that can never be sacrificed. I am simply saying that a social structure that exemplifies this value has a prima facie claim to our allegiance. If the structure does not conflict with any of the other values we deem good, it requires no further justification. A structure that deviates from that value, on the other hand, does require justification, justification in terms of other values to which we adhere. To say, for example, that material well-being is good is not to imply that the government should guarantee everyone a comfortable living. It might be the case that such a governmental program would conflict with other values we hold—economic efficiency, perhaps, or liberty. To maintain that material well-being for everyone is good is to hold a much more modest proposition: if one social structure provides a decent living for everyone and another does not, and if the first structure does not sacrifice any other of our values, then the first society is morally preferable to the second. In other words, the value commitments upon which this work is based are "weak." One need not have an absolute commitment to any of the values to which the arguments appeal to find the arguments acceptable.

Let us return to our discussion of specific values. I have already argued that economic efficiency both in its ordinary and technical sense is not a value-neutral concept; it presupposes certain value-commitments. We need not pursue this analysis further, because there is nothing objectionable about these commitments, not so long as they are understood in the weak sense just described. We can all (surely) accept material well-being as good, leisure as good; we can agree that a society should not squander scarce resources, nor require people to perform unnecessary labor. It cannot be too controversial that in general the economic output of the productive apparatus of society should reflect the desires of its citizens. And if no one would be made worse off by a shift from A to B and some people better off, then—again in general—no further justification for the shift is necessary.

Commitment to the ordinary sense of economic efficiency implies that one values material well-being, and commitment to the Pareto-optimality notion of efficiency implies that one regards the preferences of each individual as significant. Such commitments are closely linked to an even deeper value—the happiness of each individual. Indeed, there cannot be too many people today (excepting those spellbound by the darker side of Nietzsche) who do not see human happiness as good. Of course, one can go further; one can declare that human happiness is the sole or ultimate value, and that everyone's happiness counts equally. In this case, one is a utilitarian; one regards an action or institution as moral if and only if it promotes the greatest happiness for the greatest number. This position is more controversial.

Now I must confess to being drawn toward utilitarianism, particularly as applied to social structures. If one set of institutions makes more people happier than another, then there is considerable intuitive appeal to the claim that the former set ought to be instituted instead of the latter. But philosophers are fond of counterexamples. What if the first set included a benevolent dictator, or LSD Kool-Aid for the masses? What if it involved the torturing of a minority for the gratification of the majority?[2] To avoid such problems, I will simply add the utilitarian commitment to our list of prima facie goods. If one set of institutions makes more people happier than the alternatives, and if it doesn't conflict with our other values, then we will consider it the morally preferable set.

There is one final value that needs to be discussed in conjunction with efficiency, a value that is considerably more controversial than either material well-being or happiness. It is the basic value about which classical liberals and modern liberals have such conflicting intuitions, namely, equality. Modern liberals virtually without exception regard equality as good. Most hold that the existing inequalities in Western capitalist countries are greater than they should be. All assume that inequalities of wealth and power require justification. (Need, merit, contribution and effort are commonly given grounds.[3] Modern liberals of a utilitarian bent require that inequalities promote the greatest happiness for the greatest number. Rawls is even more stringent: inequalities are justified only if they can "reasonably be expected to work to everyone's advantage."[4])

Classical liberals, on the other hand, are often skeptical that equality has even prima facie worth. Nozick writes: "The entitlement conception of justice in holdings makes no presumption in favor of equality, or any other overall end state or patterning. It cannot be merely assumed that equality must be built into a theory of justice."[5] Nozick laments the general presumption among political philosophers in favor of equality, and claims that no adequate argument has been advanced in support of this presumption.[6]

We are at an impasse of sorts. I want to list equality among the values to which our arguments can appeal, and yet I do not want the classical liberal to stop reading. Let me offer a consideration that might bring about, at least temporarily, a resolution.

It should be noted that we are considering equality here in the context of the efficiency question. By that I mean, we want to investigate the role of inequality in promoting, inhibiting or distorting the production of material goods. We are interested in inequality as incentive. We are not concerned here with the relationship between equality and such noneconomic values as liberty, democracy or autonomy. These questions will be considered in a later chapter. But if one examines the writings of prominent classical liberals, one finds that objections to equality (when not the purely formal objection that equality has not been proven good) are inevitably grounded in appeals to such noneconomic values. Hayek, for example, states:

> Whenever there is a legitimate need for governmental action and we have to choose between different methods of satisfying such a need, those that incidentally also reduce inequality may well be preferable. If, for example, in the law of intestate succession one kind of provision will be more conducive to equality than another, this may be a strong argument in its favor. It is a different matter, however, if it is demanded that, in order to produce substantive equality, we should abandon the basic postulates of a free society. . . . [7]

And Nozick:

> The major objection to speaking of everyone's having a right to various things such as equality of opportunity, life and so on, and enforcing this right, is that these "rights" require a substructure of things and materials and actions, and other people may have rights and entitlements over these. [8]

In other words, classical liberals do not so much object to equality on principle as out of a conviction that governmental measures to promote equality generally infringe on other basic values. Let us suppose for the present that these other values are not infringed upon. Let us leave such questions for later consideration. It seems, then, that even a classical liberal should be willing to grant that if two alternative structures will yield comparable economic results, and if other noneconomic values are not jeopardized, then the more equal society is the preferable one. Assent to this hypothetical proposition is all we require for the arguments in this chapter. *

Let me recapitulate briefly and draw the various threads together. The basic question to be dealt with in this chapter is the efficiency of laissez-faire capitalism as compared to worker-control socialism. Efficiency, I have noted, is a value that presupposes other values, values that vary depending on how the concept is understood. Here we will understand the efficiency question in a broader sense than economists tend to understand it, though their considerations form a part of our own. Specifically, the question will be posed as follows: given a fixed technology and known resources, which society is more likely to yield for its members the greater material happiness, where "material happiness" is the balance of consumption-satisfaction over costs, and costs comprise human labor, scarce resources and inequality.

We restrict our attention to a fixed technology and known resources in order to separate the efficiency issue from questions of innovation and growth. We focus on material satisfactions and costs to defer until later a consideration of noneconomic costs and benefits. Our formulation lacks the precision usually found in welfare economics† and is more explicitly value-laden, but this formulation is clear enough for our purposes and leads quickly to the substantive issues. Welfare economists might wince at my suggesting that satisfactions are comparable and even somewhat quantifiable, [9] and at my counting

---

*I do not mean to suggest that worthy arguments cannot be advanced in support of equality, but this is an issue our basic argument can sidestep. Personally, I believe the egalitarian dimension of my model to be quite important, because I believe that the inequalities of capitalist society have ferociously destructive consequences. If one prefers more abstract arguments for equality, there are many from which to sample. A classic version of the utilitarian argument for equality is given by Abba Lerner, The Economics of Control (New York: Macmillan, 1944) Chapter 3. A more recent, often cited essay is Bernard Williams, "The Idea of Equality," in Philosophy, Politics and Society, ed. P. Laslett and W. C. Runciman (London: Blackwell, 1962), pp. 110-31. I'd also recommend Steven Lukes, "Socialism and Equality," in Inequality, Conflict and Change, ed. A. Blowers and T. Grahame (Milton Keynes, Eng.: The Open University Press, 1976), pp. 64-84.

†"Welfare economics" is that branch of the discipline which considers, usually in a highly theoretical manner, the conditions of opti-

inequality as an efficiency cost, but such notions are most helpful in getting at the major issues of the capitalism-socialism controversy.

THE EFFICIENCY STRENGTHS OF LAISSEZ-FAIRE

In Chapter 2 I described the perfect-competition model and the associated efficiency theorem: under appropriate conditions, a perfectly-competitive, laissez-faire economy that is in equilibrium is in a state of Pareto-optimality. We observed that this theorem is not devoid of content. Its significance, however, is a matter of controversy.

Let me take a stand on the controversy. It is my judgment that the efficiency theorem is at best irrelevant to the capitalism-socialism debate; if anything, it obscures and obstructs a comprehension of the real issues. It is irrelevant for the reason most critics cite. The assumptions necessary to prove Pareto-optimality do not correlate with reality.

The most basic assumption is perfect competition itself, the case in which all are "price-takers," none are "price-makers." As Scitovsky notes, it is difficult to visualize such a situation:

> Many people in our economy regard price as given to them, but they do so, in most instances, because the price is set, either by the other party or by a third person. The difficulty lies in visualizing a price that everybody on both sides of the market regards as given, and that is determined by the "impersonal forces of the market."[10]

Scitovsky lists four conditions that must be satisfied for perfect competition to obtain:

> a) customers of the seller must be able to withdraw their custom from him without inconvenience to themselves;

---

mal social welfare. The key concept is the Pareto principle; a basic analytical tool is the social welfare function introduced by Abram Bergson in his article, "A Reformulation of Certain Aspects of Welfare Economics," Quarterly Journal of Economics, 52 (1938): 310-34 For a sampling of this material, see Economic Justice: Selected Readings, ed. E. S. Phelps (Baltimore: Penguin Education, 1973).

b) each seller's sales must be small compared to the market's total turnover;

c) all the buyers must be experts, in the strictest sense of the term, in the appraisal of the goods they buy;

d) all the buyers must know about the existence of alternative offers and all of them should be prepared to shift all their custom in response to even the smallest change in price. [11]

Obviously, these conditions hold in few if any real-world markets. More important for our argument, they could not be expected to hold for any plausible reform of capitalism. And these conditions merely establish perfect competition. Many more assumptions must be made for the efficiency theorem to follow. The economy must be in equilibrium– an assumption that abstracts from two of capitalism's most characteristic features, its continuous development and its cyclical fluctuations. Firms in the economy must be presumed to face rising marginal costs, this assumption in the face of "the belief generally held by businessmen in competitive industries that they are operating under decreasing cost conditions, that is, that they could lower per-unit costs if only they could sell a larger output." [12]

The list goes on, but I've carried it far enough. Scitovsky's Welfare and Competition, a work solidly within the neoclassical tradition, scrupulously details a great many more. Post-Keynesian critics have almost limitless lists of their own. [13]

One might well wonder at this point why there is even a controversy. Why are economists interested at all in a model with such counterfactual presuppositions? An adequate answer would require a long digression, but four factors are worth mentioning. One is ideological: it is reassuring to supporters that at least some form of capitalism is optimally efficient. Another involves professional virtuosity: to formulate a model and prove interesting theorems about it involves considerable ingenuity, and mathematical sophistication. A third factor relates to the profession's positivism: it matters not what the assumptions are, so long as the conclusions are useful in making correct predictions. [14] The fourth is the "Platonic" consideration: it is important to have an ideal standard against which to measure deviations.

Only these latter two reasons need concern us, and they need not concern us much. The positivist rationale is irrelevant to the specific question we are addressing, since the perfect-competition theorem makes no falsifiable predictions whatsoever. [15] The Platonic reason is more serious, but I find it unconvincing. It is by no means clear that the insights into the real efficiency problems suggested by the neoclassical apparatus are not as easily obtained by less "rigorous" means though they might seem less impressive divested of their undeniably elegant mathematical garb. * In any event, the entire neoclassical structure is under such heavy attack these days by Marxists and neo-Ricardians (to say nothing of the post-Keynesians) that it is not prudent to lean too heavily upon it. 16

All this is not to say that the efficiency claims of laissez-faire are a hoax. The perfect-competition theorem may not be cited as evidence for the defense, but perhaps other arguments, resting on more realistic assumptions, can be marshalled. This we must consider.

Notice, we ought not assume too hastily that monopoly is the chief culprit in undermining efficiency. This is a tempting view. We know that under suitable conditions a perfectly competitive economy is Pareto-optimal, and we also know that monopoly negates the perfect-competition condition. It is tempting to think that a successful attack on monopolies– vigorous anti-trust action, and a repeal of special privileges for labor unions– would resolve the difficulties. This, of course, is the essence of the classical liberal position—but this conclusion does not follow from the neoclassical analysis we have examined. For there are more conditions than mere perfect competition to be satisfied to guarantee Pareto-optimality– and Pareto-optimality is but one aspect of economic efficiency. Monopoly may be far from the most serious problem. (On the other hand, it is also fallacious to conclude from the implausibility of the assumptions underlying the perfect-competition theorem that the laissez-faire ideal is invalid. It may or may not be. The invalidity of the laissez-faire ideal will be established only when we demonstrate that a more efficient alternative exists which has no other overriding defects.)

Let us leave the fantasy realm of perfect competition, and consider a more plausible laissez-faire ideal. Perhaps monopoly is the

---

*It is noteworthy that Tibor Scitovsky, himself one of the foremost practitioners of the neoclassical game and a former proponent of the Platonic rationale, has abandoned this framework in his more recent work. The Joyless Economy (Oxford: Oxford University Press, 1976). I shall do the same. The arguments I make will not be couched in neoclassical terminology. As a result, some of my analysis will seem overly labored to a neoclassical economist, but I am convinced that it pays to try to see things without the neoclassical spectacles-which are sometimes helpful, but more often distorting.

problem. To judge, let's rule it out. Let us consider a capitalist
system free of governmental interference and also free of monopolies.
Workers do not threaten the collective withdrawal of labor and do not
conspire to set prices or to keep new firms from entering their fields.
If necessary, the government will intervene to enforce these conditions;
we will assume that this can be done without aggravating the condition
it is trying to remedy.*

What are the strengths of this system (the true classical-liberal
ideal) with respect to the question of economic efficiency? Three aspects would seem to be the most significant. This sort of laissez-
faire possesses (a) an effective mechanism for determining and re-
sponding to consumer preferences, (b) powerful incentives for using
appropriate technology and for minimizing material waste, and (c) an
effective mechanism for allocating labor. None of these strengths is
unconditional, but all are important.

The mechanism associated with (a) is the price mechanism.
Goods and services are bought and sold. The only alternative, under
conditions of scarcity, is physical rationing. Coupons must be issued
(or some analogous device employed) that entitle their bearers to
specific quantities of specific items. Now, one might imagine such
rationing for certain basic goods- loaves of bread or gallons of gasoline—but it is staggering to contemplate rationing all the items in an
advanced industrial society. An enormous bureaucracy would be a
necessity, serious problems of inequities would have to be dealt with-
and most serious of all, those assigning goods would have no effective
means of gauging consumer preferences. Imagine for a moment filling
out a questionnaire in which you specify how many items of each available consumer good you would like during the next month or quarter or
year, and what the strengths are of your relative preferences. (This
latter condition is necessary, since planners must set priorities.) How
many rolls of cellophane tape, and of what width will you need. and how

---

*Classical liberals tend to be ambivalent about monopolies. All
see their existence as economically undesirable, but they are uneasy
about allowing the government to intervene. (Cf. Milton Friedman,
Capitalism and Freedom [Chicago: University of Chicago Press, 1962]
pp. 119 ff. or Hayek, Constitution of Liberty, pp. 264-84. Their am-
bivalence vanishes where labor unions are concerned; these must be
curbed.) We will assume away classical liberal anxieties by assuming
that monopolies can be prevented without adverse consequences to
freedom.

important are they compared to the number of vacuum cleaner bags? When the economy can produce a great variety of items, and yet not everything everyone wants, and when desires fluctuate, then there is no feasible alternative to pricing.

In allowing people to purchase items as they please, quantities desired and relative preferences are automatically registered, and producers are provided with precise quantitative information as to what is profitable to produce. If, in addition, prices are allowed to move freely in response to market conditions, producers, given their desire for profit, will adjust production in accordance with consumer preferences. The alternative to market pricing is governmental price control, but the case for price control—under nonmonopolistic conditions (an important qualification)- is slight. Holding down prices will simply cause supplies to contract unless subsidies are supplied to producers, a desirable procedure only in exceptional circumstances

Notice, the case for market pricing does not rest on the assumption that producers raise prices when demand goes up (which they generally do) or cut them when demand declines (which they often do not). This assumption, especially the latter half, is too simple When business declines, producers often take a chance, raising prices, hoping that the per-item revenue increase will offset the decline in volume. [17] Price raising must be done cautiously, however, since higher profits attract competitors, so there is a definite check—in a competitive economy—on corporate greed. Moreover, and this is the important point, production (if not prices) moves in the desired direction. Production goes up when demand goes up, and falls when demand falls.

The major objection to allocating goods via free-market prices is the correct observation that the preferences registered are exclusively dollar-backed preferences. The market is a form of democracy in which a mandate is sent to producers, but it is a mandate based, not on one-person one-vote, but on one-dollar one-vote. The more dollars, the more votes. No dollars, no votes. This is undeniably true—but the force of this objection derives from the sense that these dollar votes are unfairly distributed. This very important issue will be investigated later in this chapter, but for now, let us assume that the distribution of wealth and income is fair. In this case, the efficiency of the price mechanism has much to recommend it, and its alternatives very little.

The second strength of laissez-faire concerns technology and material resources. Since firms aim to make a profit, and since profit is the difference between gross revenue and costs, powerful incentives exist to utilize resources and technology effectively. Both the positive attraction of personal gain and the negative fear of competitive loss are ever-present. A firm cannot afford material waste or obsolete technology.

If profit is not the goal of a productive organization, then physical output must be- and here the familiar problems surface. Even if the quotas accurately reflect consumer preferences, a firm has insufficient information to select its technology and input resources properly. To produce fine pogo sticks, one would like to use the finest technology— even though these high-quality machine tools embody much valuable labor and material that might be needed elsewhere. And how does a producer decide between steel, aluminum or copper for the handles, and wouldn't silver inlay be nice? Unless a firm strives to find the right compromise between quality and cost— and to do so, both know-ledge of costs and incentives to minimize them are needed—the re-sources of society will not be efficiently allocated. Granted, there can be abuses- shoddy merchandise deceptively marketed—but the physical planning alternative is not attractive.

The third major strength of laissez-faire is the one that re-quires the most qualification- the allocation of labor. Workers are free to seek work where they will and to negotiate the highest price they can for their services. Thus the worker has an incentive to de-velop her useful skills, and the employer has an incentive to employ those skills as effectively as possible. (The employer is encouraged to other, less desirable behavior as well, but this will be considered later.) Moreover, when demand for a product rises, the producer is motivated to expand production, and since this generally requires more labor, he attracts workers to his firm, thus effecting a labor shift commensurate with consumer preferences.

The alternative to free labor mobility is assigned labor; the alternative to unregulated wages is wage regulation. Both alternatives have their drawbacks, overcentralization being the foremost (leaving aside the noneconomic issue of freedom). Planners must decide how many people of what capabilities must be employed where. They must decide what skills to encourage (through differential wages or other means) and which to deemphasize. As always with a centralized alter-native, the problems of bureaucratic inefficiency loom large: how to collect the requisite information, how to motivate socially useful behavior, how to mediate the conflicting claims of talent, effort and need.

(It would appear that centralization of labor allocation is less problematic than centralization of either consumer-goods allocation or resources and technology. It is less complicated to decide how many machinists a society needs than how many machine screws of various styles or how many specialized machines of which type to produce them, since human beings are so much more adaptable. A lathe operator can learn to operate a drill press with little difficulty, but a nut must match a bolt precisely. Nevertheless, free movement of laborers must surely be less cumbersome—and more preferable as well on noneconomic grounds.)

We have discussed the strengths of laissez-faire: its efficiency in allocating consumer goods, resources and technology, and labor. There are also weaknesses of major proportions. But before examining them, we need to shift our attention to our competing model, for if it proves to be hopelessly inefficient, our argument need go no further.

HOW EFFICIENT IS WORKER CONTROL?

In 1920 Ludwig von Mises fired the opening salvo in what was to become a several-decade academic skirmish. Socialism, von Mises declared, is impossible: without private ownership of the means of production, there cannot be a competitive market for production goods;* without a market for production goods, it is impossible to determine their values; without these values, economic rationality is impossible.

> Hence in a socialist state wherein the pursuit of economic calculation is impossible, there can be—in our sense of the term—no economy whatsoever. In trivial and secondary matters rational conduct might still be possible, but in general it would be impossible to speak of rational production anymore. [18]

We can now see that von Mises's argument is defective on a number of counts. As our model (and Yugoslavian reality) demonstrates, private ownership of the means of production is not necessary for a competitive market in production goods. Nor is it true that without such a market, their monetary values could not be determined. (This was the main issue over which the inter-war controversy was fought.) In response to von Mises a number of economists pointed out that Pareto's disciple, Enrico Barone, had already demonstrated the

---

*By "production goods" von Mises means goods produced to serve as further means of production. He allows that a socialist society might utilize a market to allocate consumer goods.

theoretical possibility of a "market-simulated" socialism in a 1907 article. How such a solution could be approximated in practice was then much debated.[19] Though von Mises remained unrepentant to the end, it is now generally accepted that his argument miscarried.[20]

And of course we can now see that even without a competitive market for production goods or any reliance on market simulation, an industrial economy is certainly possible. As a recent textbook on the subject observes:

> The Soviet command economy has failed to succumb to alleged internal contradictions after more than half a century of operation, though at one time some prominent Western economists saw such a result as inevitable. . . . The long run ability of the Soviet system to function without private ownership of the factors of production and without profit motivation can no longer be seriously questioned. The Soviet Union has established itself as the world's second largest economic power . . . and it would now be foolish to question its economic viability.[21]

But to say that a socialist economy- indeed a variety of socialist economies—are viable is not to say they are optimal, not even from a strictly economic point of view. Socialist economies work, but how well do they work? I have already called attention to structural inefficiencies of centralized, nonmarket economies. (The Soviet Union is such an economy.) We must now ask about my own model—decentralized, market socialism with worker self-management of production units.

It should come as no surprise that our model shares some of laissez-faire's efficiency strengths, for worker-control socialism is also a market economy with profit maximization- but the attentive reader may have noted some difficulties. "Profit" under worker control is something different from profit under capitalism, since labor counts as a cost under the latter, but not under the former. This is a crucial difference, and has significant efficiency consequences. *

---

*Theorems can be proven for stylized versions of worker control, using the standard neoclassical categories, just as they can for capitalist models. Jaroslav Vanek, The General Theory of Labor-Managed Market Economies (Ithaca: Cornell University Press, 1970) provides a detailed analysis. Though Vanek is sensitive to the lack of

By far the most important consequence is that worker-managed firms, unlike their capitalist counterparts, have little tendency to expand. They are not inclined to grow under conditions of constant returns to scale; they do not expand production automatically in response to an increase in demand.

The reason for this is straightforward. When costs-per-item are constant, a capitalist enterprise can increase its net profit by enlarging the scale of its operation, and this increase accrues to the owner of the enterprise. If a hamburger stand employing twenty people nets $20,000, a second stand doing similar business will net another $20,000. So the owner has an almost irresistable incentive to expand. Under worker control, by contrast, doubling the size of the enterprise may double the net profit, but is also doubles the number of workers who share those profits. Two hamburger stands run by forty people would generate precisely the same per-worker income as one stand run by twenty. Thus, the first stand, even if successful, has no incentive to open up another- or even to take on more workers—unless increasing returns to scale make a larger operation more efficient.

The consequences of this structural difference are many and significant. Benjamin Ward has suggested that they might be extremely perverse. He has argued that a worker-managed firm might even contract its supply and employment in response to an increase in demand, on the grounds (technically demonstrated) that per-worker income would thus be maximized.[22] Vanek and others have disputed this result. In Vanek's words,

> How can one reasonably expect that a working collective
> will mutilate itself (discharging, say, one-tenth of its
> membership), if it has already realized a significant
> gain from a price increase, say 10 percent of income,
> for the sake of gaining an extra, say, one percent?
> Indeed, this sounds like an extract from a book of
> rules of capitalist conduct.[23]

---

realism of various neoclassical assumptions, and has penetrating things to say about the real problems of worker control, I find myself as skeptical of the value of his formal analysis as I am about such analyses of capitalism. I won't appeal to such results in what follows, though I note for the record that with suitable assumptions Pareto-optimality can be proven for worker control. (Cf. Vanek, The General Theory, p. 93ff.)

But even if we grant (as surely we must) that a worker-managed firm whose profits have increased because of a price increase would not lay off members, we must also grant that they have little incentive to expand either production or employment when demand increases. (They might decide to work longer hours, since their incomes would benefit. They might even take on more workers if they are working their equipment at less than full capacity, since these would share the burden of the capital-assets tax. But neither of these responses is assured, or even particularly likely.)

We have here an extremely serious problem, one which must be handled if our model is to have any claim to reasonable efficiency.* The solution involves two elements. The first is educational. Firms must be made aware of their social responsibilities. If firms do not increase production when demand increases, then the economy will face problems of unnecessary unemployment and a general misallocation of resources. Thus firms must be encouraged to interpret a demand-generated price increase, not as an eternal blessing, but as a temporary compensation for the inconvenience of bringing new workers into the firm to expand production. Since all firms are public property, and hence all books open to public inspection, the community at large can be expected to exert significant pressure on firms experiencing windfall profits to "do their duty." They would probably wish to establish an employment agency (not to be confused with its capitalist namesake) to keep up-to-date records on profit figures and salary structures in order to guide people seeking work into the appropriate areas. This agency would attempt to persuade reluctant firms to take on more workers—though it should not be empowered to force them to do so.

A stick lies behind the carrot of moral suasion. The government, recall, controls new investment. If the profit-per-worker ratio in a given industry is substantially higher than average, then there exists a prima facie case for investment in that area. This is not necessarily a punitive measure. It may well be that the firm has expanded to the limit of its physical capacity. But in such a case, an investment bank has good reason to grant funds to workers desirous of setting up competing firms in such a profitable area. (This mechanism—the setting up of new firms in profitable areas—is a key feature of our model. It

---

*Yugoslavia has not dealt adequately with this problem, and thus faces more serious unemployment and inequality difficulties than it should. Cf. Vanek, The Labor-Managed Economy, pp. 64-73 His recommendations are similar to the arrangements of our model.

serves not only to induce firms to behave in the socially responsible manner; it also serves to inhibit the formation of monopoly power, and to equalize incomes throughout the various industries. It is a mechanism of great importance to the viability of worker control.)

If worker-managed enterprises respond to demand increases with increased production and to demand declines with production cutbacks (there is no problem here, since firms will not produce what they cannot sell), then it is easily seen that the worker-control economy shares the efficiency strengths of laissez-faire. The price mechanism is in effect, so the economy allows consumer preferences to be expressed effectively; individual firms have concrete incentives to produce with the appropriate technology and with minimal waste of resources; and labor allocation is reasonably efficient. Thus the economy suffers no major efficiency weaknesses in comparision with laissez-faire. As we shall soon see, it exhibits a number of efficiency strengths that its rival does not share. It is to these matters we now turn.

A COMPARISON: UNEMPLOYMENT

It had long been a postulate of neoclassical theory* that a free, competitive, capitalist economy inevitably gravitated toward full employment. It was granted that "frictional" unemployment might exist, unemployment due to people leaving one job in search of another, or to temporary imbalances between openings and skills as a result of individual miscalculation or unforeseen changes in demand. But it was generally denied that "involuntary" unemployment was possible when the economy was in equilibrium, that an equilibrium situation could exist in which unemployed people were willing to work for the prevailing wage or even less, but employers were unwilling to hire them.

---

*In this section the term "neoclassical" will designate the pre-Keynesian version of the theory, the version still adhered to by many classical liberals. Keynesian liberals, as we remarked earlier, also adhere to the neoclassical paradigm, but in a form (allegedly) compatible with Keynes's theory. Generally the term "neoclassical" refers to both schools, but here I will restrict the usage. Keynes himself designated his immediate predecessors "classical," but that term is now usually reserved for Smith, Ricardo, Marx, Mill and others who preceded the "marginalist revolution."

As is well known, John Maynard Keynes's General Theory of Employment, Interest and Money is a sustained attack on precisely the full-employment postulate. The volume of employment generated by an economy, he argues, is determined by the relationship of the "propensity to consume" to the rate of investment, and this volume need not correspond to anything like full employment. Equilibrium might be established at any level of unemployment.[24]

It might seem odd to common sense, especially to a common sense which remembers the decade-long Great Depression, that anyone could maintain that full employment is inevitable under free-market laissez-faire. But the economists had an answer, the only possible answer given the assumptions of their theory: depressed capitalist economies must be unfree. Labor unions in particular were singled out for blame. These "coercive" monopolistic organizations were charged with blocking the movement of the economy toward full employment by holding wages above their appropriate level.

This pre-Keynesian position is still maintained by many classical liberals, among them Hayek, who writes: "Unions that had no power to coerce outsiders would thus not be strong enough to force up wages above the level at which all seeking work could be employed, that is, the level that would establish itself in a truly free market for labor in general."[25]

Hayek, of course, is scarcely unaware of the Keynesian argument, but he is unpersuaded. He sees the argument as this:

> The development of Lord Keynes's theory started from the correct insight that the regular cause of extensive unemployment is real wages that are too high. The next step consisted in the proposition that a direct lowering of money wages could be brought down only by a struggle so painful and prolonged that it could not be contemplated. Hence he concluded that real wages must be lowered by the process of lowering the value of money. This is really the reasoning underlying the whole "full-employment" policy now so widely accepted. If labor insists on a level of money wages too high to allow of full employment, the supply of money must be so increased as to raise prices to a level where the real value of the prevailing money wage is no longer greater than the productivity of the workers seeking employment.[26]

This, it must be said, is a serious distortion of Keynes's argument. First of all, Keynes does not hold that increasing the money supply will cause prices to rise and hence increase employment, since he does not hold that the level of real wages determines the level of employment, but precisely the contrary—that the level of employment determines the real wage rate.[27] Second—and one is tempted to call this distortion outrageous—Keynes does not maintain that it is labor's insistence on too high a money wage that causes unemployment. The whole of the General Theory's Chapter Two is an attack on precisely this presumption:

> It is not very plausible to assert that unemployment in the United States in 1932 was due to labor obstinately refusing to accept a reduction in money-wages or to its obstinately demanding a real wage beyond what the productivity of the economic machine was capable of furnishing. Wide variations are experienced in the volume of employment without any apparent change either in the minimum real demands of labor or its productivity. Labor is not more truculent in the depression than in the boom—far from it. Nor is its physical productivity less.[28]

Keynes maintains, as Hayek surely must know, that the level of employment is not determined by the wage bargain struck between employees (unionized or not) and employers, but by other basic forces in the economy, the most critical being the level of investment and the quantity of savings, variables far removed from union control.

Of course, Keynes's saying it's so doesn't make it so, and Hayek's misrepresentation of Keynes does not invalidate his own contention that free laissez-faire tends to full employment. What we need to examine are some arguments.

The neoclassical argument, though not often explicitly stated,* is not difficult to reconstruct. Suppose there are unemployed workers desirous of work. If they are allowed to compete freely with the rest

---

*Keynes made this observation in his General Theory (p. 258), and it remains true today. One searches in vain through Hayek's Constitution of Liberty for a statement of the argument— though attacks on labor unions abound. (Some classical liberals, Friedman among them, have abandoned the full-employment argument and now maintain that there is a "natural rate of unemployment." Government and labor unions are now denounced, not for interfering with the economy's natural tendency toward full employment, but for interfering with the natural rate of unemployment. Plus ça change, plus c'est la même chose. More on the natural rate argument later.)

of the workforce, they will force wages down, thus reducing production costs. Now according to neoclassical theory a firm adjusts its production to bring the marginal cost of its product (the cost, assumed to be rising, of producing one more item) into equality with the product's market-given price. Hence, a drop in costs signals an expansion in production, and this expansion provides jobs for the "temporarily" unemployed.

Now this argument, we observe, depends on three crucial suppositions—that a firm can expand production, that a firm will expand production, and that it will be able to sell its increased output at the anticipated price. Let's examine these.

We note, as a preliminary observation, that it is always possible for a firm to take on more workers, since it can always spread around the existing volume of work by reducing the hours of some (or all) of its employees. But of course such actions will not be taken voluntarily, since neither the employer nor the current employees stand to benefit. So a firm will hire more workers only if hiring them will increase production. But to increase production, more than just labor is needed. Tools, raw materials and workspace are needed as well. If production goods and production facilities are not available, then employment will not be increased, no matter how low competitive bidding forces wages. The economy cannot expand production.

The neoclassical Weltanschauung assumes that this situation will not arise, that it is always possible to add more labor to the existing stock of capital to increase output. This assumption would seem unrealistic as a general assumption, especially when applied to underdeveloped countries, but it does not seem inappropriate to an economy operating at less than full capacity or to one capable of expanding its productive capacity with relative ease, as modern industrial economies generally are.

But if firms can expand production when labor costs decline, will they? That they will is a basic assumption of the perfect competition model, but does it hold in reality? Under perfect competition, a firm assumes that it can sell at the going price all that it can produce; under more realistic conditions, firms are less sanguine. An employer will certainly be delighted to talk to workers willing to work for less, but he might simply replace his current employees with cheaper ones (or use the threat of doing so to drive down their wages). If this happens, neither production nor employment increases, though profits might.

Then again they might not, not even if production is expanded—for goods produced must be sold. But when wages decline, so does worker purchasing power, and if this is not offset by an increase in investment, total demand declines.* In such a case, firms may find themselves unable to sell as much as they did before, let alone more, and so they respond—by cutting production and further <u>reducing</u> employment.

In short, a competitive economy might respond to an increase in unemployment, not by restoring employment to the previous level, but by cutting back even further. The fact of the matter is, there are no forces in a free-market economy which guarantee that investment decisions (the key variable in the above analysis) will be precisely (or even roughly) those necessary to offset the decline in wage-goods demand. Hence there is no reason to assume that an equilibrium, if reached at all, will be a full-employment equilibrium.

It should be noted that the above argument undercuts the classical liberal contention that labor unions (and minimum-wage laws—another oft-cited factor[29]) are responsible for unemployment. Quite the contrary. Insofar as labor unions and minimum-wage laws (and also various welfare provisions) prevent demand from falling as low as it might otherwise go during a slump, they apply a brake to the downward spiral. Far from being <u>responsible</u> for unemployment, they actually mitigate it.

We must conclude that there are no theoretical reasons or empirical evidence to support the contention that a laissez-faire economy tends to full employment.† This is a <u>fundamental</u> efficiency defect (one well-recognized by modern liberalism) of the classical-liberal ideal. If unemployed workers face idle factories, because effective demand is lacking to stimulate employers to hire them, the system does not even yield Pareto-optimality, let alone the greatest happiness for the greatest number.

---

*The traditional argument invoked Say's Law at this point. Investments <u>will</u> increase, since lower costs mean greater profits, greater profits mean greater savings, and greater savings mean greater investment. Keynes denied—correctly—the necessity of this latter clause. The forces and motivations governing saving are quite distinct from those governing investment; there is no reason why these quantities should coincide. (Cf. Keynes, <u>General Theory</u>, pp. 19-21, and Books III and IV.)

†When the Chilean junta instituted Chicago School economics (dismantling welfare programs and curtailing union activities) to restore the free market so "disrupted" by Allende, unemployment rocketed to 18 percent. (Cf. Michael Moffitt, "Chicago Economics in Chile," <u>Challenge</u> 20 [September-October 1977]: 34-43.)

(There is one "empirical" argument in support of the claim that capitalism always provides jobs for those who want them that I would think too crude to mention, were it not for the fact that one of my students reports having been subjected to it by his economics professor. The professor in question allegedly brandished a copy of the local newspaper's help-wanted section as proof that there is no involuntary unemployment. Needless to say, this "proof" means nothing in the absence of a correspondence between the number of jobs advertised and the number of unemployed—to say nothing of a correspondence between required and available skills. Try telling an employment-hungry philosopher that the "numerous" listings in Jobs For Philosophers proves that there is no involuntary unemployment in the profession.)

We've argued that laissez-faire is likely to experience unemployment inefficiencies. There is no reason to suppose they will not be severe. We must now ask about worker control. Interestingly enough, that feature of worker control that pointed toward inefficiency—the reluctance of a firm to employ more workers when demand for its product increases—has a more desirable counterpart relative to demand decline. For if a firm is hesitant to take on more workers when times are good, it is also reluctant to reduce its ranks when times are bad. The face-to-face democracy within an enterprise sharply mitigates against shifting the burden of a business slump onto a few, especially if the slump is likely to be temporary. (This solidarity could even be backed by a law prohibiting the dismissal of a worker simply for reasons of financial exigency. Considerations of equity and efficiency coincide here, since Pareto-optimality requires full employment.[30])

Of course if the demand drop proves to be more than temporary, the incomes of everyone will decline, and workers will have an incentive to seek employment in more profitable concerns. This is as it should be. Some will shift toward areas where demand is stronger, thus allowing the incomes of those remaining to rise again. Labor reallocates itself smoothly, without the violent disruptions of involuntary unemployment.

Note, too, this burden-sharing, which is natural to worker control, is far from natural to capitalism. Capitalist firms generally negotiate a wage contract that guarantees a wage rate but not employment. When demand declines, an employer has little choice but to lay off workers, since it is not open to her to abrogate the wage contract. (This is not an inevitable feature of capitalism, but one that is likely to prevail under laissez-faire. The employer has no incentive to apply "share-the-burden"; individual workers have little incentive, since, in the absence of worker-democracy, they have little motivation to concern themselves with their more expendable "comrades.")

Worker solidarity in the face of a business slump prevents a sharp drop in employment, but it does not guarantee full employment, for there are always new workers entering the labor force—young people in particular, but also refugees from firms that can no longer stay afloat. More active governmental intervention is needed to cope with this problem.* The key mechanisms are the ones already discussed in connection with enterprise behavior in the face of rising demand. The government must actively encourage enterprises to take on new workers who want employment with them, and it must also manage its investment policy appropriately. The government should make funds available to people desirous of setting up firms in areas where there is sufficient demand; it should initiate new industries if private initiative is not forthcoming. Since the government controls all new investment, it will presumably give priority, not only to especially profitable ventures, but also to those that provide needed jobs in areas where unemployment is high.

The conclusion of this section is obvious. Laissez-faire capitalism cannot guarantee full employment; it can only hope that an equilibrium approaching full employment will occur. Being laissez-faire, it opposes all governmental intervention to reduce unemployment. By contrast, our model incorporates governmental policies aimed at securing employment for everyone who wants to work, and in addition it has a structural feature that gives those who do have work considerable job security. It cannot be claimed that there will be no involuntary unemployment under worker control, but unemployment should not be the pervasive problem it is under laissez-faire.

There remains one classical-liberal objection for us to consider. It is almost always argued that attempts to secure full employment by governmental intervention lead inevitably to inflation.[31] It must be said that there is considerable validity to this charge when directed, as it usually is, against Keynesian liberalism. This we shall see in Chapter 5. But it has none vis-a-vis our model. There is no reason whatsoever why governmental spending of funds collected by taxation

---

*This lesson is confirmed not only by theory but by Yugoslavian experience. Yugoslavia, I have already mentioned, is virtually laissez-faire regarding employment and suffers a serious unemployment problem as a result. Branko Horvat, the preeminent Yugoslavian theoretician of self-management, remarks, "Strange as it may sound, there is no fiscal policy in Yugoslavia." The Yugoslav Economic System (White Plains, N.Y.: International Arts and Sciences Press, 1976), p. 249.

for the purpose of financing new enterprises should be inflationary. The classical-liberal critique of full-employment policies focuses on deficit spending, but deficit spending is not the unemployment remedy we propose.

MORE TROUBLE: THE SALES EFFORT

If an economy is to function efficiently, it must not under-employ available resources, in particular its labor supply. But the full-employment assumption is not the only problematic assumption underlying the laissez-faire case for efficiency. Another quite basic—and quite controversial—assumption is that of "consumer sovereignty." As we remarked earlier, the consumer is king in the neoclassical conception of laissez-faire; the economy exists to respond to his desires. Since it is true that the market signals consumer preferences with great facility and provides incentives for their summary satisfaction, it is tempting to conclude that the market is optimally efficient in promoting each consumer's well-being, at least within the constraints imposed by the income distribution.

But this conclusion follows only if the consumer really is king—in control of the market and of himself. It must be assumed that satisfaction of preferences expressed by market purchases do in fact promote an individual's well-being. If the consumer behaves irrationally or if his preferences are significantly manipulated, he is not really sovereign, and the system may not be efficient.

Of course, the consumer-sovereignty condition will not strictly obtain in any realistic market system. Minimal criteria (physical health, for example, or an individual's retrospective self-evaluation) suggest clear counterexamples. On the other hand, an argument such as ours cannot insist on strict compliance, since no system that allows consumers any freedom of choice can guarantee that there will be no self-destructive consumption or ignorant or soon regretted purchases. The relevant questions concern the relationship of consumer sovereignty and its failure to the structural features of laissez-faire.

If one steps from the mainstream of contemporary economics, one encounters a great many critics of the consumer-sovereignty assumption. From a Marxist perspective Baran and Sweezy write: "The preferences of consumers, in other words, are not generated by confronting him with a choice of genuinely different products but rather by the employment of increasingly refined and elaborate techniques of suggesting and 'brainwashing': this too has become a matter of common knowledge."[32]

Galbraith, a post-Keynesian, is equally insistent:

The control or management of demand is, in fact, a vast
and rapidly growing industry in itself. It embraces a
huge network of communications, a great array of mer-
chandising and selling organizations, nearly the entire
advertising industry, numerous ancillary research,
training and other related services and much more. In
everyday parlance this great machine, and the demand-
ing and varied talents that it employs, are said to be engaged in selling goods. In less ambiguous language, it
means that it is engaged in the management of those who
buy goods.[33]

To insist on consumer sovereignty, Galbraith declares to his
colleagues, is to turn away from "a remarkably obvious question:
Why does the modern consumer increasingly tend toward insanity, increasingly insist on self-abuse?"[34]

Such criticisms are not suffered lightly by those at the center of
the profession. The usual response is to raise the specter of repression. MIT's Robert Solow erupts at Galbraith: "The attack on consumer
sovereignty performs the same function as the doctrine of 'repressive
tolerance'. If people do not want what I see so clearly they should want,
it can only be because they don't know what they 'really' want."[35]
Friedman writes in a similar vein: "Indeed, a major source of objection to a free economy is precisely that it does its task so well. It
gives people what they want, instead of what a particular group thinks
they ought to want."[36]

This charge of elitism and intolerance is inappropriate; it seems
to rest on a conceptual confusion. The consumer-sovereignty assumption is the empirical claim that people's purchases tend to maximize
their well-being; it is not the normative claim that people ought to decide for themselves what is good for them. One can well maintain
the latter position and still deny that consumer sovereignty obtains
in a particular market system. One might wish to see the system reformed so as to restore market power to the consumer. One might
even want to maintain the system as is, because of other overriding
ethical considerations. None of these normative views embodies
elitism or intolerance. To infer intolerance from a denial of consumer
sovereignty is to confuse an empirical claim with a normative one.

But all this is mere charge and countercharge. The conventional
response to the attack on the consumer-sovereignty assumption may
be wide of the mark, but that does not end the matter, especially for

us, who are concerned with an ideal and not with present-day capitalist reality. We must inquire more carefully into structural relationships.

One fact is quite clear. Just as capitalism provides strong incentive for innovation, efficient management and close attention to consumer demand, it also encourages the <u>stimulation</u> of demand. Though we tend to take demand stimulation for granted, this feature is in fact rather peculiar, absent from many earlier (and some later) modes of production. No one in a primitive or feudal economy save a few traders has any reason to entice people to consume more. Neither the serf nor her lord has the slightest economic interest in persuading people to eat more bread or drink more wine. Nor does the production manager in a command economy, since quotas are set by an independent agency. In a market economy, however, the situation is different. With financial reward tied to sales, there exists a pronounced tendency toward "salesmanship."

The strength of this tendency is not uniform. It varies considerably with particular circumstances. In the early stages of capitalist development, when emerging capitalist farmers and manufacturers engaged in successful competition with small farmers and craftsmen, there was little need to stimulate demand. The market was there, to be captured by offering goods at lower prices. But as traditional markets saturated and capitalist production transformed the peasant and artisan classes into wage-laborers, pressures intensified to develop new markets, new products—and new sales techniques. More and more people, more and more resources, came to be devoted to the <u>selling</u> of goods.*

---

*In 1867 $50 million was spent on advertising in the United States. By the turn of the century the sum had risen to $500 million. By 1967 the total was in excess of $17 billion. (Julian Simon, <u>Issues in the Economics of Advertising</u> [Urbana, Ill.: University of Illinois Press, 1970], pp. 188-89.) And Simon estimates that total promotional expenditures, including advertising but also "most of what salesmen do . . . , window displays, publicity, and the display of goods so that customers can examine them, including trade fairs" is roughly three times advertising expenditures alone. This puts the promotional bill in 1967 at $51 billion. (Ibid., pp. 25-27.) That is about half of the <u>total</u> spent in the United States that year on food and beverages for personal consumption and <u>three times</u> what was spent on gasoline and oil. (U.S., <u>The Economic Report of the President</u> [Washington: United States Government Printing Office, 1973], p. 207.)

If it is clear that the market encourages the development of sales techniques, it is also clear that there is nothing in the structure of laissez-faire to inhibit this development. To the contrary, if a technique proves effective, competitive pressures insure its adoption. For a capitalist firm to forego an effective technique would be to deny itself potential profits and to subject itself to the risk—should its competitor adopt the technique—of serious loss.

But if it is clear that a large sales apparatus is likely to develop under laissez-faire, it is less clear that this is <u>detrimental</u> to the economic well-being of society. The sales effort has its defenders. One, for example, concludes his study with the assessment that "on balance, it seems clear that advertising makes a major contribution to our national economic well-being and to the competitive nature of our economy."[37] A more common (and more cautious) view is expressed by Solow:

> No one who believes, as I do, that profit is an important
> business motive could possibly argue that advertising
> has no influence on the willingness of consumers to buy
> a given product at a given price. After all, how could I
> then account for the fact that profit-seeking corporations
> regularly spend billions of dollars on advertising?
>
> But I should think that a case could be made that
> much advertising seems only to cancel other advertising,
> and is therefore merely wasteful. I should think it obvious
> that this almost has to be true—for otherwise there would
> be nothing to stop the cigarette industry and the detergent
> industry from expanding their sales to their hearts' desire
> and the limit of the consumer's capacity to carry debt. . . .
>
> It is open to legitimate doubt that advertising has
> a detectable effect at all on the sum of consumer spending,
> or, in other words, on the choice between spending and
> saving.[38]

Let us consider Solow's position for a moment, since it is both common and influential. Solow's conclusion comes to this: advertising affects how people spend their money, but not how much they spend; most advertising is self-cancelling and thus merely wasteful.

The first thing we notice is that his argument that advertising almost has to be self-cancelling, "for otherwise there would be nothing to stop the cigarette industry and the detergent industry from expanding their sales to their hearts' content . . ." is a <u>non sequitur</u>. To say that advertising can increase total consumption is not to say that consumption can be increased indefinitely—anymore than to say that fertilizer makes petunias grow larger is to say that they can be grown larger than sunflowers. The inference is invalid.

There is a deeper problem with Solow's analysis. Whether the sales effort shifts the volume of consumption or merely consumption patterns is not the relevant ethical question. Of course, if the sales apparatus has little quantitative or qualitative effect on consumption, then it is certainly wasteful and hence detrimental to efficiency. The people and resources so employed could be put to better use. But if sales techniques do have an effect—and surely they must, or else, as Solow correctly observes, those billions of dollars would not be spent—then the crucial question is whether the effect is to make people better off. Whether people consume more and save less as a result of the sales effort, or consume more of Brand X than Brand Y is irrelevant as such. What we need to know is the effect of such behavior on well-being.

As might be expected, given the difficulty of constructing controlled experiments in this area, to say nothing of the profession's reluctance to tackle normative questions, there is little empirical data to go on.[39] But if we simply pose the question properly, we can venture an answer. We begin by asking whether there are any reasons for thinking that the sales effort is likely to bring people's actual purchases into better alignment with maximal well-being. Are there any "invisible hand" forces at work that tend to produce this result?

We notice at once that an invisible-hand explanation is necessary, since the direct, conscious intention of the owners of means of production is not to maximize consumer well-being, but to make things that will sell and to sell things that have been made.[40] If we assume that the only things that will sell are those that maximize well-being, then, of course, an invisible-hand explanation presents itself immediately. But is such an assumption plausible? The twin phenomena of salesmanship and sales resistance suggest that consumers often perceive their own interests as distinct from the interests of those with products to sell. On the other hand, a sale cannot be consummated without the buyer's consent. No one is compelled to buy.

Now if a person can be convinced only by a demonstration that the purchase of the product in question is in his rational self-interest, then the assumption that only those things that will profitably sell are those that maximize well-being is firmly grounded. In this case, the sales effort consists in conveying true and complete information concerning the advantages and disadvantages of the commodity in question, so that the consumer may make as rational a choice as possible.

It is obvious that our discussion has strayed into Fantasyland. Rational demonstration is not the only sales technique. No one who has watched an hour or two of commercial television could have any doubts. Nor anyone who has read any of the popular paperbacks decrying the more esoteric practices.[41] For additional evidence, one can turn to the former head of a major advertising agency:

Claude Hopkins, whose genius for writing copy made him
one of the advertising immortals, tells the story of one of
his great beer campaigns. In a tour through the brewery,
he nodded politely at the wonders of the malt and hops, but
came alive when he saw that the empty bottles were being
sterilized with live steam. His client protested that every
brewery did the same. Hopkins patiently explained that it
was not what they did, but what they advertised they did
that mattered. He wrote a classic campaign which proclaimed "OUR BOTTLES ARE WASHED WITH LIVE STEAM!"
George Washington Hill, the great tobacco manufacturer,
once ran a cigarette campaign with the now-famous claim:
"IT'S TOASTED!" So, indeed, is every other cigarette,
but no other manufacturer had been shrewd enough to see
the enormous possibilities of such a simple story. Hopkins,
again, scored a great advertising coup when he wrote:
"GETS RID OF FILM ON YOUR TEETH!" So, indeed, does
every toothpaste.[42]

Thus we see—and of course we knew it all along—that nonrational
sales techniques are available to those who want to use them (and can
afford the price).* We can presume they are effective; if they are not,
then the most sophisticated enterprises of modern capitalism must be
indicted for awesome stupidity. But if they do work, and if the producers in a competitive capitalist economy have little direct, conscious interest in promoting consumer well-being, then the invisible-
hand argument can be saved only by a bizarre assumption: one must
assume that the only commodities people can be persuaded to buy—by
rational or nonrational means—are those that do in fact maximize
well-being. Without this assumption—which is patently false—one
cannot conclude that laissez-faire is efficient in optimizing consumer
well-being. A major countertendency is present.

(This argument does not presume that producers are smart and
consumers are stupid. But producers are likely to be more rational

*By "nonrational sales techniques" we are to understand those
that deviate from the ideal of supplying the consumer with that information (and only that) relevant to his making a rational decision about
a purchase. Needless to say, there is nothing irrational, from the
point of view of the producer, in employing nonrational techniques.

in the pursuit of their goal [selling their products] than consumers are in theirs [maximizing well-being]. A sales project is a consciously undertaken venture with clearly defined success-failure criteria; since it often involves considerable expense—and promises significant gains—it is carefully evaluated, often with the help of expert [and expensive] personnel. The consumer's project exhibits sharply contrasting features. The goal is less precise and is rarely consciously aimed at in day-to-day purchasing; purchases tend to be made piecemeal, not as part of a coordinated plan, and they do not ordinarily involve sufficient expense to warrant expert advice.* The consumer is not helpless; she must, after all, be persuaded to buy. But the sales effort pursues its goal with considerably more rationality than the consumer hers. To the extent that success correlates with rationality, the producer has a decided advantage.)

The case against the optimality of laissez-faire would seem to be a strong one—but my argument has neglected a vital, perhaps decision-reversing, consideration: worker-control socialism is also a market economy; it also relies on profit-maximization, and so it also harbors a tendency toward nonrational sales persuasion.

I wish I could say that this were not so, but of course I cannot. However—and this is the important point—the tendency toward serious nonrational distortion is significantly weaker under worker control than under laissez-faire. Not all market economies are the same. Let me offer three reasons in support of this claim.

First of all, our model shares an advantage with modern liberalism. Since we are not committed to laissez-faire, we are not averse to regulating or barring certain techniques judged immoral or offensive, or to prohibiting the marketing of products that seriously threaten health and safety. Unlike laissez-faire, we need not rely on caveat emptor.

---

*Staffan Linder cites two studies, one showing that in 1959 50 percent of consumer purchases could be classified as impulse purchases—up 12 percent from 1949, the other showing that even in the area of durable goods "only about a fourth of . . . [the] buyers displayed most of the features of deliberate decision-making—planning, family discussions, information seeking, as well as choosing with respect to price, brand and other specific attributes of the commodity." (Staffan Linder, The Harried Leisure Class [New York: Columbia University Press, 1970], p. 68.)

A second reason is more directly related to a specific feature of our model. Consider an aspect of laissez-faire problematic even apart from its relation to the sales effort: the inability of workers to effect with ease a labor-leisure tradeoff. This difficulty (along with many others) is assumed away in the perfect competition model, but it cannot be dismissed in any realistic model of laissez-faire. In a competitive, laissez-faire economy I am quite free to alter the qualitative pattern of my consumption or my consumption-saving ratio. There are no institutional barriers to my doing so. If my taste shifts from apples to oranges, I go to the market and buy oranges instead of apples. If I want to cut my consumption a quarter to save more, I simply spend less and deposit the remainder in my savings account. But what if I decide that I want to work only six hours a day instead of eight, and consume a quarter less? Do I notify my employer and come in the next day at ten instead of eight? Do I find another job just like the one I have, only with six-hour shifts instead of eight? Obviously the owner of a facility would be less than enthusiastic about such flexibility, and would have little incentive to institute it.

And yet, without the availability of a labor-leisure tradeoff, the system is less than ideally efficient, on the neoclassical's own grounds. For if a person prefers to work an hour less, his productive output will decline by precisely the amount his income declines (at least according to neoclassical theory). Thus his opting for less work would make him better off and no one else worse off. [43]

I'm not sure that this argument should be taken too seriously. (The argument, for one thing, depends heavily on the neoclassical assumption that wages reflect the marginal contribution of labor.) But the absence of a labor-leisure tradeoff is quite significant in connection with sales-effort inefficiencies. If a person has money, and little to do with it but spend it on consumer goods, he is particularly susceptible to the blandishments of an aggressive sales apparatus. And for the vast majority—at least in any existing capitalist society—that is precisely the situation. One can save instead of spend, but this is simply the choice to consume later instead of now. The situation is different for the wealthy. If one has a large quantity of discretionary funds, then saving—and investing—have tangible benefits quite distinct from future consumption: one can increase one's power, prestige and influence by purchasing productive assets; one can even avoid labor altogether by "putting one's money to work." But for the majority the only attractive alternative to consumption is leisure—and that is not available. So one must spend, now or later, on things that are by no means guaranteed to enhance well-being.

Under worker-control socialism, the labor-leisure option is a more realistic possibility. To be sure, one cannot come in at ten instead of eight at will. But since workers control democratically the conditions of their work, a majority vote is all that is needed to reduce the working day, or to allow some members greater flexibility in return for lower incomes. The labor-leisure choice is more than an abstract possibility when a forum exists for the presentation of one's case, and an accessible number of sympathizers all that is needed to effect a change. And with leisure a genuine alternative, one's sales resistance is likely to increase, making rational consumption more probable.

One might imagine that increased sales resistance would inspire firms to greater heights of persuasive sophistication. But this is unlikely under worker control for another reason, the third (and perhaps most significant) on our list. Nonrational persuasion should be less troublesome under worker control than under laissez-faire because the worker-managed firm has little interest in expansion. This peculiar feature of our model—its lack of a growth imperative—has already been discussed, but its full significance has not yet been elaborated. A worker-managed firm is less inclined to grow, recall, because growth includes more workers with whom the extra profits must be shared. Under constant returns to scale a worker-managed firm has no incentive at all to expand, whereas a profitable capitalist firm will expand indefinitely. Thus a capitalist firm has a strong incentive to increase sales, whereas a worker-managed firm has little, and so the former has a much stronger motivation to put effort into selling. A worker-managed enterprise does have a keen interest in maintaining demand, for if sales slip, incomes suffer. So one should not expect the disappearance of image making and planned obsolescence. But a major motivation underlying the most aggressive (and often most offensive) capitalist sales efforts is lacking—the desire to grow. So, since a worker-managed firm is less motivated to advertise (and will probably have fewer means, since firms are likely to be smaller than their capitalist counterparts), the sales effort can be expected to be less intense.[44]

Let us briefly recapitulate the long argument of this section. Any market economy will exhibit a tendency to employ nonrational sales techniques that are undesirable from a social point of view. This tendency is quite pronounced in existing capitalist societies, and there is no reason to suppose it would be any less under laissez-faire. On the other hand, it should be less pronounced under worker-control socialism. The firms themselves have less incentive to use nonrational techniques, since they have little interest in growth. The consumers should be better able to resist them, since they have a genuine alternative to consumption. And finally, if problems persist, the government can actively intervene. A sales effort will persist (by no means a wholly negative phenomenon, since consumers do need to know what is available and why it is useful), but it should be significantly less than the epic efforts of contemporary capitalism.

THE DISTRIBUTION OF INCOME

The question under consideration in this chapter is the comparative efficiency of worker control and laissez-faire, where efficiency is defined in terms of maximizing the consumer-satisfaction of the greatest number, while minimizing costs. Costs, it should be recalled, comprise human labor, scarce resources, and inequality. This formulation is essentially utilitarian in that it involves summing satisfactions and weighing the result against disutilities.* Inequality is counted as a cost, at least to the extent that if two societies provide essentially the same average material satisfaction and at the same cost of labor and resources, then the more egalitarian society will be considered more efficient.

Both laissez-faire capitalism and worker-control socialism rely on the market mechanism to accomplish the distribution of goods and services. This is an effective mechanism for registering consumer preferences and for transmitting this information to the productive apparatus. It has, however, one glaring deficiency: preferences are registered by purchases, and purchases require money. Those who have much are able not only to consume more of the goods at hand but also to signal strongly by their purchases that the economy produce more of what they desire. Those who have little income, by contrast, consume little and have little effective input into production decisions. Thus the anomaly of a "free," nonauthoritarian society directing resources and labor to the production of luxury goods for some, while other citizens lack basic necessities—necessities that will not even be produced in sufficient quantities because of deficient demand.

One should not conclude too hastily, however, that the market is nonoptimal, for to be consumed, goods have to be produced, and production involves costs. If resource costs were the only costs, if consumer goods were all effortlessly produced, then a good case could be made for a strictly egalitarian distribution of wealth. The market would be fully democratic and might very well yield the greatest happiness for the greatest number. [45] But material costs are not the only costs; goods are not effortlessly produced. Production involves "production-pain"—the discomfort, sometimes mild, sometimes

---

*Adding up satisfactions is of course problematic, but some such procedure is necessary to do justice to our moral intuitions and to move us beyond the sterility of Pareto-optimality.

severe, experienced by human beings who are actively engaged in the productive process. Production requires the expenditure of human energy; it involves mental and physical tension. In general, people must be enticed (or coerced) to produce.* Thus an economic system must concern itself with incentives to work.

Once again we find empirical data lacking. Scitovsky writes:

> To find the best compromise between maximizing the
> national income and equalizing its distribution seems
> like a typical problem of economic analysis. Unfor-
> tunately, we lack the information to resolve it, knowing
> next to nothing about the effectiveness of individual income
> as a spur to the individual's economic activity, and nothing
> about the cost of a marginal addition to the national income
> in terms of the increased inequality this would require.[46]

We note that Scitovsky presumes that greater inequality would increase production. Keynes, by contrast, suggests the opposite: "Thus we might aim at a practice . . . which allows the intelligence and determination and executive skills of the financier, the entrepreneur et hoc genus omne (who are certainly so fond of their craft that their labour could be obtained much cheaper than at present) to be harnessed to the service of the community on reasonable terms of reward."[47]

This disagreement as we shall see, is not central to our argument, and so we shall not be unduly hindered by the lack of data. If we clarify the question properly, we will be able to see the answer. We should begin by distinguishing several sorts of incentives. Insofar as we are assuming throughout this chapter a fixed technology, we need not be concerned with incentives to innovate; that will come later. What we must investigate are incentives for undesirable work, additional work and work that involves special talents and skills.

It seems clear that it is more efficient to entice people to work than to coerce them, particularly if the work involves judgment, care, and initiative. Slave labor has never been notable for its efficiency. It is also clear that monetary incentives are simple and effective— though nonmonetary incentives (pride of workmanship, a sense of community service, etc.) play a role in all economic systems.

---

*This should not be taken as a claim about "human nature," but as an assessment about people as they are now and are likely to be in the reasonably foreseeable future. How this might change will be described briefly in our concluding chapter.

Now it does not seem objectionable on general utilitarian grounds to grant higher incomes to those who do the work others prefer not to do, or who work longer hours or several jobs. Granted, some equality is sacrificed, but there is a substantial gain in consumer satisfaction. Granted also, the higher incomes of some give them greater weight in shaping the productive output of society, but such people demonstrate by their choice of higher pay over less arduous or less noxious work a greater concern for material goods. If differential incomes are not permitted, then fewer persons will work at the unpleasant jobs, and output shortages will develop in these sectors.* Since the demand for the output is there, and since people are willing to supply that demand if sufficiently compensated, it does not seem unreasonable to allow a market equilibrium to be established.

The question of unequal talents is more troublesome. Utilitarian considerations can be brought to bear on both sides. If we assume that people's needs and desires are more or less independent of their talents, and also that these needs and desires tend to diminish as incomes rise, then it would seem that jobs which involve equal production pain should be rewarded equally, regardless of the talent involved. For if incomes are unequal, a greater total satisfaction could be obtained by taking a dollar from the more affluent and giving it to the less. On the other hand, it is in the best interests of society to have people cultivate socially desirable talents and employ them where they will do most good. Coercive pressure is unlikely to be effective here, and nonmonetary incentives may not be sufficient. Moreover, to the degree that monetary inequalities reflect the marginal value to society of different occupations, educational and other policies can be more precisely formulated to increase the skills in short supply.

Actually we need not settle this question in order to proceed, because the issue of compensating talent—and also extra effort—does not bear substantially on our basic concern: the choice between laissez-faire and worker control. For both systems employ the market mechanism, both offer monetary incentives, both can be expected to generate income inequalities relative to production-pain and skill. Questions concerning the just compensation of talent and effort are relevant to

---

*I am assuming here that the less desirable work cannot be eliminated through job redesign or rotation. While some advances can surely be made in this direction, I do not think the goal is completely attainable in the foreseeable future.

comparisons of market and nonmarket economies, but not to the comparison we are making.

(At least not substantially relevant. Worker control would seem to have a certain advantage. Since income inequalities are subject to democratic approval, experiments with work rotations and skill up-grading—to mitigate against having to pay a higher share of the revenue to certain members—might be more widely pursued. As we shall see more clearly in a later chapter, the owner or manager of a capitalist concern has fewer incentives to undertake such experiments.)

In light of the similarities of their market structures, one might suppose that the structure of inequalities would be essentially the same under laissez-faire and worker control. This supposition, however, is quite false—for a major character has been overlooked: the capitalist herself. We have argued that inequalities relative to productive output do not necessarily conflict with (egalitarian) efficiency; in fact, a good case can be made in their favor. But no such case exists for property income, for income generated by ownership of means of production. The reason is simple. Property ownership is not a pro-ductive activity. This, remember, was a principal conclusion of Chapter 1. Providing capital or providing land is not an activity related to either talent or production-pain; it is merely an act of granting per-mission. Hence there is no good reason (relative to efficiency) for tolerating inequalities based on property ownership.*

Friedman asserts in his defense of capitalism that "payment in accordance with product is necessary in order that resources be used most effectively, at least under a system depending on voluntary co-operation."48 This, we know, is the neoclassical formulation, and it glosses (as usual) the all-important distinction between a productive factor and its owner. It is true that both land and capital are scarce resources; efficient allocation requires that users pay a charge, re-flecting the "opportunity cost" of the factor. But it is by no means true that the payment need accrue to a factor owner. As our model demonstrates, one can have an efficient economic system based on voluntary cooperation without any private individual receiving income on the basis of ownership of a productive asset.

---

*Such inequalities are by no means insignificant in capitalist economies. In the United States the distribution of total output between property income and wages is approximately 25%-75%, and has re-mained relatively constant throughout this century. (Cf. Paul Samuel-son, Economics, 9th ed. [New York: McGraw-Hill, 1973], p. 537.)

This is extremely significant. The acquisition of productive property, the making of money with money, is the major path to large-scale accumulation under capitalism. (Popular consciousness may associate spectacular income with athletic prowess or entertainment talent or a medical degree, but the big money flows through different channels.)[49] Without property income, with only inequalities of income due to effort or talent, massive accumulation is virtually impossible. To accumulate—without the magic of compound interest—a half-billion dollar fortune during a fifty-year working lifetime, one would have to save ten million a year.* To accumulate even a million, one would have to sock away $20,000 a year. (In 1962 there were 80,000 millionaires in the United States.)[50] Why one would want to save so much is hardly clear, since—unlike the situation under capitalism—there is little to do with money but spend it on personal consumption. One cannot purchase the power and prestige of owning productive wealth, nor can one avoid labor by "putting one's money to work."

These theoretical arguments might be more convincing were it not for the undeniable fact that substantial inequalities continue to exist in countries that have abolished private property. The Soviet Union is perhaps the most conspicuous example.†

---

*McDonald's hamburger entrepreneur Ray Kroc, ranked among the five richest men in America, is said to be worth over $600 million. Leading the list is Daniel Keith Ludwig (shipping and real estate) with $3 billion. (Newsweek, August 2, 1976, p. 56.)

†Comparative estimates of inequalities are notoriously difficult to establish. An ambitious attempt by Peter Wiles indicates that, though inequalities are quite severe, they are not as great as many commentators suggest. If one compares the average income of the top 10 percent with the average income of the bottom 10 percent, one gets a ratio of 7.0 for the U.S. in 1968 and 3.7 for the USSR. (Distribution of Income: East and West [Amsterdam: North-Holland, 1974], p. 48.) Moreover, whereas inequalities have remained substantially unchanged in the U.S. for decades (cf. James Smith and Stephen Franklin, "The Concentration of Personal Wealth, 1922-69," American Economic Review 64 [May 1974]: 162), they have come down substantially in the USSR during the Brezhnev era: "The statistical record since Stalin is a very good one indeed. I doubt if any other country can show a more rapid and sweeping progress toward equality." (Wiles, Income Distribution, p. 25.)

To this objection, we must observe that private property is not the only institution conducive to sharp inequalities of wealth. The historical record shows it to be an important one. The historical record shows an authoritarian political structure to be another. But the socialism I am advocating is a democratic system without private property. The Soviet Union can no more be cited as evidence that extreme inequality is inevitable under socialism than the United States is proof that it is inherent in a market economy. One must point to structural tendencies.

The equalizing tendency of political democracy is not insignificant. It is reflected even in a society such as the United States, where large fortunes do not contradict the prevailing ideology, and large salaries are regarded as essential to good management. Even in this society the salaries of top public officials are far from sufficient to allow for a large accumulation of wealth. Politicians become rich, not by saving a large fraction of their salaries, but by dabbling (legally or otherwise) in the "free market." A society that combines a democratic ideology with a socialist one—both exerting pressure toward equality—and has excised major mechanisms of wealth accumulation promises to be a more egalitarian society (primitive communism excepted) than any yet seen.*

----

*The egalitarian influence of socialist ideology may exert an influence even in the absence of democracy. The secrecy shrouding many of the institutions of privilege in the Soviet Union, and the decided lack of conspicuous consumption, suggests an uneasiness on the part of the elite at being so at variance with the socialist ideal. A joke that reportedly circulated among the Moscow intelligentsia a few years back is revealing: "Brezhnev wanted to impress his mother with how well he had done, and decided to invite her up to Moscow from their home in Dneprodzerzhinsk in the Ukraine. He showed her through his ample intown apartment, but she was nonplussed, even a little ill at ease. So he called the Kremlin, ordered his Zil, and they sped out to his dacha near Usovo, one used previously by Stalin and Khrushchev. He took her all around, showed her each room and the handsome grounds, but still she said nothing. So he called for his personal helicopter and flew her to his hunting lodge at Zavidovo. There he escorted her to the banquet room, grandly displaying the big fireplace, his guns, the whole bit, and unable to restrain himself any longer, he asked pleadingly, 'Tell me, Mama, what do you think?'

" 'Well', she hesitated, 'It's good, Leonid. But what if the Reds come back?' " (Hedrick Smith, "How the Soviet Elite Lives," The Atlantic Monthly [December 1975]: 46.)

Some concluding remarks are in order, regarding the arguments
for inequality. Classical liberals, we know, are not enamored with
equality. While they generally claim to favor egalitarian measures so
long as they do not conflict with liberty, they regard the absence of
conflict rare. They also profess to see some genuine merit to inequality, some good utilitarian consequences. Apart from the Friedman
argument just considered, which connects inequalities to allocative
efficiency, two others have a certain prominence. Hayek offers one:

> The contention that in any phase of progress the rich, by
> experimenting with new styles of living not yet accessible
> to the poor, perform a necessary service without which
> the advance of the poor would be very much slower will
> appear to some as a piece of far-fetched and cynical apol-
> ogetics. Yet a little reflection will show this is fully valid
> and that a socialist society would in this respect have to
> imitate a free society. It would be necessary for a planned
> economy (unless it could simply imitate the example of
> other more advanced societies) to designate individuals
> whose duty it would be to try out the latest advances long
> before they were made available to the rest. . . . A
> planned economy would have to provide for a whole class
> or even a hierarchy of classes, which would then differ
> from that in a free society merely in the fact that the
> inequalities would be the result of design and the selec-
> tion of particular individuals or groups would be done
> by authority rather than by the impersonal process of
> the market and accidents of birth and opportunity.[51]

We need not spend much time on this. I must confess to being
among those it strikes as "a piece of far-fetched and cynical apologetics." First of all, the choice need not be between capitalism and a
planned society that specifies a hierarchy of classes. As our model
demonstrates, it is possible to have a market economy without
massive planning or an exceedingly wealthy upper class. Nor does the
existence of some inequality in a socialist society make it functionally
equivalent to capitalism. One can have some inequality—and hence a
market for consumer goods more costly than everyone can readily
afford—without an inequality structure homologous to that which tends
to prevail under capitalism. (It is worth noting, for the benefit of anyone unaware of the magnitude of contemporary inequality, that in the
United States 1.5 percent of the adult population owns more than a
quarter of all privately owned wealth.[52])

Nor is it clear that the very rich provide the essential market
for experimental goods. It is true that some goods and services were

once available only to the rich and are now mass-produced (automobiles, televisions); it is also true that some will never "trickle down"
(servants, palatial estates).[53] And it should not be forgotten that the
industrial revolution itself was based on goods that were mass-produced from the start (textiles, agricultural products). It is not self-
evident that even those items that did in fact accrue first to the rich
would have spread more slowly in the absence of such a class—or that
society would have suffered grievously if they had. Hayek's argument
rests on a particular view of social evolution that sees the wealthy as
the vanguard blazing the trail for the masses to follow.[54] This perception is surely too simplistic to ground a major argument for the
desirability of capitalistic inequality.

If progress is sometimes seen as an accompaniment of inequality, envy is also seen in its absence. Nozick counters the claim that
equality is important to self-esteem by suggesting that a reduction of
inequality might make matters worse. This is because self-esteem is
based on differentiating characteristics (he says) and because

> some simple and natural assumptions might even lead to
> a principle of the conservation of envy. And one might
> worry, if the number of dimensions is not unlimited and
> if great strides are made to eliminate differences, that
> as the number of differentiating dimensions shrinks, envy
> will become more severe. For with a small number of
> differentiating dimensions, many people will find they
> don't do well on any of them.[55]

One might worry about such things. One might worry instead
about the kind of mind that thinks up such arguments. What Nozick
seems to be suggesting is that if inequalities of income are reduced,
then one who is ugly, ignorant and untalented would really be miserable
(and hence envious), since he could not even compensate by becoming
rich.

I don't think such an argument can be taken seriously. There is
no evidence for a "principle of conservation of envy." And if there
were such a principle, then reducing inequalities could not make envy
any worse, since ex hypothesis the quantity is unchangeable. And of
course self-esteem is not so much based on differentiating characteristics as on the way one is treated by others. (At least Hayek worried
aloud about his argument sounding like "far-fetched and cynical
apologetics.")

On this polemical note I will close this chapter. I have compared
laissez-faire capitalism with worker-control socialism, assuming a
fixed technology and no conflict between socialism and liberty. My
concentration has been on efficiency, and my conclusion is that the

socialist alternative is decidedly preferable. It promises less unemployment, fewer problems with the sales effort and more material equality. We must now ease away from some of our restrictive assumptions in order to bring other issues into focus.

NOTES

1. "Erst kommt das Fressen, dann kommt die Moral." Bertolt Brecht, Die Dreigroschenoper in Gesammelte Werke, Stũke 1 (Frankfurt: Suhrkamp Verlag, 1967), p. 458.
2. Cf. Nicolas Rescher, Distributive Justice (Indianapolis: Bobbs-Merrill, 1966), Chapter 2, for a more detailed analysis.
3. Cf. Joel Feinberg, Social Philosophy (Englewood Cliffs, N.J.: Prentice-Hall, 1973), pp. 111-17.
4. John Rawls, A Theory of Justice (Cambridge, Mass.: Belknap Press of Harvard University Press, 1971), p. 60.
5. Robert Nozick, Anarchy, State and Utopia (New York: Basic Books, 1974), p. 233.
6. Ibid.
7. Friedrich A. Hayek, The Constitution of Liberty (London: Routledge and Kegan Paul, 1960), p. 88.
8. Nozick, p. 238.
9. Not all economists are so squeamish about interpersonal comparisons. Cf. Julian Simon, "Interpersonal Comparisons Can Be Made—And Used for Redistribution Decisions," Kyklos 27 (1974): 63-98.
10. Tibor Scitovsky, Welfare and Competition, rev. ed., (Homewood, Ill.: Richard D. Irwin, 1971), p. 15.
11. Ibid., p. 16.
12. Ibid., p. 389.
13. Any post-Keynesian reference I've given so far will contain examples, as will virtually anything written by Joan Robinson.
14. See Milton Friedman's "The Methodology of Positive Economics," in his Essays on Positive Economics (Chicago: University of Chicago Press, 1953) for a full statement of this position.
15. For an excellent critique of the positivist justification of neoclassicism, see Martin Hollis and Edward Nell, Rational Economic Man: A Philosophical Critique of Neoclassical Economics (Cambridge: Cambridge University Press, 1975), especially Chapter I.
16. For a good introduction to the Marxist and neo-Ricardian critiques, which overlap somewhat with the post-Keynesian ones, see A Critique of Economic Theory, ed. E. K. Hunt and Jesse G. Schwartz (Baltimore: Penguin Books, 1972). A seminal work is Piero Sraffa, Production of Commodities by Means of Commodities (Cambridge: At the University Press, 1960). A crucial controversy is the "Cambridge

Controversy." (See G. C. Harcourt, Some Cambridge Controversies in the Theory of Capital [Cambridge: At the University Press, 1972].)

17. See Rolf Wild, Management by Compulsion (Boston: Houghton Mifflin, 1978) for an insider's account of business practices and their variance from the perfect-competition assumptions. See especially pp. 45-55.

18. Ludwig von Mises, "Economic Calculation in the Socialist Commonwealth," reprinted in Collectivist Economic Planning, ed. F. A. Hayek (New York: Augustus M. Kelley, 1935), p. 92.

19. A translation of Barone's article appears in Collectivist Economic Planning, pp. 245-90. The principal attack on von Mises was made by Fred Taylor and Oscar Lange, whose important essays on the subject are collected in On the Economic Theory of Socialism, ed. Benjamin Lippincott (Minneapolis: University of Minnesota Press, 1938). His principal defender was Hayek.

20. Von Mises insisted, as late as 1954, that "socialism is unrealizable as an economic system because a socialist society would not have any possibility of resorting to economic calculation. This is why it cannot be considered as a system of society's economic organization. It is a means to disintegrate social cooperation and to bring about poverty and chaos." The Anti-Capitalist Mentality (South Holland, Ill.: Libertarian Press, 1972), p. 102. For the prevailing view, see Abram Bergson, Essays in Normative Economics (Cambridge, Mass.: Belknap Press of Harvard University Press, 1966), p. 193.

21. Paul Gregory and Robert Stuart, Soviet Economic Structure and Performance (New York: Harper and Row, 1974), p. 2.

22. Benjamin Ward, The Socialist Economy: A Study of Organizational Alternatives (New York: Random House, 1967), p. 190.

23. Jaroslav Vanek, The Labor-Managed Economy (Ithaca: Cornell University Press, 1977), p. 20. Ward's result, clever though it is, is a good example of a mis-insight suggested by neoclassical analysis. The argument is as follows: If we assume declining marginal productivity, then each additional worker added to a firm will diminish gross income per worker; hence, the profit-per-worker would be maximal when the firm employs one worker—except for the fact that fixed costs per worker also decline when additional workers are added. So employment stabilizes at a level higher than unity, but behavior is still perverse; a price increase makes the per-worker loss due to the last employee increase, and so he will be laid off, whereas, if prices fall, the per-worker loss is less, and so another will be taken on. This argument is technically correct, given the assumption that firms maximize per-worker income (and also the declining marginal productivity assumption), but the behavior it implies strains credulity.

24. Cf. John Maynard Keynes, The General Theory of Employ-

ment, Interest and Money (New York: Harcourt, Brace and World, 1936), pp. 27-32 for a summary of this employment theory.

25. Hayek, Constitution of Liberty, pp. 270-71.

26. Ibid., p. 280.

27. Keynes, General Theory, p. 30; cf. also Chapter 21.

28. Ibid., p. 9.

29. Cf. Friedman, Capitalism and Freedom, p. 180: "The state can legislate a minimum wage rate. It can hardly require employers to hire at that minimum all who were formerly employed at wages below the minimum. . . . The effect of the minimum wage is therefore to make unemployment higher than it otherwise would be."

30. Cf. James Meade, "The Theory of Labor-Managed Firms and of Profit Sharing," Self-Management: Economic Liberation of Man, ed. Jaroslav Vanek (Baltimore: Penguin Education, 1975), pp. 414-15. for more on the economic desirability of "institutionalized solidarity."

31. Hayek, Constitution of Liberty, pp. 280-81 and 324-39; also F. A. Hayek, A Tiger by the Tail: the Keynesian Legacy of Inflation (Tonbridge, Kent: Institute of Economic Affairs, 1972). Also Friedman, Capitalism and Freedom, p. 76.

32. Paul Baran and Paul Sweezy, Monopoly Capital (New York: Monthly Review Press, Modern Reader Paperbacks, 1966), p. 121. Their entire Chapter Three, "The Sales Effort," is recommended to anyone interested in the Marxist approach. So also is Stewart Ewen, Captains of Consciousness: Advertising and the Social Roots of Consumer Culture (New York: McGraw-Hill, 1976).

33. John Kenneth Galbraith, The New Industrial State (Boston: Houghton Mifflin, 1967), p. 200.

34. John Kenneth Galbraith, "Power and the Useful Economist: Presidential Address to the 85th Meeting of the American Economics Association," American Economic Review, 63 (March 1973): 3.

35. Robert Solow, "Science and Ideology," in Capitalism Today, ed. Irving Kristol and Daniel Bell (New York: Basic Books, 1970), p. 105.

36. Friedman, Capitalism and Freedom, p. 15.

37. Jules Backman, Advertising and Competition (New York: New York University Press, 1967), p. 160. (Is it inappropriate to note that Backman was aided in his work by a grant from the Association of National Advertisers?)

38. Robert Solow, "The Truth Further Refined: A Comment on Marris," The Public Interest (Spring 1968): 48.

39. Cf. Robin Marris, "Galbraith, Solow and the Truth about Corporations," The Public Interest (Spring 1968): 38. "After a quarter of a century during which advertising has become one of the outstanding features of our economic life, and scientific economics has been intensively developed, the relevant experiments have not been tried." Cf.

also, James Ferguson, Advertising and Competition: Theory, Measurement and Fact (Cambridge, Mass.: Ballinger, 1973), a defense of advertising on the grounds that a defendant must be assumed innocent until proven guilty.

40. "It is not from the benevolence of the butcher, the brewer, or the baker that we expect our dinner, but from their regard to their own interest. We address ourselves, not to their humanity but to their self-love, and never talk to them of our own necessities but of their advantage." Adam Smith, An Inquiry Into the Nature and Causes of the Wealth of Nations (New York: Modern Library, 1937), p. 14.

41. Among the best-sellers are Vance Packard, The Hidden Persuaders (New York: Pocket Books, 1958) and The Waste Makers (New York: D. McKay Co., 1960); also William Key, Subliminal Seduction (Englewood Cliffs, N.J.: Prentice-Hall, 1973) and Media Sexploitation (Englewood Cliffs, N.J.: Prentice-Hall, 1976).

42. Rosser Reeves, Reality in Advertising (New York: Knopf, 1961), quoted by Baran and Sweezy (Monopoly Capitol) p. 129.

43. Cf. Scitovsky, Welfare and Competition, pp. 87-95, for the full-blown technical argument.

44. Vanek gives a technical argument for this conclusion. See his General Theory, pp. 120-24, and his Labor-Managed Economy, pp. 232-37.

45. See Abba Lerner, Economics of Control, pp. 23-40, for an elegant version of the classical argument. A.K. Sen mathematizes Lerner's argument and provides one of his own in On Economic Inequality (Oxford: Clarendon Press, 1973), pp. 83-87.

46. Scitovsky, Welfare and Competition, p. 288.

47. Keynes, General Theory, p. 376.

48. Friedman, Capitalism and Freedom, p. 166.

49. See Ferdinand Lundberg, The Rich and the Super-Rich (New York: Bantam Books, 1968) for an eye-opening account. For a briefer but wonderfully graphic depiction, see "A Parade of Dwarves (and a few Giants)" in Jan Pen, Income Distribution: Facts, Theories, Policies (New York: Praeger, 1971), pp. 48-58.

50. Lundberg, Rich and Super-Rich, p. 27. By 1968 millionaires had become so plentiful that Fortune could proclaim, "The U.S. has become so affluent that there is no longer any great prestige in being a mere millionaire. The very word 'millionaire' is seldom used nowadays; indeed it has an almost quaint sound. It belongs to the era some decades back when a net worth of $1 million was considered a 'fortune'; a millionaire was a member of a small class, and therefore a natural object of curiosity. To have a net worth of $1 million today is to be, much of the time, indistinguishable from members of the omnipresent middle class." (Arthur M. Louis, "America's Centimillionaires," Fortune, May 1968, p. 152.) The same article identified 153

centimillionaires (and not a movie star, professional athlete or physician in evidence). In an earlier article <u>Fortune</u> listed 76 of the nation's largest fortunes, of which 41 were mainly by virtue of inheritance and 23 were linked to oil. (Richard A. Smith, "The Fifty-Million Dollar Man," <u>Fortune</u>, November 1957, p. 177.)

51. Hayek, <u>Constitution of Liberty,</u> p. 45.

52. <u>Lundberg, Rich and Super-Rich,</u> p. 9.

53. For a sophisticated analysis germane to this point, see Fred Hirsch, <u>Social Limits to Growth</u> (Cambridge, Mass.: Harvard University Press, 1976).

54. "In a progressive society as we know it, the comparatively wealthy are thus merely somewhat ahead of the rest in the material advantages which they enjoy. They are already living in a phase of evolution that the others have not yet reached." Hayek, <u>Constitution of Liberty</u>, p. 44.

55. Nozick, <u>Anarchy, State and Utopia,</u> p. 245.

4

CAPITALISM OR SOCIALISM: GROWTH

There are difficulties with laissez-faire. This we have seen. It is vulnerable to unemployment, to the emergence of a massive apparatus of nonrational sales persuasion and to inequalities unconnected with ability or effort. But its defenses have not been completely breached. For it is open to an advocate of laissez-faire to counter with the claim that these difficulties, real though they may be, pale in the face of capitalism's stunning accomplishment: its unparalleled record of innovative growth. Whatever its faults, she might say, capitalism has been and remains a remarkable engine of progress; to discard it would be idiotic and disastrous. This is the issue we must now join. Our fixed-technology assumption has kept the question at bay; that assumption must be dropped. We must begin a serious investigation of the connection between capitalism and growth.

This, of course, is as much an ethical inquiry as our investigation of efficiency, and it will also involve an appeal to values. We need not expand our list. The arguments in this chapter will invoke material well-being and human happiness. There will be some reference to equality, but not so much as in the last chapter. We will encounter democracy in this chapter, but it need not be considered here a distinct value with intrinsic worth. Democracy is a value, like equality, about which classical liberals have reservations. Especially in the nineteenth century these were frequently expressed.[1] Contemporary classical liberals appear to have fewer reservations; they are generally willing to concede democracy instrumental, if not intrinsic, value. For the arguments in this chapter, that is all we need. Hayek's judgment that "[h]owever strong the general case for democracy, it is not an absolute value and must be judged by what it will achieve"[2] need not be disputed.

To plunge into the growth issue, we might begin by asking whether it can be <u>proven</u> that the investments of capitalist entrepreneurs generate optimal expansion. Cambridge University's Marxist economist, Maurice Dobb, finds such a suggestion incredible: "Only myopic concentration upon stationary equilibrium could breed the supposition that there is even a <u>prima facie</u> case for regarding long-term investments under free-market constraints as optimal."[3] To be sure, one can construct a formal proof if one makes the appropriate assumptions, but these assumptions do not pretend to even rough correspondence with reality. Phelps provides a typical list. Not only must a perfectly-competitive equilibrium be attained (no mean condition in itself), but also

(1) there is perfect information about current and future prices (including interest rates and wage rates) over the lifetime of the population and also perfect information about current and future supplies of public goods;
(2) producers have perfect information about current and future technology over the lifetime of the population;
(3) there are no externalities of production;*
(4) consumers have perfect information about current and future tastes over their lifetime, and their preferences are unchanging over time;
(5) there are no externalities of consumption other than public goods whose production we take as given.[4]

It is obvious from this list that we need not concern ourselves with formal proofs—but it is also plain, upon reflection, that formal proofs are not the real issue. Dobb's remark seems hyperbolic, for there is a <u>prima facie</u> case for capitalism: the empirical record of its accomplishments. Even Marx and Engels were impressed.† As one writer has put it:

> Judged solely by [economic] standards, it would seem that history has already awarded the contemporary rivalry to private capitalist enterprise. In all the statistical rankings of nations according to their accumulated wealth or per capita income, those which have fostered capitalism occupy the top positions on the list.[5]

---

*"Externalities" will be discussed below.
†Recall the quote on p. 47.

An empirical argument such as this must be approached cautiously. Even if one waives reservations about statistical indicators—why was per capita income selected and not rate of growth? Why was it not noted that the capitalist projects had substantial head starts?—one must be on guard against the logical fallacy, post hoc ergo propter hoc. The reign of capital may be contemporary with technical innovation and the rise of material prosperity, but are these phenomena causally linked? Temporal coincidence suggests a prima facie connection, but it also suggests prima facie connections between capitalism and the African slave trade, global imperialism, and the most destructive wars known to humanity, connections which proponents of capitalism would presumably call accidental. What we must ask about are the structural features of capitalism (laissez-faire in particular, since that is the ideal we are investigating) that are conducive to innovation and growth.

But these structures are surely no mystery. Advocates of capitalism will immediately point out that capitalism encourages individual initiative, that it gives free reign to that "entrepreneurial spirit" which seeks out and transforms into reality new ideas for products and technologies, that it provides, via competitive pressure and the lure of great gain, a relentless stimulus to innovative growth.

Yes, but is this stimulus optimal? It might be suggested that capitalism gives maximal encouragement to initiative, but that claim is open to dispute. For if we compare laissez-faire with our model of worker control, we see that both are competitive and both allow "entrepreneurs" to appeal to institutions for funds for new projects. Capitalism also allows the investment of one's own savings, while worker control does not (at least it does not allow one to collect interest or dividends on one's savings), but this structural difference admits no inference as to the relative quantity of investment funds available under the two systems. By taxing themselves, the people of a socialist society can decide on any level of investment consistent with their physical capabilities, for less or for more than the capitalist total.

It can be urged in support of capitalism that individuals need not go through an institutional bureaucracy to begin a project. This is true, but its significance is questionable. In contemporary capitalist societies few investment projects are unmediated by institutions similar in bureaucratic structure to a socialist investment bank. Small entrepreneurs usually appeal to lending institutions, which carefully scrutinize their proposals; large corporations, even when financing experiments internally, submit project proposals originating in one department to other departments for evaluation. And even if it is granted that bureaucratic encumbrances are significantly less under laissez-faire, this difference must be sufficient to counterbalance two structural advantages of worker control. First of all, under worker control, anyone with a good idea can request funds; he need not have personal savings or even collateral. This would seem to allow for greater initiative than under capitalism, where the risk of failure, particularly to a small business, is so high. Secondly, and perhaps more significantly, there is far more room for individual initiative within a worker-managed firm than within a capitalist one. Since workers have a direct stake in the successful operation of the enterprise and a democratic forum to present their ideas, individuals have both the incentive and the opportunity to initiate changes—including changes that might make work more satisfying. (As we shall see in the next chapter, changes of this sort are especially problematic for capitalism.)

A proponent of capitalism might respond to these observations by modifying her claim. She might wish to claim, not initiative maximization for capitalism, but initiative optimalization. She might wish to maintain that initiative under worker control would be excessive, that too many people would request funds, generating a bureaucratic quagmire, and that too much workplace democracy would degenerate into inefficiency and chaos.[6] One can make such claims, but one can do little to back them up. The empirical record, especially with respect to workplace democracy, is certainly not supportive.[7] Worker-managed firms are not without internal tensions, but they do seem to work.

An alternative response in defense of capitalism is to claim that the considerations advanced in favor of worker control are insufficient to counterbalance the major advantage of capitalism: the motive force of the possibility of great wealth. Opportunities for innovation might exist under worker control, but these opportunities are less likely to be realized, since a crucial incentive is lacking.

This claim cannot be answered so simply. We cannot say a priori which system provides the greater stimulation for innovation. Nor should we be too quick to appeal to comparative statistics—for that would involve rushing past an important consideration. A defense of capitalism based on its ability to motivate economic growth presupposes that the innovative growth of the kind produced by capitalism is a good to be maximized; it presupposes that an alternative society should strive to equal or surpass such growth. But such presuppositions are less than self-evident. A deeper analysis is in order.

WHAT KIND OF GROWTH?

Objections to the kind of growth, to the specific products and technologies, generated by laissez-faire are not unfamiliar. Economists themselves have long pointed out that "externalities" or "neighborhood effects" render certain market transactions nonoptimal. When a transaction affects others than those directly involved, either positively or negatively, the market mechanism does not give an accurate account of costs and benefits. [8] Environmental deterioration is a commonly cited example. The costs to a community of air pollution are not reflected in the free-market price of commodities produced by a highly polluting technology. If two technologies are equally costly to the producer, one more polluting than the other, he has no immediate economic incentive to select the less polluting one. Thus the market neither encourages the development of low-polluting technologies nor thwarts the development of high-polluting ones, and so technologies evolve in a nonoptimal manner.

Production externalities force laissez-faire growth away from optimality, but these difficulties are widely recognized, even by classical liberals. Governmental intervention here is at least grudgingly sanctioned. [9] Consumption externalities, however, present a deeper problem for classical liberalism (and for capitalism generally), problems less amenable to simple reform. A basic assumption of neoclassical economics is that an individual's consumption is a private matter affecting only herself. This, of course, is manifestly untrue in a large number of cases. The decision of my neighbor to buy beer in disposable bottles has consequences that affect me: a rise in litter, a decline in the natural resources available to my children, a rise (eventually) in the cost of municipal waste treatment. The private decisions of separate individuals to buy automobiles instead of horses changed the physical and social structures of continents—for those who purchased them and for those who did not.

At issue here is something other than unforeseen consequences, a difficulty from which no social system can hope to be immune. (To foresee the effects of disposable bottles is scarcely beyond the power of the human mind.) In a free-market economy the collective effect of new consumption patterns are consequent on major investment decisions, and investment decisions fall within the "private" sphere, outside the democratic process. In most cases citizens are not even aware of these decisions until long after they have been made.

After the decisions have been made, and after their effects have been felt, political action is possible (if we assume for a moment that political action regarding a free-market response to consumer preference is not ruled out of court by classical liberalism), but by then the context has altered significantly. When investment decisions have solidified into brick and steel and have engaged the livelihood of thousands, the moral as well as physical environment has shifted. Bottle companies are not wrong to appeal to the human sacrifice involved in reconverting plants, in laying off workers, in rupturing old habits— moral considerations that would not have applied when the decisions were originally made.

Individual action—refusing to buy—is also possible under capitalism, and is the response much preferred by classical liberalism, but individual action has even less chance of success. As Sen's "Isolation Paradox" demonstrates, the very logic of individual decision making is different from that of collective choice.[10] When confronted as an individual consumer with the option of buying an eight-pack of beer in disposable bottles, I might well decide that the convenience is worth the disutility, the latter being the effect on the environment of eight more bottles. Confronted with the analogous choice in a political context, however, I might decide—without any inconsistency—that the convenience of disposable bottles is not worth the disutility, for now the option is an environment free of disposable bottles. It follows that a society of quite rational people, all of whom prefer a litter-free environment to the convenience of disposable bottles, might well find themselves inundated anyway—if they allow the market to effect the decision. Such an outcome is clearly not optimal, not even in terms of the individuals' own preferences. (We see here the logical fallacy of blaming consumers for the deleterious effects of many contemporary developments. What we get is not necessarily what we want, nor what we would have chosen had the alternatives been differently posed. Macroscopic outcomes do not reveal the preferences of even quite rational consumers.)

The problem here (called by some the "tyranny of small decisions")[11] is not confined to beer bottles:

[P]urchase of books at discount stores eventually removes the local bookshop. Yet bookbuyers can never exercise a choice as between cheaper books with no bookshop and dearer books with one. The choice they are offered is between books at cut price and books at full price; naturally, they take the former. The effective choice of continuance of a bookshop at the expense of dearer books is never posed. Everyone has the choice of living in the city as it is or in the suburb as it is, but not between living in the suburb and the city as they will be when the consequences of such choices have been worked through. The house in the suburbs appears desirable in itself (just like the lower price tag on the book). Whether its attractions outweigh the subsequent deterioration of suburban amenities and perhaps the effective destruction of the city, which this choice in company with other people's carries in its train, is never put to the test.[12]

As these cases make quite clear, the market determination of investment decisions is not always preferable to a political determination. One should not too hastily conclude, however, that it never is. Even apart from the fact that it would be impossible in practice for votes to be taken on every investment choice, it is by no means evident that if some people want hula hoops or digital watches or anchovies on their pizzas, then the community should decide. Democratic decision making has drawbacks of its own, among them time-consumption, a bureaucratic tendency, and a "tyranny of the majority" possibility to set beside the "tyranny of small decisions."*

In light of these considerations the case for the superiority of the investment mechanism of worker control is plain to see. Investments under worker control are neither left to the market nor made irrespective of market considerations; they are neither made on a one-person one-vote basis, nor independently of the democratic process. Investment funds are generated by taxation. Plans—guidelines for their dispensation—are drawn up by local, regional and national investment boards, which set general priorities and specify those projects that will require large commitments of resources. Once these plans have been approved by the appropriate legislatures, the funds are given out by investment banks to those proposals that are economically feasible and within the scope of the guidelines. Given this structure, small-scale, experimental projects are likely to be funded primarily on the basis of projected profitability. If there is a significant demand for a product, even if only by a small minority, then a proposal to meet that demand will appear economically attractive, and thus a good candidate for funding. On the other hand, if an

---

*Social decision making is beset with theoretical difficulties that have occupied much attention since the publication of Kenneth Arrow's celebrated "impossibility theorem." (Kenneth Arrow, Social Choice and Individual Values [New Haven: Yale University Press, 1951].) Arrow proved that if one wants a procedure for ranking alternatives that is "rational" (i.e., transitive, reflexive and complete over an unrestricted domain), unaffected by "irrelevant alternatives," and reflective of individual preferences (at least to the extent that one state of affairs will be more highly ranked than another if everyone prefers it), then the only possibility is dictatorship. Neither majoritarian democracy, nor any other mechanism will suffice. We will not concern ourselves with Arrow's result, since it, quite unlike the "tyranny of small decisions," has no practical bearing on the issues at hand. (See A. K. Sen, Collective Choice and Social Welfare [San Francisco: Holden-Day, 1970] for a good account of the various facets of the impossibility controversy.)

experiment has proven successful and many proposals to expand the experiment are submitted to investment banks, then the matter begins to impinge itself on the investment boards (which hold public hearings about priorities and major projects) and upon the legislative bodies (which must pass on the investment plans). Thus the political community has a forum for debate and a decisive voice, regarding the direction of major economic change. And it exercises this influence before the large-scale commitment of labor and resources.

This mechanism is not fool-proof. A significant segment of investment—that carried out with depreciation funds—is outside the planning authority. This is both a strength and a weakness. It enhances the autonomy of the individual enterprise and mitigates against heavy-handed impositions of majoritarian values; on the other hand, coordinated planning is more difficult, and community control is weakened.* Nor can the mechanism guarantee that consequences will always be foreseen correctly and that investment mistakes will not be made. Post factum corrections may well be required. What the mechanism does do, however, and this is its fundamental strength vis-a-vis laissez-faire, is provide for conscious debate and democratic control over major economic developments. And it does so without choking off experimentation or exposing itself (unduly) to the risk of majoritarian or bureaucratic "tyranny" over individual wants and desires. Granted, economic change might not take place so rapidly, since a democratic decision procedure injects a note of caution, but this, in light of the "tyranny of small decisions" is by no means an unambiguous disadvantage.

Planned investment exhibits another important advantage over laissez-faire over and above its ability to better cope with externalities of production and consumption. It is widely recognized by economists that if investment projects are not coordinated, then growth will not be balanced, in which case potential profitability will not

---

*As I remarked earlier, the distinction between new investment and that from depreciation funds is somewhat arbitrary. Firms could be required to turn over all or part of these funds to the investment boards. This would strengthen the ability of the boards to plan coherently—but it would also concentrate their power. This question—the optimal degree of investment autonomy—cannot be settled abstractly. It seems desirable to give firms some autonomy with respect to investment, but by no means the autonomy of capitalist (or Yugoslavian) firms.

reflect social desirability. The Marxist Dobb quotes with approval the liberal Scitovsky:

> Only if expansion in the . . . industries were integrated and planned together would the profitability of investment in each of them be a reliable index of its social desirability. . . . Complete integration of all industries would be necessary to eliminate all divergence between private profit and public benefit. . . .[13]

The reason for this is easy to illustrate. Suppose, at given market prices, new housing looks highly profitable. Investments will flow into this area, creating a sharp increase in the demand for building materials, and consequently a rise in their prices. But this makes housing less profitable, and so some construction is halted, and investment funds are shifted toward building materials enterprises instead. This process clearly involves a degree of waste that could have been avoided had coordinated investment channelled funds simultaneously into housing construction and the building materials industries.

Projected profitability in the above example overstates the economic desirability of a particular type of investment. In other cases it understates it (e.g., when a new technique reduces costs of intermediate goods). In either case deviation from optimality occurs that is not due to random acts of nature or unpredictable changes in consumer preferences, but to a lack of communication among decision makers. Such deviations can be eliminated only by comprehensive, coordinated planning.

This defect can be (and is) mitigated somewhat under capitalism by the collection and dissemination of information by governmental and private agencies and also by the integration of independent firms into single corporations. This latter movement, with its tendency toward monopoly, is scarcely an unmixed blessing, especially to a classical liberal. The former is hampered by the sharp separation under capitalism between public and private sectors. If a decision is made to locate a plant in a particular area, then investments should be made not only in the raw materials industries serving the plant, but also in housing for the workers, in power and sewage facilities, etc. The market mechanism <u>sometimes</u> produces these results. If an entrepreneur decides to locate a plant in a particular region and if he pays his employees enough to generate a demand for new housing, then housing will eventually be constructed. And if the tax base is sufficiently increased, social services may be increased also. These developments might follow—but then again they might not. The U.S. inner-cities testify to alternative possibilities. To cite a much-quoted Galbraithian passage from the late 1950s:

The family which takes its mauve and cerice, air-con-
ditioned, power-steered, and power-braked automobile
out for a tour passes through cities that are badly paved,
made hideous by litter, blighted buildings, billboards
and posts for wires that should long since have been put
underground. They pass on into a countryside that has
been rendered largely invisible by commercial art. . . .
They picnic on exquisitely packaged food from a portable
icebox by a polluted stream and go on to spend the night
at a park which is a menace to public health and morals.
Just before dozing off on an air mattress beneath a nylon
tent, amid the stench of decaying refuse, they may reflect vaguely on the curious unevenness of their bless-
ings.[14]

Under worker control, so sharp a separation between public and
private does not exist. One can distinguish between enterprises that
generate income by selling services and products on the market, and
those—police, fire departments, highway maintenance units, etc.—
that are funded directly by the government. But the former are not
"private" since the community "owns" the facility, and the latter, as
well as the former, acquire their capital from the same source, namely the investment fund. Since the funds which finance new schools, new
sewers, new roads come from the same place as those that finance new
factories, there is no structural difficulty in coordinating development.* Balanced growth, though of course not inevitable, is far more
likely than under laissez-faire.

---

*How will salaries for governmental employees be generated?
By taxation, of course, but of what sort? Investment funds come from
taxes on capital assets. These taxes could also be used to generate
the revenue for all public expenses, but that would probably be unwise,
since too high a tax on capital assets would unduly restrain their being
acquired. The best solution would likely be an income or sales tax
for general governmental expenses, the capital tax restricted to generating investment funds. A coordination problem of sorts presents
itself, since investment in a governmental facility must coincide with
an allocation for the salaries of those who will operate it—but since
the legislature decides on both the investment plan and the current
budget, the problem should be manageable.

Laissez-faire thus founders on the shoals of externalities and unbalanced growth. These factors rip through the claim that the profitability of an investment measures its social utility. So too does a third factor, an objection from the last chapter now transposed to the dynamic setting. If balanced growth and the absence of externalities are necessary for private profitability to reflect social desirability, so too is an equitable distribution of wealth. Since projected profitability is based on a survey of <u>dollar</u> votes, a misallocation of income will not only misallocate existing consumer goods, but also those investment projects designed to increase consumer goods in the future.

The classical liberal might object that this argument is circular. It was conceded at the beginning of this chapter that laissez-faire admitted inequalities unrelated to effort or ability, but it was urged that this defect was more than counterbalanced by the system's capacity for growth. Now I seem to be arguing that this growth is nonoptimal because the distribution of wealth is nonoptimal—but how can I say that the distribution of wealth is nonoptimal until I have shown the growth to be nonoptimal? Of course I have offered two independent arguments that growth under laissez-faire is nonoptimal, but there is a point to the classical liberal's complaint. I have argued that the <u>kind</u> of growth that takes place under laissez-faire is nonoptimal, whereas the classical liberal is speaking of <u>rate</u> of growth. In Hayek's words, "The rapid economic advance that we have come to expect seems in large measure to be the result of this inequality and to be impossible without it. Progress at such a fast rate cannot proceed in a uniform front but must take place echelon fashion, with some far ahead of the rest. . . ."[15]

I have already disputed Hayek's particular view that a special class is necessary to try out the goods and services that will eventually become the province of all, but the more general argument is not without plausibility. I have not yet established the ethical nonoptimality of laissez-faire distribution or laissez-faire growth, since all factors have not yet been considered. I have merely established <u>prima facie</u> nonoptimality. The argument I must confront is that the rate of capitalist growth under laissez-faire is such as to more than compensate for the <u>prima facie</u> inequity associated with income distribution and the other factors discussed in the last chapter and for the <u>prima facie</u> nonoptimality just discussed regarding externality difficulties and lack of balance experienced by laissez-faire. Of course one could retort, not without justice, that the rate of growth is irrelevant if the kind of growth is grievously distorted. More of a bad thing is not good. But this is not the response I will make. Not only am I unpersuaded myself that negative effects of capitalist growth outweigh the positive, but I think that much can be learned by examining the rate question separately.

HOW FAST TO GROW?

Let us assume throughout this section that the kinds of investments made under laissez-faire are not problematic, that the goods
and services produced have no serious externality effects and are produced in balanced proportions unskewed by an inequitable distribution
of income. Even with these assumptions it does not follow that maximal growth is desirable. In fact, it is not clear precisely what "maximal" growth means, since production involves resource and leisure
costs. At minimum, "maximal" is subject to the proviso that the
future remain open, that resources not be recklessly squandered. It
must also be qualified—to the point that the term "maximal" is inappropriate—by reference to labor time. If people work sixteen-hour
days, they will produce more than if they work eight. The optimal
rate of growth must involve a balance of consumption now versus consumption later, and also consumption now versus leisure now.

One of the arguments of the last section against the kind of
growth is also an argument against the rate of growth. Balanced
growth is more efficient than unbalanced growth; it will accomplish a
given end with less sacrifice of leisure and resources. Since balanced
growth is more likely under worker control, if all else is equal, then
its growth rate will be higher.

But of course all else is not equal, far from it, and that brings
us to a more fundamental objection to the rate of growth under capitalism. If we ask how the growth rate is determined, we see at once
that it is not the outcome of a democratic procedure. To be sure, no
society can determine in advance exactly how fast it will grow, even
if a consensus were reached as to how fast it should grow. Growth
depends significantly on primary uncertainty, especially on technological innovation. A society can, however, make decisions that affect the
growth rate in important ways. It can decide, for example, what percent of its human and natural resources is to be devoted to research
and development, and to the establishment of new production facilities
embodying the latest technology. Such decisions allocate a certain
portion of the labor force and a certain portion of the nonhuman resources of society to the production of things that are not for immediate consumption. Such allocations involve a tradeoff (at least under
conditions of full employment), a sacrifice of either consumer goods
or leisure now so as to have more at a later date.

Under worker control, the decision most relevant to the growth
rate is the decision concerning the tax on capital assets, for this tax
is the source of new investment funds. It is this decision that determines the portion of the national product to be devoted to the expansion
of the economy. It is a decision that must be made consciously by the
national legislature.

Under capitalism the analogous decision is not made by a democratic assembly, nor is it the outcome of consumer preferences as revealed by their market purchases. Under capitalism the macrosopic decision as to how much to invest is made consciously by—no one. The societal decision is the unplanned outcome of the individual decisions of firms and entrepreneurs who have (or can lay hands on) something to invest. The nondemocratic character of this decision is well illustrated in Keynes's description of pre–World War I capitalism:

> The immense accumulations of fixed capital which, to the great benefit of mankind, were built up during the half century before the war, could never have come about in a Society where wealth was divided equitably. The railways of the world, which that age built as a monument to posterity, were, not less than the Pyramids of Egypt, the work of labor which was not free to consume in immediate enjoyment the full equivalent of its efforts.
>
> Thus this remarkable system depended for its growth on a double bluff or deception. On the one hand the laboring classes accepted from ignorance or powerlessness, or were compelled, persuaded or cajoled by custom, convention, authority and the well-established order of Society into accepting a situation in which they could call their own very little of the cake that they and Nature and the capitalists were cooperating to produce. And on the other hand the capitalist classes were allowed to call the best part of the cake theirs and were theoretically free to consume it, on the tacit underlying condition that they consumed very little of it in practice. The duty of "saving" became nine-tenths of virtue and the growth of the cake the object of true religion. . . .[16]

If this account acknowledges the nondemocratic character of capitalist growth, it also suggests a defense, a defense Keynes makes more explicit in the next paragraph:

> The cake was really very small in proportion to the appetites of consumption, and no one, if it were shared all round, would be much better off by the cutting of it. Society was not working for the small pleasures of today but for the future security and improvement of the race, — in fact for "progress."[17]

What we have here is a utilitarian defense of a nondemocratic procedure much like the standard defense of Stalin's forced industrialization: the people, if allowed to choose, would not choose wisely. One who values democracy must look with suspicion at such a defense, but the defense cannot be dismissed out of hand. If one's commitment to democracy is less than absolute—as is mine and classical liberalism's (and according to Schumpeter everyone else's[18])—one must remain open to the possibility that there are overriding factors to be considered.

But the factors cited by Keynes, the smallness of the cake and the need to enlarge it rapidly, would hardly seem relevant to a modern industrialized nation. The cake now is quite large.* There is no overpowering need for increase; nor is overwhelming sacrifice required if growth is pursued. Conditions seem to be quite favorable to a democratic determination. Can it seriously be maintained that the unplanned outcome of decisions taken by a small class of people answerable only to themselves (and stockholders) would more likely accord with what the majority of the populace need or want than would a democratic decision?

Perhaps. A classical liberal counterattack is possible on two fronts. First, it might be conceded that worker control can generate an investment fund as large as laissez-faire's, but it might be denied that this fund would be as effectively utilized. For lacking is a major motive force, the possibility of an entrepreneurial bonanza. But this objection lacks theoretical or empirical support. As noted earlier, worker control provides a variety of motivations for the socialist entrepreneur. Moreover, the growth rates of most socialist countries testify to the fact that the capitalist incentive (the possibility of a perpetual bonanza—not to be confused with mere monetary incentive) is not essential to growth.

Another objection might be raised. Classical liberals are fond of stressing the depths of human ignorance and our inability to subject everything to human reason.[19] So they might well deny that people can make an intelligent decision about the rate of investment; they might well maintain that such a decision would be arbitrary, in no way comparable to the rate achieved under capitalism.

To analyze this charge, we must consider what is involved in reaching the investment decision under worker control. The initial

---

*The total personal income of the 217 million citizens of the United States was $1530 billion in 1977; that is more than $7000 for every man, woman and child (United States Department of Commerce, Survey of Current Business [January 1979], p. S-2).

rate, of course, is rather arbitrary; a society would have the historical investment rates of capitalist and socialist societies to go by, but the precise figure (the tax rate on capital assets) can be no more than an educated choice. Subsequently, the legislature must decide whether this rate is satisfying expectations. If not, it may be raised or lowered.

What exactly is the effect of a vote to increase or decrease the investment rate? How is it felt by the populace at large? A vote to increase (at least under conditions of full employment) is a vote to decrease present consumption. Taxes will rise, and the proceeds will go to channelling workers into research and development and into new construction, activities that promise to increase the quality of life at a later date. Demand for consumer goods will drop somewhat (since taxes are up) and so will supply (since some workers are lured out of consumer goods industries). Of course, if there is less than full employment, consumption need not suffer. Taxes increase, but so do sales (since newly employed workers become consumers) and so, therefore, does production. But in general an increase in investment will entail a drop in consumption.

A vote to decrease the investment rate, on the other hand, is a vote to increase leisure (and also some consumption), but at the cost of decreasing funding for research and construction that promise more goods or leisure later. The increase in leisure is felt immediately in those sectors of the economy most dependent on demand generated by new investments. There "leisure" will not likely be regarded as an unmixed blessing. Construction workers, building-materials suppliers, etc., must cut back production, and decrease the length of the working day (or week, or year, or whatever the firm democratically decides). If the decline in income is too severe to be compensated for by the increased leisure, some workers will seek employment elsewhere—in those firms not immediately affected. The workers in these latter enterprises, whose incomes have just increased as a result of the tax cut, are thus in a position (and under pressure) to take on these workers, with the result that the workload per person declines in these enterprises as well.

(This dislocation and movement of workers is, of course, similar to what occurs under capitalism when investments decline. The socialist response compares favorably on two counts. The investment decline is a democratic decision, well publicized, and thus capable of being planned for by firms likely to be affected. Retiring workers, for example, would not be replaced. Secondly, the response to demand decline in a particular area is a decline in the working hours for everyone, and not, as is usual under capitalism, the laying off of part of the workforce.)

This analysis of investment-rate decisions brings into view a striking feature of worker control. There is no particular bias in the direction of a high rate of investment. From the perspective of the voter, there are advantages to be had from a high rate and also from a low rate. Which set the electorate would prefer (and vote to accomplish) cannot be predicted a priori. Laissez-faire (and capitalism generally) contrasts sharply on this point. As Keynes observed, "the growth of the cake [is] an object of true religion." And Marx: "Accumulate, accumulate! That is Moses and the prophets!"[20] In a capitalist climate investment is imperative. The profit of a firm (at least a substantial share) will likely be reinvested, for size enhances a firm's ability to act aggressively against competitors and to resist their threatening moves. Nor is investment a painful necessity to the individual capitalist. Investment increases her real wealth and also her power and prestige. Consumption has its rewards, to be sure, but so does investment, all the more so since it does not foreclose the consumption option, but merely (risks aside) extends it.[21]

So we see, our critic is right. There is no reason to assume that the rate of investment under worker control will approximate that achieved under capitalism. A vote to increase the investment rate does not insure that the funds will go to one's own firm; they might, but they might also go to one's competitor. This latter occurrence is not terribly threatening, however, since that firm has little incentive (as we've repeatedly noted) to expand rapidly and thus to threaten the existence of the other. Nor does a vote to invest more immediately enhance the power and prestige of the voter; the well-being and prestige of the community might be enhanced if investments are well made, but the positive effects will be felt only later. In general, the motivational forces that strongly incline (wealthy) individuals in a capitalist society to invest are absent under worker control, and that absence is filled by quite different forces.

So our critic is right- about the fact, but not about its significance. It is true that capitalist and socialist growth rates are likely to be different—but it hardly follows that this conclusion favors capitalism. Since the rate of investment in a capitalist society is in no way subject to popular approval, what can be the grounds for concluding that the investment rates of capitalism are optimal? Especially under laissez-faire, one gets what the invisible hand decrees—but the market reflects no societal preference whatsoever here.* (The

---

*The market, which can be legitimately regarded as a quasi-democratic mechanism for registering societal preferences for various sorts of consumer goods, has no such legitimacy as an indicator of societal preference for a rate of investment. It is not implausible

fact that people do not rebel is scarcely relevant, since by that criterion most nations at most times in human history have been optimal. The fact that political administrations continually plump for growth is no proof either, for, as we shall see in the next section, growth is essential to <u>capitalist</u> stability, and instability is a politician's bane.)

Our critic, who is not overly concerned with democracy anyway, has one final retort: growth, rapid growth, is good, whether people want it or not. Hayek seems to be of this opinion. The "free" society, he says, is the maximally progressive one. It is irrelevant, he continues, whether we would be happier if we stopped today or had stopped a hundred years ago; the point is not to stop:

> What matters is the successful striving for what at each
> moment seems attainable. It is not the fruits of past
> success but the living in and for the future in which
> human intelligence proves itself. Progress is movement
> for movement's sake. . . .[22]

However, he notes a few pages later,

> we must also admit that it is not certain whether most
> people want all, or even most of the results of progress.
> For most of them it is an involuntary affair which, while
> bringing them much they strive for, also forces on them
> many things they do not want at all. . . .
> And I have yet to learn of an instance when the
> deliberate vote of a majority (as distinguished from the
> decision of some governing elite) has decided on such
> sacrifices in the interests of a better future as is made
> by a free-market society.[23]

This argument leads us to the threshold of a major contemporary controversy: the desirability and possibility of continual economic

---

to say that a person who buys apples is expressing a judgment as to how many apples he would like in the future; hence, the aggregate of consumer purchases is a reasonable approximation of what people would like to have produced. But it is totally implausible to suggest that a person who saves a hundred dollars is expressing a judgment as to how much investment he would like society to undertake. (See Sen, "Optimizing Saving," for further discussion of this point. Collective versus individual logic is at issue.)

growth. As we have seen, laissez-faire is structured to encourage a high rate of growth. This rate is independent of perceived needs, desires or wishes of the general populace, arising as it does from competitive pressures and the desire to make money with money. Worker control, by contrast, is less growth-oriented. Individual firms have little natural tendency to expand; investment and growth must be the conscious decision of the electorate. If growth really is of overriding importance to society, and if human shortsightedness will often fail to perceive this, then there is indeed a case to be made for capitalism.

We will not concern ourselves here with human shortsightedness, beyond noting the irrelevance of Hayek's concluding observation. A serious canvass of majoritarian decisions would likely reveal self-chosen sacrifices, but even if not, the issue is not settled. For it is by no means clear how much "sacrifice" high investment poses on the population of an affluent society (how much pain we suffer in not being able to consume even more than we do already), nor is it clear—Sen's paradox comes into play here—how much collective sacrifice the electorate would be prepared to make if given the choice.

The other premise of the procapitalist retort is more crucial: the alleged importance of economic growth. Fortunately we need not go all the way into the thicket of the contemporary growth controversy, since the issue for us is not growth versus no-growth, but the likelihood that optimal growth is rapid growth. But we do need to survey certain issues and arguments.

First of all, we should note that the value Hayek places on "successful striving" is not a value essentially related to economic growth. Economic growth, the growth toward which capitalism is oriented, is material growth, the expansion of the material goods and services available to the populace. But surely one can strive and learn in the absence of material advance. (Moral excellence was once thought to be a worthy goal.) One might even argue—and many have—that beyond a certain point material advance might be a hindrance to the pursuit of higher goals. One need not be an ascetic to see that certain kinds of striving require unharried leisure, and that, since consumption takes time, material wealth can sometimes conflict with leisure.[24]

Frankly, it has always astonished me that serious thinkers should worry about the boredom of a nongrowing economy. The tradition goes back to Adam Smith. ("The progressive state is really the cheerful and hearty state of all the different orders of society. The stationary state is dull."[25]) But even so serious a critic of growth as Kenneth Boulding can write:

> Perhaps the most fundamental and intractible problem of
> the stationary state is, as Adam Smith saw so clearly,
> that of dullness. The second law of thermodynamics,

the principle of increasing entropy, is a special instance
of a much more general principle which might be described as the "second law of practically everything." This is
the principle of the exhaustion of potential, that once a
potential has been realized it is "used up" and cannot be
realized again. . . .

One could postulate a second law of cultural dynamics, that creative acts are essentially non-repeatable,
that once they have been done they cannot be done again. . . .
The progressive state, however, puts a high value on
creativity which is the main reason why it is cheerful and
hearty. In the stationary state creativity may become
pathological.[26]

I don't understand such arguments. To me, they reflect a failure
of logic—to say nothing of imagination. A stationary economy is one in
which the average material standard of living does not decline. Of
course if that standard is quite low (as it was in Adam Smith's day),
a stationary state is no happy prospect. But if stabilization occurs at
a much higher level, it is by no means clear that it should be dull.
Why should it be duller or less creative to work merely to maintain
one's material living standard—and perhaps to have the leisure to
develop the skills, to read the books, to visit the places, to cultivate
the friends, that one always wanted to—than to increase consumption?
A human being, after all, is unlikely to reside on this earth for more
than three-quarters of a century, and that residence is all new to each
newly born individual. Are more gadgets really necessary to keep
boredom at bay? Might not gadgets be part of the problem?[27] (If we
are really concerned about dullness, we might declare a moratorium
on para-scientific laws. Boulding's "second law of cultural dynamics"
is no brighter than Nozick's "law of the conservation of envy.")

Advocates of growth are likely to respond to these musings that
increasing leisure also requires growth. Robert Solow—who can always
be counted on for a clever defense of orthodoxy—defines "the pro-
growth-man [as] someone who is prepared to sacrifice something useful and desirable right now so that people should be better off in the
future."[28] But this definition distorts the whole issue. The anti-growth
forces also call for current sacrifice (a slowdown in material consumption) for the sake of future generations. The distortion is particularly
acute relative to our concern, since capitalism is structured to promote the growth of material production, and not, as we have seen, the
growth of leisure. Worker control is far more conducive to that kind
of "growth."

If rapid growth is unnecessary, is it perhaps also harmful? If
so, the case for capitalism further deteriorates. There are two major

arguments against material growth that should be considered. The first, and most often heard, concerns the rapid depletion of irreplaceable resources, and the rapid increase in air, water, noise and other pollutions that has accompanied industrial growth. To the depletion charge the growthmen reply that we have far more resources than we are led to believe by the antigrowth people, that new resources are constantly being discovered, and that new substitutes are constantly being found.[29] Against the pollution argument it is urged that environmental protection, though far from costless, is well within the capabilities of the industrial countries doing the most damage.[30]

This latter response, if true, is certainly hopeful. Unfortunately it might not be true. As arch-antigrowthman Ezra Mishan points out, "the fact is, that knowledge of the effects of pollutants, and potential pollutants, on human health and the environment generally comes to light slowly and haltingly. . . . If . . . no action be taken to control production of an item until evidence of deleterious effects has been established, the evidence may come too late to avert a disaster. . . . [D]ecades must pass before the ecological and genetic side effects of many thousands of new chemicals, drugs and food additives are understood."[31]

The antidepletion claim is also hopeful, but it by no means implies that current growth rates are indefinitely sustainable. Boulding is said to have remarked that anyone who believes exponential growth can go on forever in a finite world is either a madman or an economist.[32] The growthman is certainly not a mathematician. A 3 percent rise in real gross national product per year (which is less than the United States's average annual rate, going back as far as reliable statistics will take us)* means a doubling every twenty-five years, a sixteen-fold increase per century. It is true, resource consumption need not rise as rapidly as GNP. Solow notes that whereas the real GNP of the United States roughly doubled between 1950 and 1970, the consumption of primary and scrap iron increased by only 20 percent and of copper only a third.[33] That of course, is some consolation—but scarcely a counter-argument.

A second major argument against material growth has been advanced recently by Fred Hirsch, who took his cue from a little-noticed

---

*The yearly average in the U.S., between 1840 and 1960, was 3.56 percent, declining from 4.03 percent in the 1840-80 period to 3.15 percent in the period 1920-60: growth rate per capita was 1.26 percent per year in the 1840-80 period, 1.81 percent in the 1920-60 era. (Simon Kuznets, Economic Growth and Structures [New York: W. W. Norton, 1965], p. 305).

essay by Roy Harrod.[34] Though certain consumer goods might be capable of indefinite increase (what Harrod calls "democratic" wealth), others ("oligarchic" wealth) are either scarce in some absolute or socially-imposed sense, or subject to congestion and crowding (e.g., rare art works, top positions in a hierarchical social order, private automobile transportation). These latter goods cannot be indefinitely expanded. But as material wealth increases, Hirsch argues, it is these latter kinds of goods that come increasingly into demand. Since this increase cannot be satisfied—the game is zero-sum—more and more time, effort and resources are wasted by individuals in pursuit of goods that any one might obtain, but which cannot be obtained by all. Symptomatic of such social waste are excessive educational requirements for certain positions (which serve merely to screen applicants), the self-defeating exodus to the "uncrowded" suburbs, and of course traffic congestion. Growth exacerbates, rather than solves, these problems. There are social, as well as physical, limits to growth.

One need not go all the way with Hirsch or with the doomsday scenario of resource depletion[35] to recognize that both point to things important in their own right and important to our argument. If either is even partly right, the argument for worker control is enhanced. So long as material growth is a pressing social need and requires serious sacrifice for its "take-off," a case can certainly be made for non-democratic implementation. Stalin's supporters argued such a case; so did many nineteenth-century defenders of capitalism. Perhaps they were right. I am not wholly convinced. But clearly no such case for growth now exists in the advanced regions of the world. The growthmen score effectively against many of the antigrowth arguments and proposals (some of which, it should be said, are sharply at variance with democratic and egalitarian values),[36] but they have little to say in favor of growth—apart from a concern for boredom and some fatuous pronouncements about the fate of the poor, underdeveloped countries if we do not grow.* But if this is so, then there is little justifica-

---

*Solow, to his credit, notices, "If economic growth with equality is a good thing, it doesn't follow that economic growth with a lot of pious talk about equality is a good thing" (Solow, "End of the World?" p. 41). More to the point, however, one should notice that if growth trends continue, the gap between developed and underdeveloped nations will not close and will likely widen. (Cf. Wassily Leontief, "Observations on Some Worldwide Economic Issues of the Coming Years," Challenge 21 [March-April 1978]: 22-30.)

tion for a nondemocratic procedure, and even less for an economic arrangement internally structured to press incessantly for expansion. The balance tilts sharply toward worker control.

INSTABILITY

I have argued that the case for rapid economic expansion is less than impressive. But I have omitted one class of pro-growth arguments that are frequently advanced: the destabilizing effects of an economic slowdown.[37] I have not omitted them because they are trivial, much less because they are invalid. In fact many of them are sound. As we shall see, steady, sustained growth—whether desirable or even possible—is necessary for stability. Capitalist stability, that is. This conclusion does not bode well for capitalism, since steady, sustained growth (as we shall also see) is far from inevitable under laissez-faire, and the instability its lack engenders has painful consequences.

Instability arguments are commonly and rightfully associated with Marx: the "laws of motion" of capitalist development lead the system to self-destruction. Though Marx offers no comprehensive crisis theory, still less a fully-developed breakdown theory, he provides numerous suggestions, partial arguments and insights that are important to an understanding of capitalist instability.[38] Non-Marxist economic theory, on the other hand, virtually ignored the crisis question until the Great Depression and Keynes forced a reconsideration.* Keynes, for his part, dealt with the problem of short-run instability, but the Keynesian Roy Harrod took up the question of long-range stability. Harrod's instability arguments produced a debate that still continues, pitting neo-Marxists and post-Keynesians against the neoclassicists. Mathematical models, and accompanying theorems, have proliferated.[39]

Models are, in fact, quite useful for analyzing stability issues. Drastic simplifications must be made in order to bring the essential elements into focus. It won't be necessary for us to analyze the highly mathematical, highly complex models that abound in the current

---

*This is an overstatement. Not all pre-Keynesian economists were untroubled by the received view that the system would automatically and appropriately adjust to equilibrium disruptions, but their criticisms had little effect on mainstream opinion. (See Alvin Hansen, A Guide to Keynes [New York: McGraw-Hill, 1953], Chapter 1, for documentation.)

literature, since we will not be aiming at mathematical theorems, but it will be helpful to construct simple models to illustrate the relevant variables and to demonstrate graphically the macroscopic movements of people, products and resources associated with saving, investment and growth.

A basic aim of our inquiry is to identify the necessary conditions for capitalist stability. (What I mean by stability and instability will become clear as we proceed.) One such condition, which will be invoked repeatedly in what follows, is a steady or rising average rate of profit. Since Keynes it has become a commonplace that healthy capitalism requires investor confidence. If confidence declines, so does investment. A decline in investment lowers aggregate demand, which in turn produces layoffs, which reduce demand further, which provokes further layoffs, and so on, the all-too-familiar recessionary spiral. Now, the "animal spirits" (Keynes's characterization) of investors are influenced by many variables, one of which certainly is the expected rate of profit. So if the system experiences a prolonged period of declining profits, investor confidence is certain to be shaken, thus making recessionary instability highly likely.

Declining profits are also destabilizing in another way, more often stressed by Marxian thinkers. A decline in profits tends to intensify class antagonisms, as individual capitalists (or their managerial representatives) seek to fend off the decline by increasing the pace of work, lowering wages and extending the length of the working day. (Class struggle manifests itself variously, depending on the specific features of a society. In the present-day United States, for example, wages are not lowered directly, but efforts are bent to hold wage gains below the inflation rate; the working day is extended through increased mandatory overtime.)

Such instability is not the logical consequence of declining profit; the "necessity" I speak of here is not logical necessity, but rather "very high probability." It could happen that the profit rate declines so gradually that it does not upset investor confidence or class relations. It could happen that the decline is gradual and uniform, reducing profits to the point where all excess is consumed by the capitalist class, and none at all (beyond depreciation funds) invested. The resulting economy would be a no-growth stationary state.* Such

*This scenario was envisaged by many classical economists. "It must always have been seen, more or less abstractly, by political economists, that the increase in wealth is not boundless; that at the end of what they term the progressive state lies the stationary state"

an evolution could happen, but its likelihood seems minimal. Profit rates are not ordinarily uniform, and so a general decline in the average rate of profit would likely result in a period of widespread business difficulties, bankruptcies, and economic disruptions, a period of recessionary nonoptimality wherein idle workers confront idle plants while labor is intensified in others.

It is unlikely that any present capitalist economy could gradually evolve to a stationary state via a gradual decline in the rate of profit, but even if one did so, it would not be free from instability. To see this, and to begin our model building, let us suppose that society is composed of two classes, capitalists, who own the means of production, and workers, all of whom are employed by the capitalists. For now we may think of the capitalist class as embodied in a single capitalist. Let x_i represent the total output of the i'th production period. We can think of the production period as a year and its output as some uniform consumer good, say wheat. Let w_i be the wage bill (in bushels of wheat) for the i'th production period, advanced to the workers at the beginning of the period. Let r be the (constant) rate of profit.

A stationary state may be described in these terms as follows. A capitalist begins with x_0 bushels of wheat. (Where he got them need not concern us.) He advances them to his workers; thus, $x_0=x_1$. The return to him $x_1=(1+r)x_0$ bushels of wheat at the end of the first production period. The capitalist consumes the surplus rx_0 bushels. He again advances x_0 to the workers, and the cycle repeats. It can continue indefinitely, each x_i equal to x_1, w_i always equal to x_0.

Or can it continue indefinitely? The case appears economically stable, since the profit rate is steady and no other problems are evident. But politically there is a problem, for here we have modelled a

(John Stuart Mill, Principles of Political Economy, in Collected Works of John Stuart Mill, Vol. 3 [Toronto: University of Toronto Press, 1965], p. 752). Mill, unlike most of his predecessors (and, as we have seen, many of his successors) did not view this prospect with alarm. "I am inclined to believe that it would be, on the whole, a very considerable improvement on our present condition. I must confess I am not charmed with the ideal of life held out by those who think that the normal state of human beings is the struggle to get on; that the trampling, crushing, elbowing, and treading on each other's heels, which form the existing tempo of social life, are the most desirable lot of human kind, or anything but the disagreeable symptoms of one of the phases of industrial progress" (ibid., p. 754).

society (not unlike a feudal society) where one class of people live without laboring, while another labors indefinitely without any improvement in their condition. (At best there is no improvement; if the population is increasing, there is impoverishment.) It must be doubted that such a society could long persist in the absence of a rigid, hierarchical tradition or a totalitarian government. Free and effective communication would certainly be troublesome. Such a society might persist if indoctrination and propaganda are sufficient to keep people content, but Robert Heilbroner's suggestion seems nearer the mark:

> Why societal peace persists in the face of an outlandishly skewed distribution of income is a perennial puzzle, especially in a democratic society. . . . To the extent that environmental and other difficulties require a slowdown in the pace of economic growth, this struggle for place is apt to become more marked . . . [and we are apt to see] a reappearance of the "vanished" problem: Disraeli's War Between Two Nations—the Rich and the Poor.[40]

If capitalism is not stable without growth, let us build growth into our model. Let us drop the assumption that the capitalist consumes the surplus, and replace it with the assumption that he invests it. For simplicity we will assume that he invests all of the surplus and consumes nothing, though nothing hangs on so drastic an assumption.

We find ourselves confronted with a puzzle. What exactly does "investment" mean in the context of our model? Our capitalist at the end of year one has $x_1 = (1+r)x_0$ bushels of wheat, x_0 of which he must set aside for his workers's wages. But what can he do with the surplus rx_0 so as to increase production to $x_2 = (1+r)x_1$ at the end of the second year?

One solution is to do what he did before, but on a wider scale. This requires the hiring of more laborers. Since we have assumed full employment, growth in this manner (i.e., without technical progress) requires a growing population. If all workers are equally productive, and there are no diminishing returns to scale, stability (i.e., maintaining a profit rate r) requires that $n_i = (1+r)n_{i-1}$ where n_i represents the number of workers available for period i. (If we allow for diminishing returns, then n_i must be greater than $(1+r)n_{i-1}$.) Now, if population growth satisfies this condition and productivity remains constant, the system would appear to be stable. It is economically stable, since the profit rate is maintained, and politically stable, since the capitalist is not consuming the surplus, but investing it. Individual workers are not improving their condition over time, but at least there is no impoverishment. Nor can their condition be readily blamed on the (nonconsuming) capitalist, who appears instead as a paragon of social virtue.

The problem with this case, of course, is its reliance on a geometrically expanding population. In reality the capitalist cannot continue indefinitely "doing what he did before, but on a wider scale." He can for a while. This model is not inappropriate for certain periods of capitalist development. The population of Europe more than doubled, and that of North America sextupled, between 1750 and 1950. World population increased 6.4 percent per decade during this period, in contrast to about 6 percent per century between 0 and 1750 A.D.[41] But as anyone who has ever thought about it knows (if she has taken an elementary calculus course, she can draw the terrifying graphs), exponential population growth cannot go on forever. If capitalism requires a geometrically expanding population for its stability, then capitalism is not stable.*

But there is a way out. Capitalists need not "continue what they were doing." They can act out their historical role by inventing, innovating, revolutionizing the means of production. Let us model this sort of growth. Let us reverse the population assumption of our second model and assume that the workforce is constant. This is a simplifying assumption, but not an unrealistic one in light of recent population trends in industrial nations. Let us assume that all growth comes from technological innovation. To maintain the profit rate, investments must cause output to grow steadily, $x_i=(1+r)x_{i-1}$ for all i. Now, since by hypothesis our capitalist consumes nothing, this growth rate translates into a steady increase in per capita consumption, also at the rate of r per year: $w_i=x_i/n$, where n is constant and x_i is steadily increasing. This is clearly the "golden age" of capitalist development. The profit rate holds steady, keeping the capitalist happy; wages increase exponentially over time, to the delight of the workforce; and the population remains constant, to the relief of everyone. Here certainly is a case of capitalist stability.

---

*This is not strictly true, since the geometrical ratio could be so small as to be insignificant in the foreseeable future. However, in order for population growth to sustain the profit rates normally expected in existing capitalist societies (around 10 percent), it would have to far exceed demographic stability.

Such a state is logically possible. Such a state is also necessary, for the three models we have considered are the only (pure) possibilities, * and the first two are unstable. But if steady growth via technical change is both possible and necessary, is it also likely? How likely? What variables must interact and how for his happy state to persist as the unplanned outcome of a free market? (What role the government might play in securing this state will be discussed in the context of modern liberalism.)

The key variable here, obviously, is productivity: output per worker. If productivity does not rise at the rate r, then profits cannot be maintained. If x_i bushels of wheat are invested in period i, then $(1+r)x_i$ must be returned to the capitalist.† Now perhaps this steady increase in productivity can go on indefinitely. Perhaps technological innovation will always overcome the problems of diminishing returns and resource scarcity. This hypothesis is of course closely related to the growth versus no-growth controversy discussed in the last section, but an additional factor has been added—not only must resources be physically available, but technical innovation must offset their rising scarcity costs. Perhaps this can be done. But if not, then recessionary instability and an intensification of the class struggle, both triggered by declining profits, are highly likely—neither of which enhances the general happiness and material well-being of society.

(An aside is perhaps not out of place here regarding "labor productivity." In the popular mind, a decline in labor productivity is usually associated with worker laziness or incompetence or greed, the celebrated "decline of the work ethic." Now this may indeed be a part

---

*Neoclassical economists often distinguish between growth due to technological change and that which comes from simply using more capital (movement from one production function to another versus movement along a given production function). This distinction is not relevant to our purposes. Both kinds of growth (if they really can be distinguished) we call "technological" since both involve actions by capitalists to increase the productivity of labor.

†Our one-commodity world avoids—at the cost of realism—the indexing problem. (If 1000 bushels of wheat were produced in period one and 500 head of cattle in period two, how much has the economy grown? Or has it declined?) This complication, however, does not affect our basic point: the growth (measured by some suitable index) that is essential to capitalist stability requires productivity gains (measured by the same index).

of the productivity problem, but as the above model should make clear, increases in labor productivity are also—and in reality mostly—brought about by capital investment and technological innovation, the prerogatives of <u>capital</u>. When workers have little or no control over the productive process, they can be as little blamed for productivity decline as praised for increase.)

Productivity increase is the <u>sine qua non</u> of stable capitalism. It is the most fundamental of the necessary conditions—but it is not the only one. The abstractness of our model conceals several others. In actuality the increase in productivity is only one moment of a three-part movement, each moment of which must succeed in order for capitalist expectations to be satisifed and stability to obtain. The capitalist, possessing a surplus rx_i at the end of year i must find an outlet for that surplus. It will be returned to the workers <u>only if</u> they represent an investment outlet promising sufficient profit to attract the funds. This is the first moment. The funds must be <u>invested.</u> Secondly, the anticipated <u>productivity increase</u> must materialize. Thirdly, the new products must be <u>sold.</u>

The second moment we have already analyzed. The limiting factor here is technological innovation: will it be forthcoming and fast enough to overcome diminishing returns? The first moment was alluded to when we discussed "investor confidence" at the outset of this section. Investment, we know, is essentially the channelling of workers and resources from where they are less productive to where they are (expected to be) more so. If individual capitalists do not see opportunities sufficient to warrant risking their capital, they must either consume the surplus or—more likely—exercise their "liquidity preference" by holding it in wait (in a bank, of course, where it will collect interest). If this latter practice becomes widespread, aggregate demand drops and recessionary instability ensues.

Whether or not investment opportunities are really diminishing is a controversial issue. The American Keynesian Alvin Hansen advanced this "stagnation thesis" in the late 1930s. Marxist economists Baran and Sweezy revived it in the mid-1960s and made it the focus of their important and influential critique. Mainstream opinion, not surprisingly, remains skeptical.[42] For our part we need not take sides in this debate, since nobody denies that diminishing investment outlets <u>could</u> pose a problem for capitalist growth. What is important to note for our argument is that the "stagnation" problem involves two factors, one of them technological—whether and to what degree productivity increases are technically possible—and one psychosocial—whether a certain class of people will exercise their "liquidity preference." As we shall see shortly, this latter factor in particular is quite different under worker control.

The third moment essential to "golden age" capitalist stability is the <u>selling</u> of the goods produced at the anticipated prices. This condition is not captured at all by our model, where the capitalist advances the product directly to his workers. Our scenario is useful in illustrating certain relations, but it obscures the fact that in reality workers must buy the product of the capitalist, and do so with the money-wages paid to them. Thus we note two additional sources of potential instability: first, workers must <u>have</u> sufficient money to buy the capitalist's product; second, they must want to spend it. The first is the problem of aggregate demand; the second is that of "consumer confidence" and the sales effort.

In Chapter 3 we discussed at length the ethical case <u>against</u> a large-scale, sophisticated sales effort—the improbability that the needs and desires generated by nonrational techniques will genuinely contribute to individual well-being. Here we see the reverse phenomenon—the potential for economic disruption (and hence a lowering of well-being) posed by the <u>lack</u> of an aggressive sales effort. Capitalism requires growth, which in turn requires investor confidence, which in turn requires consumer confidence. If consumers stop buying in ever increasing amounts, then products remain unsold, the capitalists' "animal spirits" wane, layoffs follow, and so on. We have here another of those peculiar "contradictions" of capitalism.

The problem of aggregate demand has already been discussed in connection with the unemployment problem. So far as laissez-faire is concerned, there is nothing more to add. Laissez-faire in no way insures that aggregate demand will always be sufficient for full employment. More must be said concerning governmental intervention to maintain demand, but that topic belongs to our discussion of Keynesian liberalism. It will not concern us here. (Contemporary classical liberals generally abandon their commitment to laissez-faire at this juncture. The government must do <u>something</u> to insure adequate demand. Their favored solution is "monetarism": the government should regulate the money supply.[43] This "solution" will be discussed in Chapter 6.)

We are now in position to compare the stability of laissez-faire with that of worker control. By far the most significant factor is worker control's lack of a growth imperative. Capitalism needs to grow; socialism does not. A stationary state under worker control would not generate the peculiar political problem inherent in capitalism, for it does not contain an affluent ownership class in need of justification. This is not to say that distributional disputes will vanish under worker control. So long as there is material scarcity and also inequalities—of reward, of effort, of skill—there is potential political conflict. But what gives worker control its decisive edge is the absence of a class, plainly unproductive in a stationary economy, whose historical and contemporary justification is rooted in growth.

Worker control can function quite well as a stationary state; hence it requires neither an expanding population nor technological innovation at a pace to guarantee increased production. It can also make the transition from a growth state to a stationary state without undue disruption. If consumers begin to purchase less, the effect is to increase leisure among producers, leisure that is shared by those firms first affected, and that spreads gradually to other sections. The violent spasms of layoff-triggered layoffs to which laissez-faire is so vulnerable are absent. Nor does worker control face the threat of an "investment strike," since no class has a "liquidity" option. There is no class whose animal spirits must be sustained if stability is to be insured. Under worker control, investment funds are generated by taxation and made available to those who want them. If too few projects are proposed, the government can encourage more initiative (bonuses for successful venture, perhaps), or it can reduce the capital tax. This latter measure increases current consumption (and hence demand) and also translates into more leisure. If society does not want to grow, it does not have to. A high level of investment is not required for stability. (A positive rate of investment will always be necessary, so long as problems of resource depletion and diminishing returns persist. But the slower the growth of the economy, the less severe these problems. The greater the investment for the purpose of growth, the greater must be the research to counter diminishing returns—a paradoxical state of affairs that does not favor capitalism.)

We have seen in this chapter that relaxing the assumption that technology is fixed and allowing for the possibility of innovation and growth does little to enhance the case for capitalism. In fact, it makes it worse. The kind of growth stimulated by the free market is likely to be unbalanced, plagued by externalities, and skewed by an inequitable income distribution. The rate is also likely to deviate from optimality. Laissez-faire is structured to grow, and will grow, whether or not growth is desirable or desired, unless it runs up against destabilizing factors. These factors, however, do not brake the growth process in a smooth and natural fashion; instead they trigger recessionary unemployment and class conflict.

This is not to say that a smoothly functioning, optimal, "golden age" laissez-faire is impossible. But the golden age is not likely. There are no structural forces to keep the economy on the golden path. Reason and experience point to instability. Unless there are extremely important noneconomic considerations in favor of laissez-faire, its desirability as a societal model would seem to be outstripped by worker control.

NOTES

1. Cf. Karl Polanyi, The Great Transformation (Boston: Beacon, 1970), p. 226: "Inside and outside England, from Macaulay to Mises, from Spencer to Sumner, there was not a militant liberal who did not express the conviction that popular democracy was a danger to capitalism."

2. Friedrich A. Hayek, The Constitution of Liberty (London: Routledge and Kegan Paul, 1960), p. 106.

3. Maurice Dobb, Welfare Economics and the Economics of Socialism (Cambridge: At the University Press, 1969), p. 149. Joan Robinson is of a similar opinion. "What theory has ever been advanced of how private self-interest directs new investments into lines that best provide for the needs and desires of society as a whole?" "The Age of Growth, " Challenge 19 (May-June 1976): 9.

4. E. S. Phelps, "Growth and Government Intervention, " in Growth Economics, ed. A. K. Sen (Baltimore: Penguin Education, 1970), p. 498.

5. Joseph Monsen, Jr., Modern American Capitalism: Ideologies and Issues (Boston: Houghton Mifflin, 1963), p. v.

6. Cf. Hayek, Constitution of Liberty, p. 277: "[Industrial democracy] represents a curious recrudescence of the ideas of the syndicalist branch of nineteenth-century socialism, the least-thought-out and most impractical form of that doctrine. . . . A plant or industry cannot be conducted in the interest of some permanent distinct body of workers if it is at the same time to serve the interests of the consumers."

7. Two of the many studies one might consult are Jan Vanek, The Economics of Workers' Management: A Yugoslav Case Study (London: George Allen and Unwin, 1972) and David Garson, ed., Worker Self-Management in Industry: The West European Experience (New York: Praeger, 1977).

8. See A. C. Pigou, The Economics of Welfare, 2nd ed. (London: Macmillan, 1924) for an early systematic treatment of externalities by a neoclassical economist.

9. Cf. Milton Friedman, Capitalism and Freedom (Chicago: The University of Chicago Press, 1962), pp. 30-32.

10. Amartya K. Sen, "On Optimizing the Rate of Savings, " Economic Journal 71 (September, 1961): 479-95.

11. E.G., by Fred Hirsch, in Social Limits to Growth (Cambridge, Mass.: Harvard University Press, 1976), following Alfred Kahn, "The Tyranny of Small Decisions: Market Failures, Imperfections and the Limits of Economics, " Kyklos 19 (1966): 23-47.

12. Hirsch, Social Limits, p. 40.

13. Tibor Scitovsky, "Two Concepts of External Economies, "

Journal of Political Economy 62 (April 1954): 149. Quoted by Maurice
Dobb, An Essay on Economic Growth and Planning (London: Routledge
and Kegan Paul, 1960), p. 9.

14. John Kenneth Galbraith, The Affluent Society (New York:
New American Library, 1958), pp. 199-200.

15. Hayek, Constitution of Liberty, p. 42.

16. John Maynard Keynes, The Economic Consequences of Peace
(New York: Harper Torchbooks, 1971), pp. 19-20.

17. Ibid.

18. Cf. Joseph Schumpeter, Capitalism, Socialism and Democracy (New York: Harper Torchbooks, 1962), p. 242: "Let us trans-
port ourselves to a hypothetical country, that, in a democratic way,
practices the presecution of Christians, the burning of witches, and
the slaughtering of Jews. We should certainly not approve of these
practices on the ground that they have been decided on according to
the rules of democratic procedure. . . . [Nor] would we approve of
the democratic constitution itself that produced such results in preference to a non-democratic one that would avoid them. . . . There
are ultimate ideals and interests which the most ardent democrat will
put above democracy, and all he means if he professes uncompromis-
ing allegiance to it is that he feels convinced that democracy will
guarantee those ideals and interests such as freedom of conscience and
speech, justice, decent government and so on."

19. Consider Hayek, Constitution of Liberty, p. 30: "All political theories assume, of course, that most individuals are very ignorant. Those who plead for liberty differ from the rest in that they include among the ignorant themselves." Cf. his entire discussion,
ibid., pp. 22-38.

20. Karl Marx, Capital (New York: Modern Library, 1906),
p. 652.

21. Concerning the allegedly painful choice between consumption and investment, Marx remarks, "The simple dictates of humanity therefore plainly enjoin the release of the capitalist from this
martyrdom and temptation, in the same way that the Georgian slave-
owner was totally delivered, by the abolition of slavery, from the
painful dilemma, whether to squander the surplus-product lashed out
of his niggers, entirely in champagne, or whether to reconvert a
part of it into more niggers and more land." Ibid., p. 655.

22. Hayek, Constitution of Liberty, p. 41.

23. Ibid., pp. 51, 52.

24. Cf. Staffan Linder, The Harried Leisure Class (New York:
Columbia University Press, 1970). Linder argues, in detail and with
style, that rising income makes leisure scarce because the sacrifice
of potential income in terms of goods foregone increases with income.

25. Adam Smith, An Inquiry into the Nature and Causes of the

Wealth of Nations (New York: Modern Library, 1937), p. 81. Quoted with approval by Hayek (Constitution of Liberty, p. 42).

26. Kenneth Boulding, "The Shadow of the Stationary State," in The No-Growth Society, ed. Mancur Olson and Hans Landsberg (New York: W. W. Norton, 1973), p. 97.

27. See Tibor Scitovsky, The Joyless Economy (Oxford: Oxford University Press, 1976) for the more plausible argument that contemporary affluence generates boredom. Consider also Keynes's reflection on the future: "I see us free, therefore, to return to some of the most sure and certain principles of religion and traditional virtue—that avarice is a vice, that the exaction of usury is a misdemeanour, and the love of money is detestable, that those walk most truly in the paths of virtue and sane wisdom who take least thought for the morrow. We shall once more value ends above means and prefer the good to the useful." John Maynard Keynes, "Economic Possibilities for our Grandchildren" in Essays in Persuasion (New York: W. W. Norton, 1963), pp. 371-72.

28. Robert Solow, "Is the End of the World At Hand?," Challenge 16 (March-April 1973): 41.

29. For a lucid and impressive short account, see Wilfred Beckerman, In Defense of Economic Growth (London: Jonathan Cape, 1974), Chapter 8. For a more massive study reaching similar conclusions, see Wassily Leontief, et al., The Future of the World Economy: A United Nations Study (Oxford: Oxford University Press, 1977).

30. Cf. Beckerman, Defense of Growth, p. 213: "Although the data is still in a relatively primitive and crude state, since interest in this subject is of a fairly recent character, the order of magnitude of such estimates as are available tend to show that the costs of likely pollution-abatement programmes are somewhat in the region of about one per cent of the national product of the U.K. and the U.S.A."

31. E. J. Mishan, The Economic Growth Debate: An Assessment (London: George Allen and Unwin, 1977), p. 119.

32. Mancur Olson, "Introduction" in No-Growth Society, p. 3.

33. Solow, "End of the World?," p. 44. Oil consumption, however, kept pace with growth and natural gas consumption exceeded it. Ibid., p. 45.

34. Hirsch, Social Limits; Roy Harrod, "The Possibility of Economic Satiety," in Problems of United States Economic Development, Vol. 1, (New York: Committee for Economic Development, 1958), pp. 207-13.

35. Among the most widely known and cited: Donella Meadows, et al., The Limits to Growth (New York: New American Library, 1972) and J. W. Forrester, World Dynamics (Cambridge, Mass.: Wright-Allen Press, 1971).

36. For an elegant and amusing depiction of the "right-wing"

environmentalist scenario, see Hugh Stretton, Capitalism, Socialism and the Environment (Cambridge: Cambridge University Press, 1976), pp. 15-39.

37. See, for example, Roland McKean, "Growth vs. No Growth: An Evaluation," in No-Growth Society, pp. 217-23.

38. Paul Sweezy, The Theory of Capitalist Development (New York: Monthly Review Press, 1942), pp. 133-234, provides a lucid, sympathetic and well-documented discussion of the Marxian view.

39. Harrod's "An Essay in Dynamic Theory" appeared in Economic Journal 49 (March 1939): 14-33. It, and a good sampling of the subsequent debate, can be found in Growth Economics, ed. Sen.

40. Robert Heilbroner, "The Clouded Crystal Ball," American Economic Review 64 (May 1974): 123.

41. Kuznets, Economic Growth and Structure, pp. 8-9.

42. Alvin Hansen, Full Recovery or Stagnation? (New York: W. W. Norton, 1938); Paul Baran and Paul Sweezy, Monopoly Capital (New York: Monthly Review Press, Modern Reader Paperbacks, 1966). Cf. Raymond Lubitz, "Monopoly Capitalism and Neo-Marxism," in Capitalism Today, ed. Daniel Bell and Irving Kristol (New York: Basic Books, 1970), pp. 167-79, for a critique of the stagnationist thesis generally and Baran and Sweezy in particular.

43. Cf. Friedman, Capitalism and Freedom, Chapter III.

5

CAPITALISM OR SOCIALISM:
LIBERTY AND AUTONOMY

It is time to ascend from the cave, from the mundane world of efficiency and growth to the sublime realm of political virtue. We must address the noneconomic dimension of the debate. This is perhaps the most controversial part of our controversy, at least today. Arguments are still made that socialism is inefficient and (less frequently) that it can't match capitalist growth, but these arguments have receded in importance. The historical record has doubtless diminished their force. It is true that the Soviet Union produces fewer automobiles, televisions and refrigerators than the United States, but the fact remains that it has moved from an underdeveloped, semifeudal society to the world's second economic power in little more than half a century, and this in the face of economic sanctions by the West, to say nothing of a savage civil war and a World War that saw 20 million Russians die and two-thirds of the Soviet industrial capacity destroyed.[1] Such a system can surely grow, and it cannot be too inefficient to have grown so rapidly. Nor can a system be too inefficient that has released 800 million Chinese peasants from the pestilence and famine that had been their lot since recorded time. Nor a system that has increased Yugoslavian industrial output fivefold and the per-capita

---

A portion of this chapter was published originally in "Capitalism and Work: Some Utilitarian Considerations," The Philosophical Forum, Vol. X, nos. 2-3-4, 1980.

income of Yugoslavian workers three and a half times in twenty years.[2] (The Soviet, Chinese and Yugoslavian systems are of course quite different from one another, and growth rates do not, as we have already observed, demonstrate optimality. But growth and efficiency arguments have clearly receded in the face of socialist economic successes.)

"But such systems are not free! They are not democratic! The individual has become a mindless cog in a great totalitarian machine!" These charges, variously modulated, have not diminished. Some are true, some are more problematic, but we needn't go into that here, since historical specifics are not directly relevant to my argument. The socialism I am advocating is not embodied in any contemporary society, no more than the ideal of laissez-faire is embodied in contemporary capitalism. What is relevent, and what must be addressed is the charge that socialism, by its very nature, is less conducive to certain noneconomic, ethical values. It is one thing to point to specific abuses in specific countries; it is another to assert that these abuses flow from the very structure of socialism. This latter charge must be confronted.

To do so, we must first look at values more closely. My overall anticapitalist argument has so far proceeded without appealing to values unacceptable to most classical liberals. The underlying ethical commitments have been quite modest. This happy state of affairs will not persist throughout this chapter, because it will be necessary to appeal to values that differ—or are at least weighted differently—from those of many classical liberals. For example, the classical liberal conception of liberty (the "independence of the arbitrary will of another"[3]), will be accorded respect, but it will not be held to be an absolute value that can never be overridden. The ethical framework I have adopted precludes any value from such status; each is taken to be prima facie only, subject to override if considerations involving other values are sufficiently strong. A classical liberal might balk here, for liberty is (sometimes) held to be an absolute value: liberty may be curtailed only for the sake of greater liberty.[4]

If less weight is accorded liberty than is customary under classical liberalism, more weight will be given democracy. Classical liberals sharply distinguish individual liberty from democracy; they argue (as will be seen below) that it is a virtue of laissez-faire that it limits the number of issues a society must decide democratically. Democracy is conceded to have instrumental value under appropriate conditions, but little value is accorded to democracy per se. In Hayek's words, "It is probably the best means of achieving certain ends, but it is not an end in itself."[5] In Chapter 4 I remarked that democracy need not be accorded any more than instrumental value (relative to the less controversial values discussed) to suffice for the arguments of that chapter. In this chapter I shall assign it greater weight than that. I will not hold it to be of <u>absolute</u> worth, incapable of ever being legitimately sacrificed, but I will hold it to have <u>intrinsic</u> worth. All else equal, the more democratic social system is to be preferred.

A commitment to democracy is often (but not always) based on a commitment to a deeper value, to the principle that an individual has a right to participate in fashioning those human structures and rules to which she must submit. I will call this value "participatory autonomy," or simply "autonomy." A social structure that permits individuals greater participatory autonomy will be judged (all else equal, of course) a better system. This value is perhaps most closely associated with Rousseau, whose classical and controversial definition of freedom is "obedience to a law one prescribes to oneself."[6] The term itself, autonomy, is more closely associated with Kant, but Kant transposed the concept from the political realm to the realm of private morality. (Kant defines autonomy as the act of binding oneself to the moral law which is one's own law because it is the law one would legislate for all rational beings.)[7]

Our definition returns autonomy to the social realm and makes it a virtue of sociopolitical structures. This is not to suggest that the private and the political are unrelated. A case can be made that social structures that encourage active, deliberative participation of citizens will encourage the adoption of a "moral point of view." Mill, for one, has argued that democratic structures encourage a person to "weigh interests not his own, to be guided in the case of conflicting claims by another rule than his private particulars, to apply, at every time, principles and maxims which have for their reason of existence the common good."[8] There is much to be said for this argument, but I will not pursue the matter here. I'm concerned here with stating and explaining values, not with justifying them.

It should be noted that participatory autonomy is not equivalent to democracy. Eighteenth and nineteenth century political thought frequently appealed to what I have called "autonomy" to justify democracy, but twentieth-century democratic theory has taken quite a different turn. Taking their cue from Schumpeter, many theorists have concluded that premodern democratic theory, with its emphasis on a participatory "rule by the people," is unrealistic and impractical. Democracy, they argue, should be regarded as a quasi-market where politicians compete to offer their leadership services to an electorate. The essence of democracy is held to be, not the active deciding of issues by an electorate, but an institutional arrangement for arriving at political leaders by means of a competitive struggle for the people's votes.[9] The value of democracy so conceived does not lie in its enhancement of participatory autonomy. To the contrary, too much autonomy, too much participation by the citizenry, is thought to be destabilizing. [10] Democracy is held to be valuable because it checks the governors: just as the market constrains producers to seek out and satisfy consumer preferences, competitive democracy similarly constrains politicians.

To ask whether the competitive or participatory conception (and justification) of democracy is more legitimate is to ask a question too abstractly formulated to be answered. The substantive stability issue needs to be discussed, and it will be, but for now we need only inquire as to which conception is more congenial to classical liberalism. Or rather, more fundamentally, does classical liberalism value participatory autonomy? The answer, I think, is no. At least not much. The concept itself is linked with Rousseau, and Rousseau is anathema to most classical liberals. Rousseau is held to be the originator of "totalitarian democracy" and of a concept of freedom totally at odds with classical liberalism's notion of liberty. [11] Autonomy itself, the right to participate in social decision making, is explicitly attacked by Nozick:

> Others have no right to a say in those decisions which
> importantly affect them that someone else . . . has a
> right to make. . . . After we exclude from consider
> ation the decisions which others have a right to make,
> and the actions which would aggress against me, steal
> from me and so on and hence violate my (Lockean)
> rights, it is not clear that there are any decisions re
> maining about which even to raise the question of
> whether I have a right to say in those that importantly
> affect me. Certainly if there are any left to speak about,
> they are not significant enough a portion to provide a
> case for a different sort of state. [12]

Let us pause for a moment and consider this position. Nozick buttresses his argument with a series of examples. If four men propose marriage to a woman, he says, she has the right to choose; the suitors have no right to a say, though the decision importantly affects their lives. If Arturo Toscanini wants to retire, the musicians in the New York Philharmonic have no right to a veto. If you loan your bus to some friends for a year, and they come to depend on it, they acquire no rights to the vehicle, because "the bus is yours." [13]

The basic problem with this argument is Nozick's apparent assumption that rights can never conflict. If I have a right to X, then you cannot possibly have a right to X. Another problem, at least for me, is that things seem obvious to Nozick that seem far from obvious to me. Is it really so plain that the above suitors or musicians or

friends have no rights regarding their respective concerns? Not even
the right (for example) to a hearing? Might it not be better to think
that a weighting principle is involved here, that the effect on the woman, for example, of a bad marriage is so much more serious than "un-
requited love" that her right overrides her suitors' rights? No advocate of political autonomy argues that everyone ought to have an equal
say in all matters; the right to participate is always conceived as proportional to the relative magnitude of the effect of the decision.

But if weighting is involved, then it is not at all obvious—as it is
to Nozick—that "if one starts a private town, . . . persons who chose
to move there or later remain there would have no right to a say in
how the town was run."[14] More importantly, it is by no means clear
that democratic procedures are illicit with respect to consumption
externalities or the rate of investment (to cite two issues we have already discussed) or working conditions in an enterprise (an issue we
will soon discuss). But if procedures enhancing participatory autonomy
in these areas are both moral and feasible, then they might indeed
"provide a case for a different sort of state."

Let me summarize briefly before plunging into the main arguments of this chapter. The values to which these arguments will appeal
include liberty (in the classical liberal sense, i.e., freedom from the
arbitrary will of another) and autonomy (having significant input into
decisions that affect you). Democracy is held to have intrinsic worth,
since it is a particular manifestation of autonomy. Liberty is nonprob-
lematic. No one denies liberty is a value. Democracy and especially
autonomy are more controversial. I have not attempted to justify
these values, but I have tried to show that a certain argument against
autonomy fails.

My arguments will also appeal to values explicated in preceding
chapters, especially to equality and human happiness. Equality will
be taken here, more explicitly than before, to include equality of power
as well as equality of material conditions, though in this case, as in
all others, the value is prima facie only, subject to modification by
other ethical considerations. Human happiness, also presumed valuable, will be broadened here to include psychological happiness. The
preceding analysis has stressed material well-being as a good to be
optimized in a well-ordered society; here we will also refer to psychological well-being. Rawls calls it the "Aristotelian Principle":
"other things equal, human beings enjoy the exercise of their realized
capacities (their innate or trained abilities), and this enjoyment increases the more the capacity is realized, or the greater its complexity."[15] I shall not defend this principle here. (I have not attempted to
justify any of my ethical principles, beyond an occasional rebuttal to
objections; my aim is simply to state and clarify the moral values underlying my critique of capitalism before elaborating that critique.)

I will merely assume with Rawls and many psychologists that the principle states a psychological fact. [16] I am not sure that a classical liberal would agree, nor am I sure he would object. If he objects to the above-mentioned values, he will not be wholly persuaded by what follows.

LIBERTY

Liberty, for a classical liberal, is defined as absence of coercion, and "coercion occurs when one man's actions are made to serve another man's will, not for his own but for the other's purpose." [17] Liberty in this sense is associated with an assured "private sphere" wherein one is free from interference; liberty is sharply distinguished from one's ability to accomplish desired ends or from having a range of opportunities. This is a controversial delimitation, but we will sidestep the controversy. What we want to investigate is a more concrete issue: the claim that one has more liberty (classical liberal definition) under laissez-faire than under worker control.

The first thing we observe as we begin to consider this question is that a great many of the traditional arguments against socialism have no force against our particular model of decentralized market socialism. For Hayek, "the common features of all collectivist systems may be described, in a phrase ever dear to socialists of all schools, as the deliberate organization of the labors of society for a definite social goal." [18] For Friedman, "in a socialist society, there is only the all-powerful state." [19] But neither of these characterizations applies to our model. The significant enlargement of governmental control involves only new investments. Firms are controlled by their workers, not by the government. All the labor of society is not directed toward a "definite social goal" by an "all-powerful state." (Recall, in 1977, new investment accounted for less than 6 percent of the gross economic activity of the United States.*) Worker control, no less than laissez-faire, draws a line between political power and economic power, and allows one to check and counterbalance the other.

"But," a classical liberal is bound to reply, "worker control represents an <u>extension</u> of governmental power, a power that is already enormous and constantly growing. A 'mere' 6 percent increase would raise the government's total share of the Gross National Product

---

*See p. 54 for the precise figures.

to 40 percent, a frightful and frightening figure." As Hayek has argued, "Once the communal sector, in which the state controls all the means, exceeds a certain proportion of the whole, the effects of its actions dominate the whole system. Although the state controls directly the use of only a large part of the available resources, the effects of its decisions on the remaining part of the economic system become so great that indirectly it controls almost everything."[20]

To respond to this charge is not so easy. I can begin by saying that it is by no means a foregone conclusion that the government will absorb a larger share of the gross national product under worker control than it does under contemporary capitalism. It need not run to 40 percent. Many governmental programs in contemporary capitalist societies are necessitated by the underlying contradictions of capitalism. Unemployment and underemployment, for example, are more fundamental to capitalism than to worker control (more on this in Chapter 6); hence, larger, more expensive, (more divisive) welfare programs are required.

A smaller, not larger, government might be appropriate to worker control—but this response does not go to the heart of the matter. I have already argued that control of new investments, though quantitatively not large, is of strategic importance. Governmental control here does give, in an important sense, control over the whole economy. That is precisely what we want. We want political control of investment to head off the anarchy of the market, to subject the growth of the economy to human direction, to eliminate the boom-bust cycles of capitalism. The appeal here is to efficiency, material well-being and also to autonomy. Private investment decisions affect the lives of everyone in quite decisive ways; better democratic control than no control at all.*

Does this control really conflict with liberty? Is an individual's free space significantly limited? Are individuals more subject to the wills of other individuals? We observe that under worker control

---

*Such control is not synonymous with directing the labor of society to a unitary end. It is worth recalling Walter Benjamin's startling metaphor: "Marx says that revolutions are the locomotives of world history. But the situation may be quite different. Perhaps revolutions are not the train ride, but the human race grabbing for the emergency brake." (Cited by Bernd Witte, "Benjamin and Lukacs: Historical Notes on the Relationship Between Their Political and Aesthetic Theories," New German Critique [Spring 1975]: 10-11.)

people are free to seek work where they will, to change work associations if they come into conflict with its rules or personnel, not to work at all if they can find someone to support them. Worker control implies no restriction of private ownership of nonproductive property: food, clothing, shelter or the thousands of other personal possessions people might want to purchase. One's home is still one's castle.* One can even own a productive facility, so long as one works it alone or with one's family. The line, remember, is drawn at wage-labor and at the making of money through ownership rather than work. To be sure, we do not rule out laws regulating (or prohibiting) manufacture of specific items, or rental of land or dwellings, or speculation in real estate, but it is not at all evident that such laws significantly restrict an individual's free space, much less subject her to the arbitrary will of another. (It is worth noting that one of the greatest champions of individual liberty (an ardent supporter of free trade as well) did not think that the justification of laissez-faire was liberty: "Restraints [on trade] are wrong solely because they do not produce the result which it is desired to produce by them. . . . The principle of individual liberty is not involved in the doctrine of free trade."[21])

Nozick, for one, would object. Liberty is curtailed: "the socialist society will have to forbid capitalist acts between consenting adults."[22] This much-quoted conclusion is derived from the following scenario:

> Notice also that small factories would spring up in a socialist society, unless forbidden. I melt some of my personal possessions and build a machine out of the material. I offer you and others a philosophy lecture once a week in exchange for yet other things, and so on. . . . Some persons might even want to leave their jobs in socialist industry and work full time in this private sector. I shall say something more about these issues in the next chapter. Here I wish merely to note how private property even in means of production would occur in a socialist society.[23]

*Socialists have been insufficiently appreciative of the case for private housing as a component of well-being, and of the fact that private housing in no way conflicts with the basic principles of socialism. An important and articulate exception is Hugh Stretton, Capitalism, Socialism and the Environment (Cambridge: Cambridge University Press, 1976).

Despite the implausibility of this scenario, the substance of Nozick's argument has merit: certain capitalist acts will be forbidden under worker control. George Bernard Shaw has remarked, "under socialism you would not be allowed to be poor."[24] Our model is not so (severely) benevolent, but you will not be allowed to sell yourself into slavery, nor will you be allowed to agree to work at a productive facility constructed with private funds unless the owner agrees to relinquish his ownership claim and run it cooperatively.* The reason for the prohibition is not paternalism. Logic (and history) demonstrate that such seemingly innocuous acts can generate the massive inequalities of wealth and power experienced so acutely in capitalist countries today, as well as the chronic instability and other disutilities catalogued in previous chapters. This is not to say that a worker-control society would necessarily evolve into a capitalist society in the absence of certain laws. Frankly, I think that about as likely as the peaceful resurrection of the Antebellum South should the Thirteenth Amendment be repealed. Nevertheless, "capitalist acts" could generate sufficient inequalities to be destabilizing, even if the vast majority are clear in their preference for worker control and the economy as a whole far from capitalistic. A few individuals with much money can generate much mischief; the historical record is clear on that. So the legal prohibition of "wage-slavery" seems justifiable. Some liberty is sacrificed. The will of another, i.e., the majority, is imposed on that minority which might want to work for wages instead of for income shares in a worker-managed firm. The majority look at the consequences of not having such a law and decide not to take the chance.

Or so they might decide. Notice, there is nothing in the structure of our model that demands such a law. Unlike classical liberalism, which insists that certain matters are not to be subject to the democratic process, our model contains no such restriction. The establishment of a worker-control society would certainly require such a law; worker control will not evolve naturally out of capitalism (this we shall see below). But once the basic structure is in place, once the transition has been accomplished, it is at least arguable that the wage-labor prohibition would no longer be necessary—as it is arguable today that the Thirteenth Amendment is no longer essential.

---

*Actually, small-scale exceptions might be allowed. In Yugoslavia, for example, private craftsmen, restaurant owners and others can employ up to five people before becoming subject to the worker-control provision. (Rudolf Bićanić, Economic Policy in Socialist Yugoslavia [Cambridge: At the University Press, 1973], p. 34.)

This response to Nozick is perhaps less than wholly satisfying—for lurking behind his abstract argument is a more concrete (though unspoken) concern. To speak of "prohibiting capitalist acts" is to raise a specter that has long troubled people of good will: the repression of dissent in socialist societies. As anyone can observe, in (many) capitalist countries one can advocate socialism; in socialist societies one cannot advocate capitalism. This asymmetry, according to some, is no historical accident; it is an inevitable consequence of structure. Milton Friedman, for example, argues that dissent under socialism will never be as free as under capitalism, because the two systems differ in four crucial respects:

1. In a socialist society all jobs are under direct control of the government, and so an advocate of capitalism risks being denied all forms of employment.
2. To gain support for a cause, one needs funds; under socialism the only wealthy people will be government officials, whereas under capitalism there are many independently wealthy people from whom "to get funds to launch any idea, however strange."
3. In a capitalist society publishers need not agree with an advocated cause; if a book or magazine will sell, it will be published; not so under socialism.
4. In a socialist society an advocate of capitalism, even if he had the funds, "would have to persuade a government factory making paper to sell to him, a government printing press to print his pamphlets, a government post office to distribute them among the people, a government agency to rent him a hall, and so on."[25]

If we think about this argument, we see immediately that (1), (3), and (4) do not tell against worker control. Control over new investment may give the government strategic control over the economy, but it by no means gives it control over employment or printing presses. And the profit motive operates within a worker-controlled publishing house as it does within a capitalist one. If anything, dissent under worker control might be easier, since employment is likely to be more secure. Workers, we have seen, are likely to be given substantial job protection by law, since the economy will not function efficiently if a firm reduces its labor force when financial troubles occur. A capitalist employer, certainly under laissez-faire, can fire an employee for political reasons. A worker-managed firm might have more difficulty. (I am not claiming that a worker-control society would be broadminded about dissent if the social structure were seriously threatened. The historical record does not show societies of any stripe tolerant under such conditions. I am merely claiming that there is no reason to think a worker-control society would be <u>less</u> tolerant than laissez-faire, especially if constitutional provisions for freedom of speech and assembly are the same.)

If (1), (3), and (4) do not apply, what about (2)? Friedman's argument here comes perilously close to sophistry. There is no evidence to support Friedman's claim that "radical movements in capitalist societies . . . have typically been supported by a few wealthy individuals,"[26] at least regarding radical <u>Left</u> movements. The lunatic fringe on the Right, of course, is another matter.[27] On balance, the suppression of socialist agitation by the power that concentrated wealth can command has surely been more massive than its encouragement. Friedrich Engels did indeed help Marx through some bad times, and Left movements occasionally attract wealthy individuals—but this must be set beside Blackshirt, Brownshirt, White Hand and the myriad other forms of Right-wing, wealth-backed terror. The "role of inequality of wealth in preserving political freedom . . . is seldom noted," says Friedman.[28] For good reason.

So much for Friedman, but let us pursue this matter a bit further. Concern for the status of free speech and other civil liberties under socialism is by no means sophistical. No socialist society yet established has a record on civil liberties as good as the best of Western capitalism. There has been <u>much</u> suppression. Why this is so is a question of enormous importance, though one too complex to do justice to here. But let me make a couple of perhaps obvious observations and relate them to our argument.

To understand contemporary socialist societies, we must take specific historical factors into account, most notably the fierce resistance to socialism on the part of prior regimes and the capitalist world, the lack of liberal and democratic traditions, and, perhaps most important, the severity of underdevelopment in those countries where revolutions were successful. The industrial revolution in the West, it should not be forgotten, was also a brutal affair.

There are also two basic structural features of contemporary socialism that bear on civil liberties, one political and the other economic. All existing socialist societies are governed by single political parties organized according to the principles of "democratic centralism."* Most have attempted large-scale centralized planning. Under

---

*Lenin's doctrine, "freedom of criticism, unity of action" became increasingly authoritarian as the revolution progressed. In 1906 the emphasis was on "freedom of criticism." In 1917 the Sixth Party Congress proclaimed, "Party factions in state, municipal, soviet and other institutions in the capacity of Party organizations

democratic centralism information may flow from the bottom up, but authority descends from top down. This type of organization, a mass, authoritarian party, is a uniquely twentieth-century phenomenon, as is its economic correlate—centralized planning.

The two phenomena are distinct, but they are mutually reinforcing. To plan effectively, one needs authority. This, I think, is the valid core of the classical liberal's critique of socialism. Planners are neither evil beings nor inordinately selfish, but planners like to plan and planning is easier the fewer the constraints. Unhappily, democratic participation multiplies constraints. To a planner, an active citizen is a nuisance. This is not to say that planning is impossible under democratic auspices, but tensions are inevitable. Similarly, an authoritarian party can oversee a decentralized, democratized economy—as in Yugoslavia—but again there will be tensions.* But

---

subordinate themselves to all decisions of the Party and to the respective leading Party centers." A 1919 Statute declared, "The strictest Party discipline is the first obligation of every member of the Party and of all Party organizations. Decisions of the Party centers must be fulfilled speedily and accurately." (See John Resheter, Jr., A Concise History of the Communist Party of the Soviet Union [New York: Praeger, 1960], pp. 65, 131, 165.)

*Many commentators on Yugoslav society have noted this conflict. The Dean of the Faculty of Political Science of Belgrade University observed, at a conference in Santa Barbara in 1971: "A third series of difficulties stems from the contrast between the extremely large potentiality for expressing different interests at all levels of social organization, and the rather narrow channels through which these interests can be transformed into effective political demands in political decision-making. There is still a duality in our system. Self-management is fairly well developed at the grass roots level, at the level of the individual self-managed unit; but as for the global organization of society, the state still plays a very important role." Najdan Pasic, a participant in a discussion recorded in Self-Management, ed. Adizes and Borgese. (The quote is from p. 132.) It is worth noting that Yugoslavia is the only socialist country that still talks seriously about the Marxian concept, "the withering away of the state." (Cf. David Granick, Enterprise Guidance in Eastern Europe: A Comparison of Four Socialist Economies [Princeton, N.J.: Princeton University Press, 1975], pp. 327-31.)

if socialism does not involve overall central planning, and if it comes into being in an industrialized economy with deep democratic and liberal traditions, it is not unreasonable to anticipate a society very different from existing socialist states—not tension-free, but more democratic, less authoritarian, more open, than socialism or capitalism today.

One final observation is in order concerning the connection between capitalism and liberty. Those who assert such a connection—and deny that socialism is compatible with liberty— usually conflate two quite distinct features of capitalism, private ownership of the means of production and the market. But the fundamental socialist objection to capitalism is to the former (and perhaps even more to the third defining characteristic of capitalism, the commodification of labor). There are problems to be sure with the market, but since the alternative to the market is central planning, one can make a case for a connection between the market and liberty. But private property (in the means of production) is another matter. Yale political scientist Charles Lindblom has noted: "The traditional liberal argument is incomplete unless it defends private property as itself consistent with freedom, a point on which it is silent. It is simply blind to the implications for freedom of Proudhon's 'Property is theft!' as well as to the implications of less extreme interpretations of how property is established and instituted."[29]

I can do no better than to quote his argument:

In liberal thought a world of exchange is conflict-free. Everyone does what he wishes. When all social coordination is through voluntary exchange, no one imposes his will on anyone else. But how, we ask, can such a happy state be possible? It's possible only because the conflicts over who gets what have already been settled through a distribution of property rights in the society. Was that distribution conflict-free? Obviously not. Was it noncoercively achieved? Obviously not. The distribution of wealth in contemporary England, for example, is a consequence of centuries of conflict, including Viking raids, the Norman Conquest, the early authority of the Crown and nobility, two waves of dispossession of agricultural laborers from the land, and the law of inheritance.[30]

Property may not always be theft—but its correlation with liberty has been and remains less than absolute. Liberty is better off without it.

DEMOCRACY

Democracy is less highly valued than liberty by classical liberals. The "classical" classical liberals brooded that the masses might use their power to impinge upon property, the bulwark (in their eyes) of liberty.[31] Their misgivings have not been borne out. Plato presumed that the natural evolution of democracy is toward a redistribution of wealth—which provokes civil war, which, in turn, leads to tyranny.[32] It is arguable that something like this ancient scenario worked itself out in Weimar Germany and post-World War I Italy, but it has not (yet?) materialized in other liberal societies. Property holdings remain enormously concentrated; incomes are enormously unequal. Though most economists think inequalities have diminished somewhat during the course of this century, few think that there has been much change since World War II.[33] The democratic threat to property appears to have receded.

No doubt because of this, classical liberals today are more favorably disposed toward democracy. They are not committed to participatory autonomy, but they express the conviction that democracy is the best check to liberty-usurping tyranny. Moreover—and this is what we want to consider now—they have argued that only a capitalist society is compatible with democracy. A famous and forceful articulation of this thesis was given by Hayek:

> It is now often said that democracy will not tolerate "capitalism." If "capitalism" means here a competitive system based on free disposal over private property, it is far more important to realize that only within this system is democracy possible. When it becomes dominated by a collectivist creed, democracy will inevitably destroy itself.[34]

The argument for this claim is abstract but important:

> It is the price of democracy that the possibilities of consensus are restricted to the fields where true agreement exists and that in some fields things must be left to chance. But in a society which for its functioning depends on central planning this control cannot be made dependent on a majority's being able to agree; it will often be necessary that the will of a small minority be imposed upon the people, because this minority will be the largest group able to agree among themselves on the question at issue. Democratic government has worked successfully where, and so long as, the functions of government were, by a

widely accepted creed, restricted to fields where agreement among the majority could be achieved by free discussion; and it is the great merit of the liberal creed that it reduced the range of subjects on which agreement was necessary to one which was likely to exist in a society of free men.[35]

Friedman makes substantially the same allegation.

The use of political channels, while inevitable, tends to strain the social cohesion essential for a stable society. The strain is least if agreement for joint action need be reached only on a limited range of issues on which people in any event have common views. Every extension of the range of issues for which explicit agreement is sought strains further the delicate threads that hold society together. If it goes so far as to touch an issue on which men feel deeply yet differently, it may well disrupt the society. Fundamental differences in basic values can seldom if ever be resolved at the ballot box; ultimately they can only be decided, though not resolved, by conflict. The religious and civil wars of history are bloody testament to this judgment.[36]

This argument cannot be dismissed by simply pointing out that worker-control socialism is not centrally planned. The market structure of worker control deflects some of the argument's force, but the fact remains, under worker control far more questions are subject to a conscious, democratic, decision procedure than under capitalism (especially laissez-faire). But the Hayek-Friedman argument is abstract. To evaluate it, we must be more concrete. What are the specific issues that laissez-faire, but not worker control, remove from the field of free discussion? How much strain would their inclusion place on the social fabric?

First of all, there is the matter of workplace organization. Under capitalism, the capitalist (and/or management) has complete control; under worker control, the workers do. Will the latter structure involve conflict? We can hardly say no. Some workers may wish to use a technology that is boring but productive; others may have reverse priorities. More significantly (judged from the historical experience of worker self-management), those with managerial authority in a firm may often feel hampered by democratic constraints, constraints that are likely to vary markedly among enterprises, despite identical formal structures.[37] But these disputes are confined <u>within</u> an enterprise; there is neither theoretical reasoning nor empirical evidence to suggest that such local disputes might erupt into civil disorder, much less bloody civil war. To the contrary, one of the great merits of the democratic process is to allow problems to surface, to be debated, and to be dealt with, before they reach a flash point.

A second basic issue is the overall direction of economic change. Governmental control over new investment makes this decision a conscious one, subject to debate. Here again there is bound to be conflict. Consider a specific, far from fanciful issue: the question of nuclear power. A socialist society, no less than a capitalist one, must confront the energy crisis. Since nuclear power generation requires massive capital investment, the decision of a worker-control society to embark along the nuclear road must be a political decision. The national investment board must hold hearings; the national legislature must approve. Under laissez-faire, by contrast, the decision rests with the utility companies. The business of generating power is the business of business; it is not the business of government. Now it cannot be ventured, at this level of abstraction, what the outcomes of these respective procedures would be, but that is not the question relevant to our inquiry. What we must ask is which system will resolve the issue more peacefully.

It is surely not obvious that the laissez-faire solution would be more peaceful—and the lack of obviousness tells against the classical liberal view. A democratic decision would be preceded by sharp debate, and there is no guarantee that the discontented minority—if the pronuclear forces prevailed—would not engage in civil disobedience. But—and this is the crucial point—there is no guarantee that the same thing would not happen if the decision were privately made. (And their case would have even more appeal, since the populace was not consulted.) It is surely misguided to think that decisions so important to people should (or could) be kept off the political agenda. Unvented pressure cookers sooner or later explode.

Classical liberals, in fact, are not thinking of such issues as nuclear power when they make their abstract argument. Virtually all acknowledge market imperfections and neighborhood effects that necessitate some political intervention. They are thinking rather of a different issue, one that always figures prominently in their analyses. The provocative issue numero uno that must be kept from the ballot box is distribution of income. That, above all, must be handled by the market. [38]

But notice, the distribution of income under worker control is handled by the market, at least distribution among firms. The more efficient better organized firms have more income to distribute among their workers. (Distribution within a firm is done democratically). Of course, the use of progressive taxation is not ruled out, if unseemly inequalities develop, but this democratic "infringement" might not be necessary at all, since worker control, without property income, is far more egalitarian than capitalism. It is not implausible that a simple, flat-rate income tax would be quite appropriate, so long as income differentials really reflect differences in effort, burdensomeness of work and talent. The demand to reduce inequality—which keeps forcing itself onto the political agenda of capitalist societies—may well be less contentious under worker control, since the functional character of the inequalities are more transparent, not shrouded in obscurantist ideology.

Since the argument that democracy will work only under laissez-faire has failed to survive examination, it is time to reverse the question. Will democracy work at all under laissez-faire? Is there not a substance to the charge, made by Marxists (among others) that "bourgeois democracy" is a sham? To make sense out of this question, we need to clarify some terminology. Let us follow Lindblom (and Robert Dahl), and call a system whose political leaders are selected via regular popular elections from among competing candidates a "polyarchical" system.[39] Many contemporary capitalist societies are polyarchical; no contemporary socialist society is. Let us reserve "democracy" for government by the people—for a system in which the electorate comprises all sane, adult members of the society, and is "sovereign." To be sovereign, an electorate must satisfy two conditions; (1) its members must be reasonably well-informed about the issues to be decided by the political process and reasonably active in contributing to their resolution; (2) there must exist no stable minority class that is "priviliged," that is, possessing political power at least equal to that of elected officials and unmatched by any other stable grouping.[40] Democracy, in short, is a system in which a universal electorate is well-informed and active, and unobstructed by a privileged minority class. (This concept is not as operationally precise as polyarchy, and it certainly represents an ideal, but that does not render it ill-suited for our purposes. Our concern, after all, is with ideal societies.)

Our question is this: is the classical liberal ideal compatible with democracy thus defined? The historical record demonstrates that capitalism, even in its relatively laissez-faire forms, can coexist with polyarchy. No such assurances exist regarding democracy. Laissez-faire societies have never coexisted with universal suffrage—which did not come to the United Kingdom until 1929, France until 1945 or Switzerland until 1971.[41] And of course in the United States until the passage of the Nineteenth Amendment (1920) women, and until the Voting Rights Act of 1965, a substantial number of black Americans, were disenfranchised. Nor has it coexisted with a well-informed and active electorate. But above all the empirical record raises doubts concerning privilege. The case has been made by many, but most recently (and quite convincingly) by Lindblom, that business occupies a privileged position in all contemporary polyarchies.[42] Businessmen, Lindblom maintains, contribute vastly greater amounts to political campaigns than other groups, * are better organized to represent their special interests, have special ease of access to governmental officials, and are disproportionately represented at all upper levels of government. Moreover, given their control of the mass media, they are in position to exert great influence on the electorate itself. [43]

But we must remember—empirical arguments do not tell decisively against the classical liberal position. Friedman, Hayek, Nozick, et al. concede—insist—that much is wrong with contemporary capitalism. We must interrogate structures. We must ask whether the empirical reality reflects an inherent incompatibility between democracy and laissez-faire.

I think it does. My argument depends in part on conclusions already drawn. If, as I argued in the last chapter, laissez-faire is inherently unstable, then it is inevitable that a democratic government will attempt to prevent or mitigate this instability. It will abrogate laissez-faire. If the electorate is sovereign, it will refuse to allow unemployed people to face idle factories indefinitely. Laissez-faire mystification cannot contain the discontent. This is the basic incompatibility, but the argument can be continued. If the government does play a significant role in the economy, it becomes imperative that businessmen protect their interests. Thus they have a strong motive to press for political power. And they have the means. For two reasons. First, and most obvious, they have wealth. Wealth, I take it as axiomatic, implies power. Second, they occupy so strategic a position in the economy that an elected government must acquiesce to (most of) their demands.

The first reason first. To my knowledge no classical liberal has ever denied that a laissez-faire economy will generate substantial inequality—though they sometimes suggest that this will diminish over time. [44] The argument for this latter claim is invariably an appeal to "the facts," "facts" that are debatable in their own right, but in any event irrelevant to the theoretical issue, since twentieth-century capitalism has been anything but laissez-faire. From a theoretical perspective, it is hard to see how the inequality gap can fail to widen

---

*Of the $500 million spent during the 1972 U.S. presidential election campaign, unions contributed roughly $13 million. In 1956, a year for which direct union-business comparisons are possible, the contribution of 742 businessmen matched the contributions of unions representing 17 million workers. (Lindblom, Politics and Markets, p. 195.)

under laissez-faire (real laissez-faire, that is, not perfectly competitive paradise). It is a mathematical truth that if I enter a fair gam-
bling game with fewer resources than my opponent, I will probably
lose. The greater the gap, the greater the probability. If it is possible
to make money from money as well as from labor, and if a large class
save nothing, then the laws of probability and the magic of compound
interest point to a widening gap.

But even if the gap does not widen, if it merely stays wide (a
gap that is essential for progress, according to Hayek, *) the concentration of wealth surely undercuts democracy. Classical liberals are
remarkably reticent on this issue. The response, presumably, is
that government will be small under laissez-faire, and unconcerned
with economic matters, and so there would be no point to the wealthy
sector's intervening in the democratic process. But, as I have argued,
government will not likely remain small, and even if the system were
more stable than I'm convinced it would be, it takes a surprisingly
sanguine view of human nature (a view classical liberals are not
otherwise prone to take) to think that concentrated private wealth will
be either unwilling or unable to bend the political process for its own
ends.

My second reason for thinking that the owners of the means of
production in a laissez-faire society will be privileged derives from
looking at the system from the point of view of a political figure. A
politician, no less than a businessman, values economic stability.
She must pay attention to those groups that threaten that stability. Now
it is clear that labor unions and rebellious ethnic minorities can disrupt the system. But these groups must be organized to be effective,
and force can be brought to bear against them if they go too far. On
the other hand, the business community need not be organized to employ its fundamental weapon: the "investment strike." And the threat
of force is impotent against it. As we saw in Chapter 4, investor confidence is the key to capitalist stability. If a government initiates policies that businessmen perceive to be hurting their interests, they
may, with neither organization nor malice, become reluctant to invest.
The resultant outcome of such isolated acts is economic—and hence
political—instability. A government under laissez-faire (or any other
form of capitalism) must regard the interests of business as privileged. In a very real sense, what is good for business is good for the
country; if business suffers, so will everyone else.

---

*Recall p. 95.

The reader may assent—but still be troubled. Would it be any different under worker control? Is not democracy as I have defined it wishful thinking? Is it really possible to have an active, informed, sovereign electorate embracing the entire adult population? Is worker control any less incompatible with democracy than laissez-faire?

These are difficult questions. I cannot prove that genuine democracy is realizable. But some things can be said for worker control.

First, and most important, is the question of privilege. Under worker control there will be considerably less inequality and, therefore, less concentration of wealth; this I have already argued. And there will not exist a class of private individuals capable of an investment strike, since investment is an explicitly political matter. Capitalists cannot dominate the government, for there are no capitalists.

But might there not arise a "new class"? Perhaps—but what would it be? The party? A mass, majority party might well dominate the political process for a sustained period of time, but this, in itself, does not constitute an abrogation of democracy. If the electorate remains active and informed, it is not contrary to democracy that a particular party is hegemonic. Of course the party might become rigid and bureaucratic; thus popular participation might atrophy. This might happen. It might happen as well under capitalism. Democracy is no more vulnerable to this threat under worker control. (I suppose one might argue that capitalism is shot through with so many contradictions that no one political party can long remain unchallenged, whereas worker control, less unstable, is more likely to become complacent. Perhaps—but that is certainly a backhanded argument for capitalism.)

Might not the governmental bureaucracy itself become "the new class?" This indeed is a threat. It is not at all hard to imagine the civil service as "a stable class possessing political power at least equal to that of elected officials and unmatched by any other minority group." And it cannot be denied that the worker-control ideal embraces a larger governmental apparatus than the laissez-faire ideal. One might argue that given the choice of business as privileged or the civil service as privileged, society is better off with the latter. There is much to be said for this conslusion. The interests of a governmental bureaucracy are not coincident with those of the general populace, but the variance tends toward inefficiency, a problem less severe than many of those that are consequent on the pursuit of private business interest. Furthermore, the privileges of bureaucracy are more amenable to political control. In a polyarchical society, the conflict between governmental bureaucracy and popular control is widely recognized. One can expect candidates and elected officials to propose various experiments for "taming the bureaucracy"; some might even succeed.

The real choice, however, is not between business privilege and civil service privilege. The contradictions of laissez-faire necessitate governmental intervention. The more the economy develops, the greater the contradictions. The greater the contradictions, the greater the intervention. All this I have argued. So the real choice is a governmental bureaucracy with a privileged capitalist class or a governmental bureaucracy without a privileged capitalist class. A bureaucracy of some sort is inevitable, at least in the foreseeable future. In the absence of a capitalist class, that bureaucracy may or may not become privileged, depending on concrete circumstances. But unless the capitalist class is absent, democracy is a wholly idle dream.

A final candidate for the new class is the "technostructure." Galbraith has argued that managerial-technical elites dominate contemporary capitalist societies, and would as readily dominate socialist ones. [45] This is an important thesis, and it merits consideration, but the analysis belongs more properly to the critique of post-Keynesian capitalism in the next chapter. We need only note here that the charge applies as much to laissez-faire as it does to worker control. The problem is no more serious for the one than for the other.

So—is democracy more likely under worker control than under laissez-faire? I've given reasons for thinking so, but the reasons are not conclusive. An important obstacle would be removed, but others might appear that may or may not be surmountable. There remains a final observation in support of worker control. In addition to privilege (the issue with which we've been concerned), the posibility of an active and informed electorate makes the democratic ideal problematic. But one feature of worker control is important in this respect, the extension of democratic procedures to the workplace. It's an old argument, but it bears repeating: one develops democratic attitudes and skills by practicing democracy. Under worker self-management, crucial decisions that have immediate impact—organization of work and distribution of income, to name only two—must be made democratically by the individuals affected. However imperfectly the democratic structures function, they provide a greatly expanded opportunity for participation—and they close off none of the channels open to citizens of capitalist polyarchies.

I have tried to demonstrate that democracy (though not polyarchy) is incompatible with laissez-faire. The same conclusion can be drawn, we shall see, with respect to Keynesian and post-Keynesian capitalism. Is democracy possible at all? Perhaps not in its ideal form, but democratic procedures can certainly be extended. Will anarchy result? One should recall that no extension of suffrage or any move toward one-person one-vote has ever occurred without generating predictions of dire consequences. One can be "tough-minded" and predict inevitable chaos and/or the inevitable rise of a "new class, " but such predictions are based on assumed first principles and/or dubious historical extrapolations, not on sound theory or hard evidence. The fact of the matter is, no society has yet structured itself as a worker-controlled polyarchy. The historical conditions have not been ripe for the experiment; the concept itself is new. It might just be the case that democracy is more possible than we (are supposed to?) think.

CAPITALISM AND WORK

We come now to the final objection to competitive capitalism. It is perhaps the most serious of all. Capitalism, I shall argue, dehumanizes the worker. Or, to put the charge in terms of our articulated values, a capitalist organization of work runs sharply counter to the psychological well-being and autonomy of employees. The conflict is so severe that the word "dehumanization" is not inappropriate.

The neoclassical worldview that underpins classical liberalism suggests that such dehumanization is impossible, so long as competition reigns. The neoclassical conception inclines one to think that if working conditions are unpleasant and the work itself alienating, it is because workers have in some sense chosen their fate.

Marx takes a contrary view. Dehumanization of the worker is held to be a necessary feature of capitalism. What distinguishes capitalism from simple commodity production is neither private property nor the market; it is the commodity character of labor-power. Therein, Marx insists, lies the secret of capitalist production.

> The sphere we are deserting [the market] within whose boundaries the sale and purchase of labor-power goes on, is in fact a very Eden of the innate rights of man. There alone rule Freedom, Equality, Property and Bentham. Freedom, because both buyer and seller of a commodity, say of labor-power, are constrained only by their own free will. . . . Equality, because each enters into relation with the other as simple owners of commodities, and they exchange equivalent for equivalent. Property, because each disposes only of what is his own. And Bentham, because each looks only to himself.
> . . . Each looks only to himself and no one troubles himself about the rest, and just because they do so, do they all, in accordance with the preestablished harmony of things, or under the auspices of an all-shrewd providence, work together for their mutual advantage, for the common weal and in the interest of all.

> On leaving this sphere of simple circulation or of
> exchange of commodities, which furnishes the "Free
> Trade Vulgaris" with his views and ideas . . . we think
> we can perceive a change in the physiognomy of our
> dramatis personae. He, who before was the money
> owner, now strides in front as the capitalist; the pos-
> sessor of labor-power following as his laborer. The
> one with an air of self-importance, smiling, intent
> on business; the other, timid and holding back, like
> one who is bringing his own hide to the market and
> has nothing to expect but—a hiding. [46]

There are a number of questions we must ask. Is it true that
workers under capitalism receive a "hiding"? Perhaps they did in
Marx's day, but do they now? There is substantial evidence that many
workers in the United States think they do. Numerous studies indicate
a job-dissatisfaction. [47] Author Studs Terkel, who travelled the country interviewing workers, reports that though "there are, of course,
the happy few who find savor in their daily jobs,"

> for the many, there is a hardly concealed discontent. The
> blue-collar blues is no more bitterly sung than the white-
> collar moan. "I'm a machine," says the spot welder.
> "I'm caged," says the bank teller, and echoes the hotel
> clerk. "I'm a mule," says the steel-worker. "A monkey
> could do what I do," says the receptionist. "I'm less than
> a farm implement," says the migrant worker. "I'm an
> object," says the high-fashion model. Blue and white
> collar call upon the identical phrase: "I'm a robot."
> "There's nothing to talk about," the young accountant
> despairingly enunciates. [48]

The empirical question as to the extent and depth of job-dissatisfaction is of vital importance to an overall assessment of the capitalism-socialism controversy and of the possibility of change. But it is
not one that falls squarely within the purview of our analysis, since
we have chosen to focus on ideal structures. The empirical evidence
is not irrelevant. If our structural analysis points to worker-aliena-
tion, and yet no dissatisfaction manifests itself, then the analysis is
surely suspect. But our major concern is, and must be, with structural linkage. What is it about the capitalist nature of the economic
system that breeds job dissatisfaction? Perhaps the past and current
dissatisfaction is accidental—or rooted in human nature.

At first sight the causal linkage seems obvious. The owners of
the means of production or their representatives determine the organ-

ization of the workplace. That is their prerogative. Workers do not participate in such decisions; they have no autonomy in this sphere. If the workplace is dehumanizing, then the capitalists have made it so.

To this indictment there is a standard retort. Appearances, it is said, are deceptive, for the capitalist does not decide arbitrarily on the organization of work, but according to factors that allow for worker influence. If work is dehumanizing, workers have chosen it to be so, and so their autonomy has not been violated. Consider Nozick's version: Productivity, under a reorganization scheme designed to make work more meaningful, will either rise, remain the same, or fall.

> If the productivity of the workers in a factory rises when the work tasks are segmented so as to be more meaningful, then the individual owners pursuing profits will so reorganize the productive process. If the productivity of the workers remains the same under such meaningful division of labor, then in the process of competing for laborers firms will alter their internal work organization.
> So the only interesting case to consider is that in which dividing a firm's work tasks into meaningful segments, rotation of labor, and so forth is less efficient (as judged by market criteria) than the less meaningful division of labor. This lessened efficiency can be borne in three ways (or in combinations of them). First, the workers in the factories themselves might desire meaningful work. It has all the virtues its theorists ascribe to it, the workers realize this, and they are willing to give up something (some wages) in order to work at meaningfully segmented jobs. They work for lower wages, but they view their total work package (lower wages plus the satisfaction of meaningful work) as more desirable than the less meaningful work at higher wages. They make a tradeoff of some increase in the meaningfulness of their work, increased self-esteem and so forth. . . .[49]

We need not consider Nozick's other ways of bearing the lessened efficiency (consumer groups voluntarily subsidizing the less efficient firms or the government prohibiting nonmeaningful work).[50] Both are beyond the pale of standard neoclassicism, and neither is relevant to any realistic version of capitalism. His important claim concerns the first way. If a reorganization that makes work more satisfying is at least as productive as the original organization, then a capitalist pursuing his own interest will so reorganize. If it is less productive, he will still reorganize, provided the workers accept a wage reduction sufficient to maintain his original profit margin. Hence, if work can be made more meaningful but is not, it is because workers have been unwilling to bear the cost of making it so.

Of course this argument presumes that a capitalist is entitled to his present rate of profit, but we will let that pass. The essential flaw is deeper, springing from an ambiguity in the concept "choice of work packages." We must distinguish two senses: choice of occupation and choice of how a specific production process is organized. The first is available to workers under capitalism, at least in the sense that no one is legally required to pursue a particular trade. But the issue with which we are concerned is the second: the selection of one productive process from among the technically feasible alternatives. The choice of occupation is relevant only to the degree that it bears on this decision.

To assess its relevance, let us consider how workplace organization comes about. We can distinguish two cases: (1) the owners or managers of an ongoing concern reorganize their establishment; (2) owners of surplus capital set people into motion constructing a new facility. In the first case the owners have an existing workforce at their disposal; in the second, they must attract one.

Now there may be cases on record where an owner of an existing concern has approached her workforce with a proposition such as this: "I am thinking of reorganizing. This will make the work more tedious, but I will pay you more. Let us take a vote." But such cases—as the history of labor resistance to reorganization makes plain—are not paradigmatic. Other approaches are more typical.

One in particular is especially problematic: a reorganization that increases productivity by substituting lesser-skilled labor for greater. Skilled workers do not <u>choose</u> to be replaced by unskilled workers. They might be permitted to stay on, provided they change their work category and accept the same (or more likely, lower) pay. The "choice of total work packages" is not between "more meaning with less pay" and "less meaning with more pay"; it is between less meaningful work and no work at all. That, in any event, is the immediate choice. If a worker's skill is in demand, he has other options—but even so, he cannot be said, in any meaningful sense, to have chosen the reorganization.

Autonomy is not the only value at stake in such matters, of course. It might be argued that participatory autonomy is overridden in such cases by an appeal to the greater happiness of the consumer. A valuable skill is released for employment elsewhere in the economy. There is merit to this argument <u>if</u> the skill is needed elsewhere. If not, a crucial cost is incurred that should be registered in the utilitarian calculus but is ignored by the market: the skilled laborer, to be employed at all, must sacrifice her skill, and with it perhaps some income, job-satisfaction and self-respect. This is a matter of theoretical importance. The neoclassical argument for the optimality of competitive capitalism rests on the presumption that a competitive market compels those who make decisions to bear the social costs of these decisions. But here is a decision class of profound importance to individual well-being (decisions concerning skill requirements for productive processes) for which the social costs are not borne by the decision makers. The capitalist decides, and a rise in profit confirms the choice. But the market does not register the cost to the skilled worker who is now unable to exercise her skill.

We have been considering the reorganization of an existing facility. Perhaps a new facility fares better. After all, unless there is widespread unemployment, the owners of a new enterprise must entice workers away from their present employers. They might choose to do this by offering more satisfying work. It is here that a worker's freedom of occupation exerts an influence on workplace organization—and that influence rebounds to established enterprises, who must now compete to retain their workers.

One _may_ compete by offering more satisfying work. But one may also compete by offering higher wages. When wage competition is adopted, a worker's freedom of occupation has no impact at all on working conditions. The overall influence of occupational choice, therefore, depends on the degree to which owners of productive facilities, when competing for employees, emphasize qualitative differences in workplace organization rather than (or at least in addition to) wage differentials.

But under competitive capitalism the latter mode of competition will surely predominate. Wage competition is far simpler than competition based on qualitative organizational differences. Differences in wages are immediately quantifiable, no innovation is necessary, advertising costs (to attract workers) are minimal. Once an organizational format is decided, it is an easy matter to determine wage rates necessary to attract the requisite number of workers. By contrast, experiments with various formats relative to a given wage are more complex, time-consuming and costly. Until the format is decided and made operational, an employer does not really know how much or how little he will have to pay. (Henry Ford revolutionized automobile assembly; workers quit in droves—until he also revolutionized the pay scale: an unprecedented five dollars a day for factory work.[51])

The reader, especially if conditioned by neoclassicism, will likely be unhappy with this analysis. I have argued that a worker's choice of occupation has no direct impact on a firm's reorganization, nor, if wage-competition is relied on, on initial organization. Since wage competition predominates (there are, of course, exceptions), a worker's choice of occupation has minimal effect on workplace structure. To this argument, one might well object: "Wage competition cannot be separated from workplace-quality competition. The workers who stayed with Ford for $5 a day <u>chose</u> that 'total work package.' Ford's success demonstrates that autoworkers preferred an assembly line with more pay to alternative methods without."

It demonstrates no such thing. One cannot view a capitalist economy as being in static equilibrium, featuring alternative packages of work and reward. The system is dynamic, ever-changing, and the initiative lies with capital. What about those autoworkers who preferred the earlier methods, the workers Ford could not entice away from his competitors? They too soon found themselves on assembly lines (if not in the streets), for their companies could not compete with Ford unless they adopted similar technologies. The choice of <u>some</u> autoworkers to submit to Ford (and of course we can only speak of choice if employment alternatives were available elsewhere) soon altered the "work packages" available to the rest.

An objection appealing to consumer well-being is due to surface again at this juncture: Granted, capitalism circumscribes a worker's autonomy; it may even at times interfere with her psychological well-being. But the reorganizations and innovations that have taken place—even if against the will of the workers involved—have contributed vastly to the raising of living standards—for the workers as well as for the capitalists. Surely this more than counterbalances.

There is no way to <u>prove</u> that it does. The market, I have already noted, does not correctly record the costs. It might well be the case that we would be a healthier, happier society if we had fewer goods and more meaningful work. Of course one cannot prove this contention either. But then one shouldn't try, because there is an important dimension to the problem overlooked if one raises the meaningful work versus technological efficiency dichotomy so abstractly. The fact of the matter is, organizational changes under capitalism are <u>not</u> dictated by the requirements of technological efficiency. The fact of the matter is, capitalist organization and reorganization are biased in the direction of dehumanization. When faced with a choice of technologies that yield the same output and require the same outlay of capital and wages, but which differ in degree of work satisfaction, a capitalist has good reasons for preferring the less human alternative. This claim I shall try to prove. I do not claim that an owner will <u>always</u> choose the less human alternative, but I do claim that there are systematic structural features that incline him to do so regularly.

This claim might seem to contradict the assumption that the capitalist model under consideration is ideally competitive, since such competition presupposes profit maximization. If two techniques cost the same and yield the same output, a profit-maximizing capitalist ought to be neutral between them. I seem to be imputing sinister motives to capitalists or to be appealing to class interests that take precedence over individual interests (and thus exposing myself to Nozick's sneer, "And don't say it's against the class interests of investors. . . . Investors are not so altruistic.").[52] The reasons I have in mind, however, are not sinister, nor are they grounded in "altruistic" appeals to class interest. They rest on the assumption that a capitalist can distinguish his immediate short-term interests from his somewhat longer-ranged ones. I assume only that those who decide upon workplace structures possess a normal degree of rationality.

My argument will rest on certain assumptions about the nature of "meaningful" work. I do not regard "meaningful" as simply a matter of taste. I assume that a reorganization that makes work more meaningful (more human, more satisfying) will ordinarily involve one or both of the following sorts of changes: changes that allow individual workers greater exercise of their human faculties—intelligence, imagination, judgment, and so forth—and changes that give workers, collectively, more control over the work they do. By collective control, I mean a direct voice (via some democratic forum) in matters concerning what is produced, how much, and under what conditions. I do not assume that all individuals want to exercise their faculties and to have control over their work, but I do assume that workplace changes of the type described will enhance the general level of well-being. I assume, in short, that the Aristotelian Principle applies at the workplace, and that autonomy enhances satisfaction. These are not fanciful suppositions. (Paul Blumberg concludes his survey of 25 years of research on worker-participation as follows: "There is hardly a study in the entire literature which fails to demonstrate that satisfaction in work is enhanced or that other generally acknowledged beneficial consequences accrue from a genuine increase in workers' decision-making power. Such consistency of findings, I submit, is rare in social research."[53])

Now it is plain that changes that increase worker autonomy at the expense of the traditional prerogatives of ownership will be resisted, even if short-range profits are not affected. Human beings, by and large, are not indifferent to usurpations of their power. If the choice is between equally profitable techniques, one of which transfers significant power from owners to workers, and if this choice is made by the owners (or their representatives), the outcome is not much in doubt. The choice is not in doubt at all if one option jeopardizes long-term profits by closing off a major profit source—which is precisely what happens when autonomy opens onto the domain of the Aristotelian Principle, when, that is, workers decide questions concerning the replacement of skilled labor by unskilled. Here we find the interests of capital and labor in stark opposition—another basic "contradiction" of capitalism.

We have already broached the skill question. I have argued that the replacement of skilled workers by unskilled raises doubts as to the optimality of capitalism. But that earlier analysis did not go to the root of the problem; the argument was so abstract as to suggest that the factor determining the replacement of skill by nonskill (or perhaps vice-versa) is technology. But this, I now wish to argue, is not so. More precisely, I assert that technological development under capitalism is not neutral with respect to the skill question; it is biased by class interest in the direction of skill reduction. More precisely still, I claim the following: whan faced with a choice of technologies that involve different levels of skill but are equally costly in terms of capital and wage outlay, the capitalist has good reason to choose the one requiring lesser skills.

The reason is straightforward: the skilled worker is more difficult to <u>control</u> than the unskilled. The skilled worker is less dispensable, less easily replaced, and so less susceptible to workplace discipline. Moreover, the more complex the work and the more knowledge required, the more difficult it is to determine just what can be expected from a worker, just what constitutes a "fair day's work." The trouble with skill, from the point of view of the capitalist, appears not (only) on the cost side of the ledger, but on the output side as well.

The correlation between skill and intransigence has often been remarked. Marx quotes from Andrew Ure's 1835 treatise <u>The Philosophy of Manufactur</u> (sic): "By the infirmity of human nature, it happens that the more skillful the workman, the more self-willed and intractable he is apt to become, and of course the less fit a component of a mechanical system in which . . . he may do great damage to the whole."54

In this centruy the problem has not merely been recognized; a whole philosophy, science, and technology of work has developed to deal with it. This development has such direct bearing on our concern that it merits a moment of our attention.

A seminal figure is Frederick Winslow Taylor, the "father of Scientific Management." As conceived by Taylor, Scientific Management attempts to resolve "the greatest evil from which both workmen and employees are suffering," namely, "systematic soldiering." Systematic soldiering is that "loafing" which goes on not because of the "natural laziness of men," but as a result of "a careful study on the part of workmen of what they think will promote their best interests." As Taylor sees it:

> The greater part of systematic soldiering . . . is done
> by the men with a deliberate object of keeping their em-
> ployers ignorant of how fast work can be done.
>
> So universal is soldiering for this purpose that
> hardly a competent workman can be found in a large es-
> tablishment, whether he works by the day or on piece
> work, contract work or under any of the ordinary sys-
> tems of compensating labor, who does not devote a con-
> siderable part of his time to studying just how slowly he
> can work and still convince his employer that he is going
> at a good pace.[55]

Taylor's solution is justly famous. Management must take control of the workplace to a degree previously unknown. The labor-proc-
ess must be preplanned and precalculated to such a degree that the
process no longer exists as a unified whole in the mind of the workman, but only in the minds of a special management staff. As Taylor
emphasized: "All possible brain work should be removed from the shop
and centered in the planning and laying-out department."[56] To this
end, research and experimentation are necessary, for

> the managers must assume the burden of gathering togeth-
> er all of the traditional knowledge which in the past has
> been possessed by the workmen, and then of classifying,
> tabulating and reducing this knowledge to rules, laws and
> formulae.[57]

Now Taylor's is but one of a series of "philosophies of work"
that have emerged in the twentieth century, but at least in its general
formulation it may well be what sociologist and management consultant Peter Drucker calls "the most powerful as well as the most lasting
contribution America has made to Western thought since the Federal-
ist Papers."[58] To be sure, many of the specific features of Taylor-
ism have been superceded. Detailed daily instruction cards are no
longer handed out, and even time and motion studies, pioneered by
Taylor, have receded in importance. But two elements have persisted:
a preoccupation with the problem of control, derived from an explicit
or implicit recognition that the perceived interests of workers are at
variance with those of management, and an attempt to resolve the problem by reducing to a minimum the necessity for independent judgment
on the part of the worker.[59] If this is so, then it cannot be maintained
that workplace organization has been dictated by technological considerations any more than by worker choice. The organization has been
determined—and there is no reason to suppose it would have been any
different in an ideally competitive capitalist economy—by the perceived (and real) interests of capital. My conclusion thus follows: the

structure of capitalism, which sets up a real opposition between owners and wage laborers, and which grants the former effective control over the workplace, inclines organizational and technical changes in the direction of dehumanization.

A reasonable objection deserves to be heard. As any student of managerial philosophy knows, there has been considerable concern in recent years with the "decline of the work ethic," and there have emerged theories of management that appeal to precisely the values I have accused capitalism of flaunting. There are contemporary theorists who urge both job enrichment and worker participation; there are corporations that have experimented extensively in implementing such changes.[60] These changes, as well as the "dehumanizing" ones I have described, have developed within the context of capitalism. Do they not constitute a major counter-tendency to the one on which I've based my case?

My response is twofold. First an abstract consideration. Even if there exists a countertendency within capitalism, the original tendency toward skill-reduction persists. If skill-reduction leads to higher profit than job-enrichment or participation, then skill-reduction will take place. A system that does not exhibit this tendency (and we shall see in a moment that worker control does not) is thus morally preferable.

A second and more concrete consideration is that a capitalist structure places rather strict limits on the degree of participation that can be permitted. Participation and enrichment must increase profits; they often do, but not always.[61] The point, notice, is to increase profits, not merely maintain them. Management will not find palatable, for example, a reorganization scheme that reduces productivity in exchange for work-enhancement, even if the profit level can be sustained. But if a scheme is unpalatable to management, it will not be implemented, for in all the participatory arrangements seriously considered by corporations, management is firmly in control. As Richard Sennett notes,

> The experiments in cooperative decision-making make use of employee questionnaires to find out how workers want to do a job, and they set up conferences with workers on the job site. All these techniques try to create a feeling of mutual interest and good will between those who, in the end, will give the orders and those who must obey them.[62]

Nor is this likely to change. Management is well aware that too much participation can mushroom in unacceptable directions. A high-level General Motors official is quite explicit. If workers begin participating,

the subjects of participation . . . are not necessarily
restricted to those few matters that management considers to be of direct, personal interest to employees. . . .
[A plan cannot] be maintained for long without (a) being
recognized by employees as manipulative, or (b) leading
to expectations for wider and more significant involve-
ment—"Why do they only ask us about plans for painting
the office and not about replacing this old equipment and
rearranging the layout?" Once competence is shown (or
believed to have been shown) in, say, rearranging the
work area, and after participation has become a conscious, officially sponsored activity, participators may
very well want to go on to topics of job assignment, the
allocation of rewards, or even the selection of leadership. In other words, management's present monopoly
[of control] can in itself easily become a source of
contention. [63]

Indeed: So one should not count on a humanized workplace under capitalism—certainly not under laissez-faire.

There remains, it seems to me, but one counterargument to
consider. I have argued that so long as organizational initiative remains with the representatives of capital, worker participation will be
restricted, and worker choice will have little impact on the organization of work. The tendency toward meaningless work, though capable
of being checked somewhat by enrichment and participation schemes
that enhance productivity, will persist. "But even if all this were
true," it might be contended, "your case is inconclusive, since capitalists, in a free society, need not retain the initiative. If workers
are genuinely dissatisfied, there are alternatives available to them.
If they really want something better (and are willing to pay for the
loss of efficiency), then they can take the initiative. Socialist acts,
after all, are not forbidden under capitalism." Again consider Nozick:

Of course, as an altervative, persons may form their own
democratically-run cooperative firms. It is open to any
wealthy radical or group of workers to buy an existing
factory or establish a new one, and to institute their favorite micro-industrial scheme; for example, worker-controlled, democratically-run firms. . . . The important
point is that there is a means of realizing the worker-
control scheme that can be brought about by the voluntary actions of people in a free society. [64]

This argument should not be dismissed on the grounds that few workers can afford to buy their factories and that the "radical rich" is a small set indeed. Nozick's argument admits of a subtler interpretation: If workers really want worker self-management, then cooperatives will spring up, funded initially by radical philanthropists or wealthy workers. They will be few at first, as is the case with all innovative organizations, but if they are technologically and operationally viable, they will gradually attract workers away from the capitalists until the point is reached where everyone is satisfied. As a matter of fact, cooperatives have not undermined capitalism, and so they must be either nonviable economically or unattractive to workers or both. Worker self-management either doesn't work or it isn't wanted.

It is tempting to respond to Nozick by appealing to contingent historical facts to explain the failure of cooperative ventures that have appeared (not infrequently) on the capitalist stage. But such a response focuses on the wrong issue—and implicitly gives credence to an evolutionary scheme that is wholly untenable. The key issue is not the failure of specific ventures (some, in fact, have done and continue to do rather well);[65] the key question is why the movement as a whole has not expanded.

But we know the answer to that question. The reason is structural. We know from our earlier analysis that a worker-managed firm lacks an expansionary dynamic. When a capitalist enterprise is successful, the owner can increase her profits by reproducing her organization on a larger scale. She lacks neither the means nor the motivation to expand. Not so with a worker-managed firm. Even if the workers have the means, they lack the incentive, since enterprise growth brings in new workers, but does not (usually) increase per-worker revenue. Cooperatives, even when prosperous, do not spontaneously grow. But if this is so, then each new cooperative venture (in a capitalist society) requires a new wealthy radical or a new group of affluent, radical workers willing to experiment. Since such people are usually in short supply, it follows that the absence of a large and growing cooperative movement proves nothing about the viability of worker self-management nor the preferences of workers.* The

---

*Nozick refers to the "large cash reserves in union pension funds," and asks why groups of workers are not now instituting worker-control schemes (Anarchy, State and Utopia, p. 255). It should be pointed out that the Pension Fund Act of 1974 prohibits the investment of a pension fund in excess of 5 percent of the total capital of a company.

commonsense neoclassical dictum that only those things that best accord with people's desires will survive the struggle of free competition is not the whole truth with respect to consumer goods; with respect to workplace organization it is not even a partial truth.

To compare worker-control socialism with laissez-faire, little need be said beyond making explicit what was implicit in the preceding critique. Workers have far more autonomy under worker control. Workers have a democratic voice in two areas from which they are excluded under capitalism, the investment arena and the workplace. This increase in autonomy, especially at the workplace, should enhance job satisfaction. The empirical evidence points unmistakably to this conclusion; structural analysis concurs. A root problem with capitalism is its tendency to deskill labor. Labor-power is a commodity, to be purchased at the lowest possible cost, and "consumed" so as to maximize output; deskilling frequently promotes both these goals. Under worker control, the organization of work also reflects a concern for "profit," but "profit" here means the difference between total revenue and non-labor costs. Average workers have an interest in preventing any particular class of specialists from becoming so indispensable that they can demand preferential treatment, but they also have an interest in raising the average level of skill as high as possible. In fact the two interests converge, since raising the general skill level not only makes work more satisfying, but it also undercuts the argument of the highly skilled for exceptional treatment. Workers have no interest at all in turning themselves into automatons.

Worker self-management increases autonomy; it is also likely to increase productivity. Again the empirical evidence points in this direction.[66] This is not to say that there will never be conflicts between efficiency and work-satisfaction, or, for that matter, that all problems of work-alienation will vanish. Tensions can certainly arise within an organization between managers and managed, between those who want more production and those who want more leisure, between backers of this or that reorganization scheme. The values of autonomy, psychological well-being and material well-being need not inevitably conflict, but they sometimes do. And when they do, a democratic resolution of the conflict that follows from free and open debate, that expresses the will of the majority of those involved, and that leaves

---

It should also be noted that it makes little sense for a union to take the (substantial) risk of funding a new enterprise that will benefit only a small fraction of its membership when it is so much safer to go with the established giants.

open the possibility of revision and experimentation seems the best possible hope for an optimal outcome.

Thus the case for worker control.

NOTES

1. See Alexander Werth, Russia at War 1941-1945 (New York: E. P. Dutton, 1964) for a vivid account. Americans, but not Russians, tend to forget the massive destruction World War II brought to the Soviet Union.

2. Though specific estimates and statistics of socialist development are often disputed, the general picture is reasonably clear. Concerning the USSR, one might look at Alec Nove, The Soviet Economic System (London: George Allen and Unwin, 1977); concerning China, at Alexander Eckstein, China's Economic Revolution (Cambridge: Cambridge University Press, 1977). The statistics on Yugoslavia were cited by Elizabeth Mann Borgese in her introduction to Self-Management: New Dimensions to Democracy, ed. Ichak Adizes and Elizabeth Mann Borgese (Santa Barbara: ABC-Clio, 1975), p. xx.

3. Friedrich A. Hayek, The Constitution of Liberty (London: Routledge and Kegan Paul, 1960), p. 12.

4. Cf. Hayek, Constitution of Liberty, p. 6; Robert Nozick, Anarchy, State and Utopia (New York: Basic Books, 1974), p. ix.

5. Hayek, Constitution of Liberty, p. 106. What are these ends? Hayek lists three: efficiency ("it is less wasteful to determine which has the stronger support by counting numbers than by fighting"), individual liberty, and the enhancement of the general level of understanding of the population. Ibid., pp. 107-8.

6. Jean-Jacques Rousseau, The Social Contract, trans. Maurice Cranston (Baltimore: Pengiun, 1968), p. 65.

7. Immanuel Kant, Foundations of the Metaphysics of Morals, trans. Lewis Beck White (Indianapolis: Bobbs-Merrill, Library of Liberal Arts, 1959), p. 51.

8. John Stuart Mill, Considerations on Representative Government (New York: Bobbs-Merrill, 1958), p. 54.

9. Cf. Joseph Schumpeter, Capitalism, Socialism and Democracy (New York: Harper Torchbooks, 1962), p. 269.

10. For a recent statement of this view, see Samuel Huntington, "The Democratic Distemper," The Public Interest (Fall, 1975): 9-38. This view is quite popular in influential circles today.

11. Hayek, Constitution of Liberty, p. 56. Cf. also Isaiah Berlin, Two Concepts of Liberty (Oxford: Oxford University Press, 1958), p. 48. For a defense of Rousseau against this charge, see Carole Pateman, Participation and Democratic Theory (Cambridge: Cambridge

University Press, 1970), pp. 22-27.

12. Nozick, Anarchy, State and Utopia, p. 270.

13. Ibid., p. 269.

14. Ibid., p. 270. So much for the American Revolution.

15. John Rawls, A Theory of Justice (Cambridge, Mass.: Belknap Press of Harvard University Press, 1971), p. 426.

16. Rawls cites R. W. White, "Ego and Reality in Psychoanalytic Theory," Psychological Issues 3 (1963). A. H. Maslow is an even more prominent advocate of the psychological need for self-actualization. Cf. his Motivation and Personality (New York: Harper and Row, 1954).

17. Hayek, Constitution of Liberty, p. 133.

18. Friedrich A. Hayek, The Road to Serfdom (Chicago: University of Chicago Press, 1944), p. 56.

19. Milton Friedman, Capitalism and Freedom (Chicage: University of Chicago Press, 1962), p. 18.

20. Hayek, Road to Serfdom, p. 61.

21. John Stuart Mill, On Liberty (Indianapolis: Hackett, 1978), p. 94.

22. Nozick, Anarchy, State and Utopia, p. 163.

23. Ibid., pp. 162-63.

24. George Bernard Shaw, The Intelligent Woman's Guide to Socialism, Capitalism, Sovietism, and Fascism (London: Constable, 1928), p. 504.

25. Friedman, Capitalism and Freedom, pp. 16-18.

26. Friedman, Capitalism and Freedom, p. 17. This passage, in context, suggests that wealthy patrons provide the primary support; it is not the trivially true observation that some wealthy persons have supported radical causes.

27. Cf. Roland Sarti, Fascism and the Industrial Leadership in Italy, 1919-1940 (Berkeley: University of California Press, 1971), especially Chapter I, or even the relatively conservative Henry Turner, Jr., "Big Business and the Rise of Hitler," American Historical Review 75 (October 1969): 56-70.

28. Friedman, Capitalism and Freedom, p. 17.

29. Charles Lindblom, Politics and Markets (New York: Basic Books, 1978), p. 46.

30. Ibid.

31. Cf. Mill, Representative Government, p. 94.

32. The Republic of Plato, trans. Francis MacDonald Cornford (Oxford: Oxford University Press, 1941), p. 290ff.

33. Cf. Jan Pen, Income Distribution: Facts, Theories, Policies (New York: Praeger, 1971), pp. 48-75; or Martin Bronfenbrenner, Income Distribution Theory (Chicago: Aldine-Atherton, 1971), especially pp. 66-72.

34. Hayek, Road to Serfdom, pp. 69-70.

35. Ibid., p. 69.

36. Friedman, Capitalism and Freedom, p. 24.

37. Cf. Richard Farkas, Yugoslav Economic Development and Political Change: The Relationship between Economic Managers and Policy-Making Elites (New York: Praeger, 1975); and Ichak Adizes, Industrial Democracy: Yugoslav Style (New York: The Free Press, 1971). The former work is based on extensive interviews with Yugoslavian firms, one run democratically, the other in a more authoritarian fashion.

38. Cf. Friedman, Capitalism and Freedom, Chapter X; Hayek, Constitution of Liberty, Chapter 6; Nozick, Anarchy, State and Utopia, Chapter 7.

39. The term was introduced by Robert Dahl and Charles Lindblom, Politics, Economics and Welfare (New York: Harper and Brothers, 1953). See also Lindblom, Politics and Markets, Chapter 10.

40. Cf. Lindblom, Politics and Markets, p. 172.

41. Ibid., p. 133.

42. See, in addition to Lindblom: C. Wright Mills, The Power Elite (New York: Oxford University Press, 1956); Gabriel Kolko, Wealth and Power in America (New York: Praeger, 1962); G. William Domhoff, Who Rules America? (Englewood Cliffs, N.J.: Prentice-Hall, 1967); Ralph Miliband, The State in Capitalist Society (New York: Basic Books, 1969).

43. See Lindblom, Politics and Markets, Chapters 13, 14, and 15.

44. Cf. Friedman, Capitalism and Freedom, p. 169.

45. See John Kenneth Galbraith, The New Industrial State (Boston: Houghton Mifflin, 1967), especially Chapter VI.

46. Karl Marx, Capital (New York: Modern Library, 1906), p. 196.

47. The best known is Work in America, Report of a Special Task Force to the Secretary of Health, Education and Welfare (Cambridge, Mass.: MIT Press, 1973). Confirming evidence has been supplied by Harold Sheppard and Neil Herrick, Where Have All the Robots Gone?: Worker Dissatisfaction in the 70's (New York: Macmillan, 1972). See also Graham Staines, "Is Worker Dissatisfaction Rising?" Challenge 22 (May-June, 1979): 38-45. In addition to the statistical studies, there are a number of on-site, "impressionistic" studies of specific facilities that shed much light on the contemporary workplace. See in particular Göran Palm's account of his year at LM Ericsson (the largest private employer in Sweden), The Flight from Work (Cambridge: Cambridge University Press, 1977); Theo Nichols and Huw Beynon's three-year study of a British chemical company, Living With Capitalism: Class Relations in the Modern Factory (London: Routledge and Kegan Paul, 1977); and Richard Balzer's inside

look at a Massachusetts Western Electric plant, Clockwork: Life in and Outside an American Factory (Garden City, N.Y.: Doubleday, 1976).

48. Studs Terkel, Working (New York: Avon Books, 1975), p. xiv.

49. Nozick, Anarchy, State and Utopia, p. 248. (Emphasis Nozick's.)

50. Ibid., p. 249.

51. Cf. Keith Sward, The Legend of Henry Ford (New York: Rhinehart, 1948) for details. It is worth mentioning that labor's dislike of the new system was intense. In 1913, before the $5 per day, the company found it necessary to hire nine persons to get one who would stay. (Sward, Henry Ford, p. 49.)

52. Nozick, Anarchy, State and Utopia, p. 252.

53. Paul Blumberg, Industrial Democracy: The Sociology of Participation (New York: Schocken, 1969), p. 123.

54. Marx, Capital, p. 403.

55. Taylor's three principal works, Shop Management (1903), Principles of Scientific Management (1911), and the public document, Hearings Before the Special Committee of the House of Representatives to Investigate Taylor and Other Systems of Shop Management (1912), are contained in a single volume, Frederick W. Taylor, Scientific Management (New York: Harper and Brothers, 1947) and are separately paginated therein. The quotes are from Shop Management, pp. 32-33. My argument here owes much to Harry Braverman, Labor and Monopoly Capital (New York: Monthly Review Press, 1974), the work that first called my attention to Taylor and the significance of workplace organization.

56. Taylor, Shop Management, p. 98.

57. Taylor, Principles of Scientific Management, p. 36.

58. Peter Drucker, The Practice of Management (New York: Harper and Brothers, 1954), p. 280.

59. Cf. Richard Edwards, Contested Terrain: The Transformation of Work in the Twentieth Century (New York: Basic Books, 1979), for a further elaboration of this thesis. Edwards downplays the specific influence of Taylor, and sees "bureaucratic" control as superceding "technical" control in the more sophisticated corporations today. But the general result (the monotonization of work) remains the same. For empirical evidence regarding the thesis that capitalist development decreases skill levels, see Braverman's summary of the works of James Bright and others, Labor and Monopoly Capital, pp. 184-235.

60. The job-enrichment school takes its cue from Maslow (cf., for example, Motivation and Personality); among the leading participation-theorists is Yale professor Chris Argyris (cf. his Integrating the Individual and the Organization [New York: Wiley, 1964]). For a good introduction to the theories and practices of the various schools, see Management and Motivation, ed. Victor Vroom and Edward Deci

(Harmondsworth: Penguin Books, 1970).

61. In an experiment at Autonetics, a division of North American Rockwell, it was found that two-thirds of the workgroups participating in decision making increased their efficiency dramatically. Productivity rose an average of 20 to 30 percent; there was a 30 to 50 percent decrease in errors in work involving inspection. Frederick Chaney and Kenneth Teal, "Participative Management—a Practical Experience," Personnel 49 (Nov.-Dec. 1972): 8-19. On the other hand, an influential study by Goode and Fowler showed that under certain conditions workers with low morale may be highly efficient. W. J. Goode and I. Fowler, "Incentive Factors in a Low Morale Plant," American Sociological Review 14 (1949): 618-24.

62. Richard Sennett, "The Boss's New Clothes," New York Review of Books 26 (February 22, 1979): 44.

63. Thomas Fitzgerald, "Why Motivation Theory Doesn't Work," Harvard Business Review 49 (July-August 1971): 42.

64. Nozick, Anarchy, State and Utopia, pp. 250, 252.

65. For examples, see Folkert Wilken, The Liberation of Work (New York: Roy, 1968).

66. Cf. David Jenkins, Job Power: Blue and White Collar Democracy (Garden City, N.Y.: Doubleday, 1973), especially Chapter 12.

6

MODERN LIBERALISM

I have completed my case against laissez-faire, the heart and soul of classical liberalism. But there are other defendants in the dock. My j'accuse is pointed at capitalism, not merely laissez-faire. Other defendants must be brought forward.

Recall the structure of my brief against laissez-faire. I argued that its claims to greater efficiency, better growth, and more liberty than worker control are false. I countered with an eight-count indictment:

1. Laissez-faire cannot guarantee full employment.
2. Laissez-faire encourages nonrational sales persuasion.
3. Laissez-faire generates an inequitable distribution of wealth.
4. Laissez-faire promotes the wrong kind of growth.
5. Laissez-faire yields a nonoptimal rate of growth.
6. Laissez-faire is economically unstable.
7. Laissez-faire is incompatible with democracy.
8. Laissez-faire dehumanizes workers.

I contend that the same indictment will stand against other forms of capitalism. My specific targets are the modern liberal structures.

A portion of this chapter originally appeared in "Should Rawls be a Socialist," Social Theory and Practice, 1 (Fall 1978): 1-27 and is reprinted with the permission of Social Theory and Practice.

These may be less guilty on some counts than laissez-faire, but when compared with worker control, their guilt remains transparent. This I propose to demonstrate.

Let us first consider what is being indicted. What exactly is modern liberalism? I understand modern liberalism to be a reaction formation to the excesses of laissez-faire. Modern liberals, like socialists, find laissez-faire to be morally and economically unacceptable. But modern liberals, unlike socialists, judge the basic structure to be sound; they think the "contradictions" of the system can be alleviated without abrogating the institutions of private property, wage labor or the market. (They concede, of course, that modifications are in order.) How might the contradictions be ameliorated? By dropping the laissez-faire provision and allowing the government to intervene. And how should the government intervene? This question brings us to the division within modern liberalism discussed in Chapter 2. Reform proposals depend heavily on how the system itself is conceptualized. For a Keynesian liberal the (modified) neoclassical model provides the guiding insights; it illustrates the strengths, but also the weaknesses of laissez-faire, and suggests the appropriate remedies for the latter. For a post-Keynesian, the neoclassical model does nothing of the sort; the neoclassical model is seen to be part of the problem: not only does it suggest the wrong kinds of reforms, but it is part of a protective ideology that masks the real workings of modern capitalism.

An examination of the ins and outs of the Keynesian-post-Keynesian dispute would take us too far from our central topic. In my judgment there is much to be said for the post-Keynesian attack on the neoclassical paradigm, but that issue is not essential to our concern. What we must ascertain is the extent to which the reforms of laissez-faire suggested by the competing paradigms deflect the charges of my multi-count indictment. Of course the way one conceptualizes capitalism bears strongly on one's evaluation of specific reform proposals, but I think we will see, when we compare reformed capitalism with worker control, that the latter shows itself superior whichever way one conceives capitalism.

This is a strong claim, perhaps stronger than I can justify. In fact, I must immediately insert a qualification. It is beyond the scope of this work to survey the entire field of Keynesian and post-Keynesian liberalism, and to analyze the myriad reforms implemented or advocated over the last half-century. Simplifications must necessarily be made. My strategy will be to focus primarily on one major figure in each tradition who has sketched and defended a reasonably comprehensive societal ideal. Such figures are not so easy to find. Since modern liberalism has been preoccupied historically with specific, piecemeal reforms, not many thinkers have stood back and attempted a comprehensive view.

A notable exception is the political philosopher John Rawls. To be sure, Rawl's magnum opus, A Theory of Justice, is not principally a treatise on liberal capitalism. Principally it develops and defends an original "theory of justice," the point of which, says Rawls, is to describe and clarify our ordinary, considered judgments regarding justice, much as a theory of grammar describes and clarifies a native speaker's ordinary usage.[1] But these "considered moral judgments" are the value-judgments of a modern liberal.[2] Moreover, Rawls employs his theory to evaluate socioeconomic formations. Specifically, he constructs a reasonably detailed model of a "property-owning democracy," and argues that such a system would be just.[3]

It is this model of capitalism that I intend to examine, for it well represents the Keynesian-liberal ideal. Unlike most political philosophers, Rawls does not, with the usual declaration of specialty noncompetence, shy away from economic issues. And when he does confront them, he does so from the perspective of the neoclassical (Keynesian-modified) paradigm—though unlike most economists of this tradition, he insists on keeping the ethical dimensions prominently in view.

That Rawls should adopt the neoclassical-Keynesian perspective without any apparent hesitation is not surprising, given the fact that he was writing and rewriting his treatise during the middle and late 1960s. For recall, from the end of World War II until the early 1970s—and especially during the prosperity seemingly ushered in by the Kennedy-Johnson, Keynesian-liberal tax cuts*—the "new economics" of the mainstream appeared impregnably solid and irreproachably scientific. Dissent on the Right was regarded with amusement. The radical and post-Keynesian mice who had begun to gnaw at the truck of the stately, flourishing, Keynesian-liberal paradigm were barely discernible in the underbrush. Rawls was not the only one to be impressed.†

Actually one "pest" was already making noise and attracting attention-though more from the general public than from the economics profession. In 1958 "the affluent society" entered our lexicon,

---

*It was not at all respectable in those days to suggest that the prosperity was war-related.

†In those (economically) untroubled days, even Milton Friedman would declare, "We are all Keynesians now," and Richard Nixon, "I am now a Keynesian." (Quoted by Paul Samuelson, Economics, 9th ed. [New York: McGraw-Hill, 1973], p. 205.)

and the author of the book so titled, John Kenneth Galbraith, achieved a certain renown. In 1967 another of his major works, <u>The New Industrial State</u>, became an international best-seller.[4] Remarkable events—important economic treatises by a serious (albeit witty and irreverent) economist attracting such popular notice—but by no means unplanned. An earlier work, <u>The Theory of Price Control,</u> had received no such reception, and so, Galbraith says,

> I made up my mind that I would never again place myself
> at the mercy of the technical economists who had the enor-
> mous power to ignore what I had written. I set out to in-
> volve a larger community. I would involve a larger com-
> munity. I would involve the economists by having the
> larger public say to them, "Where do you stand on Gal-
> braith's idea of price control?" They would <u>have</u> to con-
> front what I said.[5]

Has his strategy been successful? Somewhat. Galbraith's books are now reviewed in the scholarly journals; he is occasionally an object of, and participant in, scholarly polemics.[6] In 1972 he was elected president of the American Economics Association. But in 1973 Paul Samuelson could still say, "Galbraith in a sense has no disciples. There are few testable, researchable propositions in his writings that could serve for the purposes of Ph.D. theses or articles in learned journals. How can a jury prove his attitudes and insights right or wrong?"[7]

The fact of the matter is, Galbraith has not had much impact on mainstream economics, and the reason is not hard to find. The Galbraithian constructions and criticisms simple do not fit the neoclassical paradigm; they cannot be incorporated. And what cannot be incorporated is not much studied in established circles.

On the other hand, Galbraith fits rather neatly into the alternative paradigm that has emerged in recent years.* Galbraith is not the

---

*Thomas Kuhn has sensitized us to the fact that scientific revolutions occur, not as the result of slow and steady accretion of knowledge nor by one theory explaining all that another explains and more besides, but by a radical shift in perspective, by a "paradigm shift," wherein one way of conceiving a subject is replaced by another, thus opening up new topics, problem areas and methodologies while relegating others to (adopting Galbraith's phrase) "the museum of obsolete ideas." Such shifts do not occur without struggle, nor does it often

founder of post-Keynesianism. Contemporary post-Keynesians generally trace their provenance to Joan Robinson and her younger Cambridge colleagues for their relentless attacks on the foundations of
neoclassicism, and to Kalecki, Sraffa, and Keynes himself.[8] But
Galbraith's perspective is much in harmony, especially with the re-
form-oriented liberalism that can be associated with post-Keynesianism. More than most post-Keynesians Galbraith has concerned himself in a systematic fashion with the question of reform, so much so
that he can be taken as the prototypical post-Keynesian liberal.

Before embroiling ourselves in reform and criticism, let us do
what we have done at the outset of each of the last three chapters. Let
us think for a moment about values. We know that all criticisms of
capitalism or socialism ultimately rest on value commitments. I've
stated the commitments underlying my critique of laissez-faire.
Some are nonproblematical, even to classical liberals—material
well-being, (voluntary) leisure, efficiency, human happiness, liberty.
Others—notably equality, democracy and autonomy—are more controversial, and so a classical liberal might balk at several of my arguments on the grounds that she does not adhere to the value-assump-
tions.

Few modern liberals can pull up this way. The values I have
articulated (with one possible exception) are as basic to modern liberalism as they are to worker-control socialism. A hallmark of modern liberalism is its commitment to reducing inequality. Few people
of any political persuasion have expressed a deeper commitment to
equality than John Rawls. Not only must society structure its institutions so as to allow fair (and not merely formal) equality of opportunity to all; they must be shaped, he insists, so that all inequalities
work to the advantage of the least advantaged. Inequalities are permitted, but only to the degree that they serve as incentives for the
exercise of talent, and only if these incentives result in sufficiently
greater efficiency and innovation that the benefits reach the least
well-off members of society.[9]

Galbraith (and other modern liberals) are perhaps less egalitarian than Rawls, but Galbraith's commitment to equality is not subject
to doubt. His reform strategy is shot through with proposals to reduce
the inequalities of modern capitalism—inequalities between workers

---

happen that an established practitioner is converted by the "evidence."
The shift occurs only when new scholars are attracted to the new paradigm. (Thomas Kuhn, The Structure of Scientific Revolutions [Uni-
versity of Chicago Press, 1962].)

and managers within modern corporations, between the "planning sector" and the market sector, between property-generated income and income from work. The efficacy of his reform-proposals may be open to question (this we shall examine below) but not their intention.

Rawls and Galbraith also share a commitment to democracy. Both presume their "ideal states" to be democratic. Neither is preoccupied with the specter of a "tyrannical majority" encroaching on the property rights of a minority. Neither is concerned to keep controversial issues off the democratic agenda. They are representative modern liberals in these respects.

As to autonomy—the value of people participating in the decisions that will affect them—the picture is less clear. Modern liberalism seems somewhat divided on this value. Certain currents are rather taken with "technocracy." Not Rawls, however. He avows a "principle of equal participation," and links it to

> the medieval maxim that what touches all concerns
> all. . . . Political liberty so understood is not designed
> to satisfy [the individual's] quest for power. . . . Nor
> does it answer to the ambition to dictate to others. . . .
> The public will to consult and to take everyone's beliefs
> and interests into account lays the foundations for civic
> friendship and shapes the ethos of political culture.[10]

That Galbraith—and post-Keynesian liberals generally—value autonomy is not so plain. There is much talk of "emancipating belief" from the neoclassical categories and of "emancipating the state" from the control of corporate interests, but there are few (if any) proposals put forth to enhance the active participation of individuals in decision-making processes. The scope of government is certainly to be broadened, but the rationale is not so much to give citizens a greater voice in shaping their collective destiny as to better enable public officials to serve the general interests. Of course it might be the case that this absence of participatory proposals reflects a theoretical incompleteness, and not a devaluation of autonomy. Perhaps such proposals will be forthcoming. But it is worth remembering that Galbraith in particular has considerable admiration for technocratic elites.[11] This admiration is by no means servile, but it suggests the view that an independent governmental elite is necessary to serve as a countervailing power to private corporate elites. And this view suggests an allegiance to the technocratic ethos—an ethos that has little use for popular participation. If Galbraith (or anyone else) has such an allegiance, he will not be moved by arguments that are grounded on an appeal to participatory autonomy. But no matter. The case against post-Keynesian liberalism is not as strong without such arguments—but by no means does it collapse.

JOHN RAWLS AND THE KEYNESIAN-LIBERAL IDEAL

In A Theory of Justice Rawls sketches an ideal property-owning system that he thinks would be just. Let us call it "Fair Capitalism." The political structure of this system is democratic; liberty of con- science and freedom of thought are taken for granted, as are the other familiar civil liberties. The economic structure is capitalist—private property, wage labor and the market—but this structure is overseen by a formidable government. Four governmental departments do the overseeing, each with a distinct set of functions. The Allocative Branch is charged with keeping the economy competitive and with using taxes and subsidies to compensate for cases where competitive prices do not accurately reflect social benefits and costs. That is, it attempts to correct deviations from Pareto-optimality caused by monopolies and externalities. The Stabilization Branch concerns itself with the macro- scopic movement of the economy. It sees to it that strong effective demand brings about reasonably full employment "in the sense that those who want work can find it."[12] Together these two branches are to insure an efficient market economy.

More directly concerned with justice are the Transfer and Dis- tributive Branches. The Transfer Branch sees to it that no individual or household falls below the "social minimum." It guarantees a cer- tain level of well-being and honors specific claims need. The Distrib- utive Branch occupies itself not with the less well-off, but with the opposite end of the income spectrum. By a judicious mix of inheri- tance, gift, and progressive income taxes, it seeks to prevent a con- centration of wealth that might jeopardize political liberty and fair equality of opportunity. (The Distributive Branch is also given general taxing powers to "raise the revenues that justice requires."[13] Rawls favors a proportional expenditure tax to this end.)

This model, we observe, is modern-liberal in its willingness to redistribute income and in its general presumption that the government has a major role to play in counteracting the harsher effects of the free market. It is Keynesian as opposed to post-Keynesian in that it takes the competitive market as its ideal of efficiency, while at the same time charging the government to deal with unemployment by maintaining strong effective demand.

So we see what the government is supposed to do. But are the institutions adequate to the intentions? How likely is it that this Keynesian-liberal economy will be able to escape the various counts of my general indictment? How likely in comparison with worker control? These are the questions we must now investigate. (Rawls himself should not object to this formulation of the problem. He ex- plicitly avows a "greater-likelihood" principle: "Suppose aims which may be achieved by two plans are roughly the same. Then it may happen that some objectives have a greater chance of being realized by one plan than the other, yet at the same time none of the remaining aims are less likely to be attained. . . . A greater likelihood of success favors a plan just as the more inclusive end does."[14])

Let us test Rawls's proposal against my eight-count indictment of capitalism. Let us take the charges one at a time. To facilitate the exposition, let me rearrange them and begin with inequality, a concept central to Rawls's concept of justice. How egalitarian is Fair Capitalism? Here a socialist can only gasp in amazement. Rawls proclaims a profound commitment to equality; his theoretical strictures on inequalities are as severe as the most ardent socialist's—and yet he defends a system that admits, indeed requires, property income, the fundamental source of contemporary inequality. Interest, rent, stock dividends, the whole gamut of income-from-ownership all persist under Fair Capitalism. To be sure, the Distribution Branch acts to dampen inequalities of income and wealth, but are its instruments suitable to insuring that these inequalities work to the benefit of the least advantaged? Notice, inheritance, gift, and progressive income taxes—the weapons of the Distributive Branch—do not discriminate as to the source of income. Income differentials that serve as incentives for the performance of onerous work or the development of needed skills are not distinguished from those that derive from no productive contribution whatsoever. Nor can they be distinguished, for Fair Capitalism relies on private savings to generate investment funds and private investment to direct economic development. When this mechanism is relied upon, property income must be permitted, or else the economy would dissolve into chaos. But as our analysis of worker control has demonstrated, a private savings-investment mechanism is not essential, even to a decentralized market economy. It is difficult to understand how a theory of justice exemplifying so strong a commitment to equality as Rawls's can remain neutral with respect to ownership-income and the savings-investment mechanism. In fact it is impossible to understand. Rawl's theory—however neutral it is intended to be—plainly favors worker control over Fair Capitalism on this point.

In the middle section of Chapter 4 I argued that laissez-faire is incompatible with genuine democracy. One of the reasons—that a concentration of wealth, inevitable under laissez-faire, brings in its train disproportionate political influence—is recognized by Rawls. Institutions that insure fair equality of opportunity, he says, "are put in jeopardy when inequalities of wealth exceed a certain limit, and political liberty likewise tends to lose its value, and representative government to become such in appearance only."[15] The Distributive Branch is specifically charged with preventing this from happening.

Now the Distributive Branch may or may not be able to keep wealth within appropriate limits, given the pressure toward inequality generated by property income, but even if it succeeds in maintaining a fairly wide dispersal of property, my second argument is not negated. A capitalist economy, Fair Capitalism included, requires investor confidence for its stability. Thus an elected administration must give special weight to the interests of investors (be they few or relatively many), whether or not these interests are in accord with the majority interests of society. Thus investors constitute a privileged class, a class that oddly fits—or rather does not fit—our concept of genuine popular rule.

Now it might be thought that the interests of investors—let me call them capitalists, for that is who the significant investors will be, even under Fair Capitalism—are never at variance with the general interests of society. But that, I have repeatedly argued, is not so. Consider the case of workplace autonomy. The empirical evidence strongly suggests that genuine productivity increases are likely to result when workers feel that they are working for themselves and not for an alien set of owners. The evidence strongly suggests that work satisfaction will also rise appreciably. Yet owners (and managers beholden to owners) will certainly resist worker control of production. The lure of greater productivity is tempting, but countervailing considerations present themselves: the infringements on their own power, and also the obstacles worker self-management presents to spurious productivity increases (the reorganization of work to better control employees so that more work can be squeezed from them). A Keynesian-liberal government might encourage greater worker participation, but it will find its efforts resisted. This resistance it ought to find dismaying, for even if productivity were to suffer somewhat, as a result of greater participation, the enhancement of work satisfaction ought—in virtue of modern-liberal value-commitments—to be overriding. For as Rawls writes,

> It is a mistake to believe that a just society must wait upon a high material standard of life. What men want is meaningful work in free association with others, these associations regulating their relations to one another within a framework of just basic institutions. To achieve this state of things great wealth is not necessary. [16]

This is a prescription for worker control, not capitalism.

The sales effort is a second area where the interests of capital and those of society conflict. Neoclassical economists tend to pay little attention to advertising and the rest of the sales apparatus, and Rawls follows suit. None of the governmental agencies of Fair Capitalism are mandated to keep nonrational sales techniques in check. This is perhaps an oversight on Rawls's part, for his careful analysis of "the good life" specifically identified goodness with rationality. A "good life," he says, is one that follows a rational plan, a plan

> that is consistent with the principles of rational choice when they are applied to the relevant features of [one's] situation, and . . . that plan among those meeting this condition which would be chosen . . . with full deliberate rationality, that is, with full awareness of the relevant facts and after a careful consideration of the consequences.[17]

Given this emphasis on rationality, Rawls must surely look askance at an apparatus that propagandizes relentlessly, with the most sophisticated psychological techniques that money can buy, on behalf of consumption. He cannot but be uncomfortable with a system in which "even minor qualities of unimportant commodities are enlarged upon with a solemnity which would not be unbecoming in an announcement of the combined return of Christ and all the apostles."[18]

Now both worker-control socialism and Fair Capitalism are market economies, and so both are vulnerable to abuses of a nonrational sales effort. Neither are as vulnerable as laissez-faire, since both allow governmental intervention to curb excesses. But the other arguments raised earlier should not be overlooked, for they are as applicable to Fair Capitalism as they are to laissez-faire. Worker control is less growth oriented than Fair Capitalism since workers have leisure options more readily available and growth is not so essential to stability. So, without the pressure to expand, enterprises are less prone to a massive sales effort, and with expansion non-essential to stability, governmental intervention to curb abuses can be less hesitatingly undertaken.

Keynesian liberalism may pay little attention to advertising, but it pays much to one of the other counts of my indictment. The name of Keyes is associated with nothing so much as unemployment— a revolutionary diagnosis and a putative cure. A remarkably simple cure at that, though paradoxical to commonsense: when times are bad, spend, go into debt, don't save! If consumers are reluctant to oblige, then the government should step into the breach, unbalancing its

budget by spending in excess of its tax revenues.* The Keynesian
remedy is simple to state, but is it effective? Can it cure unemployment without inducing other destabilizing consequences—in particular,
inflation? Let us hold this question for a moment and consider a perhaps more basic point. Suppose the Keynesian policies are able to insure full employment. Will they be implemented? Michael Kalecki,
the independent co-creator of the "Keynesian" general theory, raised
a lonely dissenting voice in 1943 against the prevailing Keynesian op-
timism. Kalecki, unlike the Keynesian liberals, saw class conflict as
a decisive factor:

> Indeed, under a regime of permanent full employment,
> 'the sack' would cease to play its role as a disciplinary
> measure. The social position of the boss would be un-
> dermined and the self-assurance and class-conscious-
> ness of the working class would grow. Strikes for
> wage increases and improvements in conditions of
> work would create political tensions. It is true that
> profits would be higher under a regime of full employ-
> ment than they are on average under laissez-faire; and
> even the rise in wages resulting from the stronger bar-
> gaining power of the workers is less likely to reduce
> profits than to increase prices, and thus affects only
> the rentier interests. But 'discipline in the factories'
> and 'political stability' are more appreciated by busi-
> ness leaders than profits. Their class interest tells
> them that lasting full employment is unsound from

---

*Though "Keynesianism" now refers to governmental monetary
and fiscal policies, Keynes himself did not hesitate to exhort the public. In a 1931 radio broadcast he urged: "Oh patriotic housewives,
sally out tomorrow early into the streets and go to the wonderful sales
which are everywhere advertised. You will do yourselves good—for
never were things so cheap, cheap beyond your dreams. Lay in stocks
of household linen, of sheets and blankets to satisfy your needs. And
have the added joy that you are increasing employment, adding to the
wealth of the country because you are setting on foot useful activities,
bringing a chance and a hope to Lancashire, Yorkshire and Belfast."
(Quoted by Elizabeth Johnson in "John Maynard Keynes: Scientist or
Politician?" After Keynes, ed. Joan Robinson [Oxford: Basil Blackwell, 1973], pp. 15-16.)

their point of view and that unemployment is an integral part of the 'normal' capitalist system. [19]

"Tough-minded" business analysts often voice similar concerns (though without Kalecki's system-critical edge):

Unemployment remains too low for the workforce to have flexibility. Anytime the jobless total is less than 2 million even common labor is scarce. Many employers tend to hoard skills. And certainly, the labor unions are in the driver's seat in wage negotiations. More workers can be had, to be sure. But at considerable cost. And they probably wouldn't be the skills most desired. There's no assurance against inflation like a pool of genuine unemployment. That's a blunt, hard-headed statement, but a fact. [20]

It is also a blunt fact that under worker control there exists no class of people with a specific interest in maintaining unemployment. Unemployment cannot generate downward pressure on wages, for there are no wage laborers; it does not enhance factory discipline, nor the power of management vis-a-vis labor unions. Since the material needs of the unemployed must be financed from the taxes of those employed, the latter have no interest whatsoever in preserving what Marx labelled the "Industrial Reserve Army."[21] (This is not to say that worker-control socialism will experience no difficulty in providing work for everyone who wants to work. The point is, the difficulty is not so systematic and structural as it is under capitalism, even Fair Capitalism.)

I've touched so far on five counts of my general indictment: inequality, democracy, work alienation, the sales effort and unemployment. A sixth count concerns the kind of growth promoted by capitalism. My critique of laissez-faire on this point developed three themes: inequalities distort development, growth is unbalanced, growth is plagued by production and consumption externalities. Rawls is not insensitive to these problems. Some income redistribution is effected by the Transfer and Distributive Branches of his model government. The Allocative Branch attempts to correct "the more obvious departures from efficiency caused by the failure of prices to measure accurately social benefits and costs" by means of "suitable taxes and subsidies and by changes in the definition of property rights."[22] But I must reply, "Too little and too late." Under Fair Capitalism inequalities are not likely to be sufficiently reduced. I've already argued that. Moreover, since investments remain in private hands, decisions will not be coordinated—certainly not if the market is to remain competitive. And externality remedies remain post factum. Investment projects are undertaken, the consequences are evaluated, and then taxes or subsidies are proposed. Society does not attempt to take conscious control of its economic development by subjecting it to plan; society remains prey to the "tyranny of small decisions" generated by the logic of the market.

Worker control does not obviate all such problems, since a significant quantity of investment funds (depreciation funds) remain under the control of individual firms—this to enhance the autonomy of workers within the enterprise and to check governmental "tyranny." But all new investment—that financed by the capital tax and aimed at increasing the country's capital stock—is coordinated by the investment boards. This strategic sector is under democratic control, and so the character of economic development becomes a matter of public debate and conscious decision. No such control, debate or decision takes place under Fair Capitalism.

Nor is control exercised over the rate of growth. Keynesian policies aim at establishing that equilibrium of savings and investment that insures full employment. When savings are in excess of investment, or vice versa, steps are taken to reduce one or increase the other. But the question is never raised as to whether the investment level sufficient to induce employers to hire all who want to work is in any way related to the socially desirable (or socially desired) rate of growth. This difficulty is not recognized by Rawls. Were it recognized, it would be most disconcerting, for Rawls treats the question of societal saving as one of great moral urgency. He discusses at length the problem of "justice between generations," and worries that a democratic electorate might "perpetrate grave offences against other generations" by choosing to save too little.[23] What Rawls overlooks completely is that Fair Capitalism provides no mechanism whatsoever for a conscious determination of the saving or investment rate. The market will decide each of these rates, and the government will intervene if there is an imbalance. (If investment is too low to sustain full employment or so high as to generate inflationary pressures, the government will step in.) But there is no room in this process for consideration of future generations, nor for public consultation. (I am assuming here that the Keynesian policies work, i.e., that no trade-off need be made between unemployment and inflation. If they do not work—more on this below—then there is room for choice, but concerning which elements of society must bear which burdens, not concerning future generations.)

Actually Rawls's concern is misplaced. He worries about insufficient savings—but the tendency of capitalism, especially Keynesian capitalism, is toward a high rate of savings. The tendency is for savings to outstrip investment, and this (as Keynes showed) causes the economy to contract—unless the government intervenes. Capitalism—

especially Keynesian capitalism—is structured to save, to invest and to grow. But it is precisely this growth that poses the threat to future generations, not the lack of saving. Capitalist "saving," when balanced by investment, involves a channelling of workers and resources into activities that promise increased consumption later. "Saving" does not involve a saving of resources or a reduction of the strain placed on the environment. This latter sort of "saving" occurs when consumption is traded for leisure, or perhaps for less "efficient" but more ecologically sound techniques, not for more consumption later. But as we have seen, it is worker control and not capitalism that allows society to decide consciously the rate and structure of its investment, and on its labor-leisure tradeoff.

If growth poses a problem for Fair Capitalism, so does its absence. In the last section of Chapter 4 I argued that without growth, laissez-faire is unstable. The argument applies to capitalism generally. If profits are merely consumed by the capitalist class, the resulting stationary state is likely to be politically unstable, since the functionless character of property ownership would be apparent to all. (At least the medieval lords could claim to be protecting those in their charge; it is unclear how a blatantly parasitical capitalist class could justify itself.) If profits are invested, however, the capitalist class appears functional. But even so, both political and economic instability are likely to ensue, if growth is not forthcoming. If growth slackens, profits decline, businesses fail, and investor confidence is shaken. A downturn in investment, we know, signals layoffs, reduced demand, and the onset of a recession. If this downturn is long-lasting, class antagonisms are bound to surface. The historical rationale of capitalism has been its ability to generate growth. Inequalities of wealth and power and the other irrationalities of the system are far less resented when one perceives one's own future as ever more comfortable. But without growth, resentments—and reactions to these resentments—must surely be expected.

So capitalism—even Fair Capitalism—must grow. But can it grow? We know that sustained growth requires three moments: investments must be made (by investors confident of gain), the anticipated productivity increases must materialize, and the products must be sold. (This latter moment depends on consumer confidence and adequate aggregate demand.) From this perspective we can view the Keynesian remedies and consider their effectiveness. They fall into two classes—monetary policies and fiscal policies (manipulation of the money supply; manipulation of taxation and governmental spending).

By now even classical liberals are "Keynesian," at least in their conviction that the government must do something to stimulate growth. Their preference is for monetary measures, measures initiated by the central bank to increase or decrease the money supply.* Friedman, for example, urges a legislative rule instructing the monetary authority to "see to it that the total stock of money [including currency outside commercial banks plus all deposits of commercial banks] rises month by month, indeed as far as possible, day by day, at a constant rate of X percent, where X is some number between 3 and 5."[24] The great merit of monetary policies, in the eyes of classical liberals, is that money is made available to individuals without governmental mediations that are likely to redistribute income or increase governmental bureaucracy.

We readily grasp the intent of this program. With loanable funds increasing, investors can finance expansion, and consumers can buy the goods produced. But is this sufficient for stability? It won't insure full employment. Friedman makes no claim that it will. There is, he says, a "natural" rate of unemployment consistent with stable prices; to try to reduce unemployment below this rate is to invite runaway inflation.[25] But unemployment aside, would such a monetary policy insure growth? "There is an unearthly, mystical element in Friedman's thought. The mere existence of a stock of money somehow promotes its expenditure." So writes Joan Robinson.[26] I can see no reason not to agree. Merely making money available does not guarantee that investors will invest, that productivity will increase, that consumers will buy. Friedman and fellow monetarists point to the historical record, but that is hardly satisfactory. A correlation between business booms and expansions of the money supply does not demonstrate causality. (Robinson notes that a sharp rise in business activity is likely to be preceded by an increase in the money supply, because a rise in borrowing for working capital will show up sooner in the statistics than an increase in the value of the output. But that does not mean that an increase in the money supply caused the production increase.[27]) In any event the historical record cannot guarantee that the necessary conditions for growth will persist.

Keynesian liberals are generally in agreement with this critique of monetarism.[28] Fiscal policy, they say, is also needed. If insuffi-

---

*The central bank has a number of tools at its disposal for doing this. The most commonly used is the buying and selling of governmental securities. Buying government bonds with newly created money expands the supply; selling them has the opposite effect. Because of fractional reserve requirements, there is a multiplier effect. (For an introduction to these mysteries, see Samuelson, Economics, Chapters 16 and 17.)

cient investment is being made by the private sector, then the government can invest directly—in armaments, public works, space shuttles, whatever—financing these programs by borrowing. Alternatively, the government can cut taxes and finance existing programs from borrowed funds. (The effect is the same, so long as the increased take-home income is spent rather than saved.) There is no need to wait for entrepreneurs or consumers to do the borrowing necessary to stimulate the economy.

Again we ask, will the advocated policies work? Their intent is to increase investment and to increase consumer spending. But as monetarists are the first to argue, government borrowing might simply drive up interest rates, and thus decrease private investment. And government spending might simply increase consumer saving rather than spending. It is not logically necessary that fiscal policies will work—and the empirical record is hotly debated. [29]

But that debate is beside the point—at least beside our point. Whether or not an appropriate mix of monetary and fiscal policies can keep investment in line with saving so as to sustain aggregate demand at an appropriately high level, the policies plainly do not impinge on the key moment of the growth process: productivity increase. Or rather, they impinge in conflicting ways. Growing aggregate demand enhances investor confidence; investments tend to increase productivity, as does direct governmental subsidy of research and development. On the other hand, a growing money supply may be diverted into purely speculative ventures (real estate, stock speculation, art, etc.) that have no effect at all on productivity, and governmental expenditures can generate ever-expanding bureaucracies, the development and deployment of ever more ferocious weaponry, and other familiarities that exert a drag on productivity. And of course when governmental stimulation fails to increase either employment or productivity, or enhances the former at the expense of the latter, the result is not growth but inflation. The (simple) fact is, neither monetary nor fiscal policies can insure growth—the growth that is so essential to capitalist stability.

Compare worker-control socialism. It doesn't need to grow. Nor is there a class of investors who must be kept confident, lest their lack of confidence spell recession. Nor is there the possibility of owner-worker class struggle, since there is no propertied class. The basic causes of capitalist instability are absent. Granted, unemployment might sometimes be a problem. This I have already discussed. Granted also, the inequalities that persist under worker control might be more seriously challenged when society slows its growth—but that is not a flaw in the system. If more egalitarian policies within a firm do not hamper productivity, then they should be implemented; if the result is productivity slippage, then workers should be free to accept the loss, to experiment with nonmonetary incentives, or to reinstate monetary differentials. There may be conflicts, but at least no spurious argument for inequality can be put forth based on the alleged "vital function" of providing capital.

We've completed our survey of the eight-count indictment originally directed at laissez-faire. I've argued that on every count Keynesian liberalism is less vulnerable on many counts than laissez-faire, since much of the former is an attempt to cope with these specific charges. On the other hand, the value-commitments prompting the Keynesian-liberal reforms are even more in line with the values underlying the case for worker control than are the value-commitments of classical liberalism. So, though the problems with reformed capitalism may be less severe than those of laissez-faire, the Keynesian liberal has fewer ethical reasons—indeed he has none—for preferring his model to worker control.*

THE POST-KEYNESIAN VISION OF JOHN KENNETH GALBRAITH

Post-Keynesianism is first and foremost a critique of neoclassicism. The concern of this work lies elsewhere. Our concern is not to judge among competing models of how contemporary capitalism works, but to compare alternative ideal societies. These concerns, however, cannot be completely separated. To understand the post-Keynesian ideal, one must have a sense of the post-Keynesian critique.

Perhaps the most characteristic and revealing feature of the post-Keynesian critique is its treatment of what is traditionally called "monopoly." Monopolies—and their close relations, oligopolies—have

---

*I'm referring here to reasons relative to the intrinsic desirability of the respective goals. I am not referring to the liklihood that they will be reached from where we stand now in the Western capitalist world. The transition problem is not my concern in this work. I realize that to speak of ends apart from means is dangerously nondialectical, but I think it important that the ethical and economic superiority of the socialist goal be plainly established at this time, a concrete goal, not an abstract utopia. We can more cogently debate political strategy when we know where it is we want to go. A few remarks on transition will be made in Chapter 7, but they are not directly relevant to my central thesis.

been regarded since the days of Adam Smith as <u>evil,</u> something to be avoided even at the cost of governmental intervention. Neoclassicism strongly reinforces this view: monopolies are not only exploitative, they are inefficient (the ultimate perjorative in strict neoclassicism). Why inefficient? The neoclassicist explains: a monopoly can influence prices by influencing the quantity of goods that reach the market—and it will use this power to keep supply short and thus drive prices up. Hence society finds itself with less of what it really wants and more of what it wants less strongly; consumer satisfaction is less than what it could be.[30]

Post-Keynesians find this analysis preposterous. The analysis follows smoothly and with elegance from the neoclassical categories, but it cannot be true, they say, for it implies that those industries at the center of contemporary capitalism—automobile, aircraft, oil, petorchemical, electronic computer, etc.—are grossly inefficient, and that the corner grocer is the model to be emulated.

> Most industrial production comes from large firms which have extreme power in the market. They are oligopolies. So the textbook finding is that the modern economy is mainly exploitative in the prices it charges, wasteful and inefficient in the way it employs resources, and challenging in the need for reform. Then comes the conclusion from the same books that the modern economy is highly efficient. . . . Detailed performance is bad but aggregate performance is excellent. To the person who insists on asking how this contradiction is resolved, the answer is that it is not.[31]

To avoid this and other anomolies, post-Keynesians declare the neoclassical categories radically inappropriate to contemporary reality. A modern capitalist economy, they insist, must not be thought of as an imperfect realization of perfect competition. Rather, it should be viewed as a <u>dual</u> economy: one sector (agriculture, much retail trade, small businesses) is subject to the market more or less as traditionally conceived, but the other sector (the modern corporate sector) is largely independent of the impersonal forces of supply and demand. The firms of this latter sector—the dominant sector—create demand for specific products, set prices to reflect their costs and investment needs, negotiate labor costs via quasi-political bargaining, and have considerable influence over the governmental policies that shape their environment. Post-Keynesians argue that notions of marginal costs, marginal product, marginal preference and the analytical apparatus that has been developed around these concepts are irrelevant to understanding this sector of the economy, and its complex relationship to the market sector and the state.

The post-Keynesian paradigm is explanatory, and like all paradigms it retains a degree of openness to normative ideals. At the same time (again like all such paradigms) it tilts in a particular direction. Which direction? When one views reality as a post-Keynesian, certain features of capitalism stand forth in such a way as to suggest governmental intervention on a scale and of a type that would not be pleasing to a classical liberal, so the tilt is Left—but how far Left? At this date I don't think a definite answer can be given. Some post-Keynesians envisage reform that is clearly modern liberal (i.e., reform that leaves intact the basic elements of capitalism), while others, particularly those more reticent about reform, seem to possess a more radical vision.

What about our representative post-Keynesian, John Kenneth Galbraith? Is his vision modern liberal or socialist? The question is more complicated than one might think. Galbraith is surely an "establishment" figure: an economics professor who taught at Harvard, a Democratic Party activist, a consultant to presidents on economic affairs, John Kennedy's ambassador to India. One expects to encounter a liberal vision when one reads Galbraith, and these expectations are generally fulfilled. And yet—in his 1973 treatise Economics and the Public Purpose, Galbraith speaks of a "New Socialism," and proposes a "euthanasia of stockholders."[32] That's not the stuff of modern liberalism. If the major corporations that dominate an economy were taken over by the state, then the institution of private property would be so severely altered that I don't think the system should be called capitalist. I would call it socialist—though not (in lieu of that reform) worker-control socialist. *

---

*Terminological disputes (not without substance) abound here. Many would argue (Marx, I would venture) that socialism without worker control is not socialism (where "worker control" is understood as something more general than the specific institutional arrangement I've proposed). Many think "state capitalism" better designates a nationalized but not worker-controlled economy, but that term too is problematic, since the structure and dynamic of such a system might be vastly different from a capitalism rooted in private property. These issues are not without importance, but I won't pursue the debate, since I don't think it relevant to the specific concern of this work.

In Chapter 7 I will comment briefly on Galbraithian "techno-cratic" socialism, but for now I propose a different tack. Galbraith is rarely interpreted as a socialist. His earlier works steered clear of (or disparaged) the socialist alternative,[33] and these earlier works, especially The Affluent Society and The New Industrial State, have been more widely read than Economics and the Public Purpose. I propose to read Galbraith as a liberal, to examine the ideal model that emerges from his writings if one ignores his "euthanasia" suggestion. This model does justice, I believe, to the post-Keynesian liberal current of contemporary thought (if not complete justice to Galbraith himself), and that, after all, is what we are concerned with here.

Let me call the Galbraithian liberal ideal the Ideal Industrial State. At first sight this model is reassuringly familiar. The bulk of the economic activity is carried on by private enterprises, which range from small, family-run businesses to corporate conglomerates. A large and active government oversees the economy: it insists on a high minimum wage and a guaranteed minimum income for all; it finances its programs with a sharply progressive income tax; it enforces environmental guidelines; it engages in deficit spending when the econ-omy threatens to slump, and it increases taxes when demand becomes excessive.[34] So far, so good. Classical liberals scream, but Keynes-ian liberals smile contentedly.

But suddenly they grow uneasy. Something is missing. There is one major Keynesian-liberal action that the government does not take in. It makes not even a pretense at enforcing antitrust laws; it pays not even lip service to keeping the economy competitive. In fact it does the opposite. It proclaims the imbalance between the market sector of the economy and the "planning" sector* to be an important source of inequality, so it encourages market-dominated businesses to undertake joint action to stabilize prices and production, and to regulate entry into their industry in order "to give the small business-man (and his workers) something of the security in prices and income, and therewith in investment and planning, that the large firm (and its employees) enjoy as a matter of course."[35]

If the government does not attempt to discipline the economy by making it more competitive, it has no intention of letting the economy run itself. The government of the Ideal Industrial State will go through

---

*This is Galbraith's terminology for the dominant corporate sec-tor. "Oligopolic" might be a more accurate designation, since firms in the market sector also plan, but "oligopoly" has pejorative conno-tations that post-Keynesians prefer to avoid.

the factory gates and intervene directly, not only to enforce rigid
health, safety, and environmental codes, but also to encourage
labor unions to bargain about income differentials between management
and labor. And if such bargaining is not sufficient to dampen top
salaries, the government will impose some limitations of its own.
Labor unions are also urged to bargain for more labor-leisure options—
more flexible hours, 20-hour workweeks for those who want them,
readily available leaves-of-absence. On the other hand, labor is not
free to negotiate any wage-settlement it can manage. Wage controls
are a permanent feature of the Ideal Industrial State, and (and this cuts
neoclassicism to the quick) so are price controls.*

Finally, one notices more public corporations in the post-Keynesian ideal state than in Fair Capitalism. The Keynesian-liberal penchant
is for putting purchasing power in the hands of the needy (via social
security, medicare, food stamps, etc.) and letting the private sector
provide the goods. The post-Keynesian response is to provide services directly in areas where the private sector has been inadequate.
Thus we see a nationalized health care industry, large inter-state
transportation corporations running railroads, buses, urban mass
transit; we see governmental housing authorities and well-funded
public broadcasting. These corporations are given substantial autonomy, so that they can plan effectively. They are treated, in fact, like
private corporations and are expected to behave similarly. They are
expected to develop the technical and organizational expertise of private corporations, and they are expected to follow (as reluctantly as
private corporations) governmental environmental, wage and price
guidelines.

This is a sketch of a post-Keynesian ideal. We will not examine
its merits vis-a-vis the classical-liberal or Keynesian-liberal
ideal—though there is much that could be said in its favor. Instead we
will ask the question more germane to our project: how does it compare with worker control? More specifically, how does the Ideal
Industrial State fare with respect to the eight-count indictment I have
leveled against laissez-faire and Fair Capitalism? (Some of the following arguments are by now familiar and need be only briefly remarked.)
Let us proceed.

---

*Post-Keynesians are not unanimous in urging price controls.
All agree that an "incomes policy" is needed to supplement the usual
Keynesian instability-remedies, but some hold back on price control.
(Cf. John Cornwall, "Post-Keynesian Theory: Macrodynamics,"
Challenge 21 [May-June 1978]: 11-17, for a view contrary to
Galbraith's.)

Count One: Unemployment. Galbraith's ideal does not aim at full employment. Keynesian remedies, even when supplemented with wage and price controls, will not guarantee a job for everyone. Galbraith admits this. The fact of the matter is, he says, many people "for reasons of educational disqualification, location in an urban ghetto or rural slum or because of race . . . are not readily employable . . . [except] in numerous ill-paid services of the more derogatory sort—the men who shine shoes in a hotel or airport or tender towels in a washroom."[36] The proposed solution: a minimum wage high enough for a decent living and a guaranteed income modestly below that. True, some jobs will disappear if a high minimum wage is enforced, but "this should be viewed not as a loss but as a modest advance in the general state of civilization."[37]

My criticism here is almost classical-liberal: with welfare so pleasant, who would want to work? Given the boring, dehumanizing character of so much work under capitalism—and as we shall see shortly, Galbraith proposes little that would alleviate this problem—the welfare rolls would likely surge. Not only would this be economically destabilizing, but it would doubtless provoke a sharp reaction on the part of those who do work. The scenario is not so pleasant to contemplate. Worker control, by contrast, aims at employing everyone. Governmental agencies encourage firms that are doing well to take on workers who want to work there; they are to share the work if production cannot be expanded. New investment is managed with employment priorities in mind. Welfare provisions are of course made for those unable to work, but full employment is a societal goal.

(The case for full employment can be made on purely utilitarian grounds, but an even stronger case can be made by appealing to another value. Socialists, especially those from the Marxist tradition, tend to regard work as a central element of human well-being. It is through [unalienated] labor that a person actualizes herself, develops her capabilities, makes her contribution to society, and experiences her "species being."[38] Rawls would likely accept this value;* it is not so clear with Galbraith.)

Count Two: the Sales Effort. Few people have written with more wit and scorn about the "organized public bamboozlement" rampant in our society than Galbraith.[39] So one is surprised by the remedy he proposes: "one does not prohibit advertising; one resists its persuasion."[40] The call is for a heightened consciousness—an astonishingly feeble response to what Galbraith himself describes as a multi-billion

---

*Cf. p. 141.

dollar "great machine engaged in the management of those who buy goods."[41]

Yet if we probe further, we see the necessity for so feeble a remedy. Galbraith finds organized public bamboozlement despicable, but he also recognizes, quite explicitly, that the health and survival of contemporary capitalism depend on it. Unless corporations can be sure that they can induce the public to buy what they produce, they will not undertake the long-range planning and massive capital outlay necessary to bring new products to market. And if corporations do not invest, the economy will slump. But if contemporary capitalism requires a massive sales effort to stay healthy, so does the Ideal Industrial State. Both depend on private investment, which depends on investor confidence, which depends on growth, which depends on relentless propaganda on behalf of consumption. Therefore, Galbraith must propose (almost against his will, one suspects) a solution that is not really a solution—a call to consciousness that will be answered slowly if at all.

A proponent of worker control faces no such "contradiction." Worker control does not need to grow, does not require investor confidence, is not internally structured for relentless expansion. A proponent of worker control can decry public bamboozlement without having to concede its necessity.

Count Three: Inequality. In many respects Galbraith's attack on ownership has affinities with my own.

> In its mature form the corporation can be thought of as an instrument principally for perpetuating inequality. The stockholders, as we have seen, have no function. They do not contribute to capital or to management; they are the passive recipients of dividends and capital gains. As these increase from year to year, so, effortlessly, do their income and wealth.

His solution, I have already noted, is euthanasia:

> A solution would be to convert the fully mature corporations—those that have completed the euthanasia of stockholder power—into fully public corporations. Assuming the undesirability of expropriation this would mean public purchase of the stock with fixed interest-bearing securities. This would perpetuate inequality, but it would no longer increase adventitiously with further increases in dividends and capital gains. In time inheritance, inheritance taxes, philanthropy, profligacy, alimony and inflation would act to disperse this wealth.[42]

As I mentioned earlier, we are not going to take Galbraith's euthanasia proposal to be a feature of the Ideal Industrial State, since it transgresses the limits of liberalism, but the proposal is worth considering for a moment. Galbraith's conceptualization of the problem is revealing. The stockholders of a fully mature corporation do not contribute to capital, he says. What does this mean? Galbraith seems to be calling attention to something neoclassical analysis obscures, namely that purchasing stock need not add a penny to a corporation's capital. Textbook neoclassicism pictures savers supplying money directly to entrepreneurs, whereas in reality the vast majority of stock purchases are from other stockholders, not from corporations themselves. And yet only the sale of new issues adds to corporate coffers— a form of financing far less significant to a mature corporation than reinvesting profits or borrowing from banks. So the stockholder in a mature corporation is functionless. His purchase has contributed something to a former stockholder, but nothing to the enterprise itself.

This line of reasoning is not without validity, but it does not touch bottom. The impression persists that those who purchase new shares or who loan money to a corporation do contribute to production. But this, I have repeatedly argued, is false. Money does not create goods. Human labor, mental and manual, interacting with nature creates goods.* Worker control recognizes this truth, and is designed to block all making-of-money-from-money. The Ideal Industrial State is not so designed. Ownership-income persists: stock dividends (at least from nonmature corporations), interest, land-rent—multiple sources of inequality that are absent under worker control.

Count Four: Kind of Growth. The Ideal Industrial State is concerned about the kind of growth generated by unregulated private enterprise. When the divergence of private purpose from public interest becomes acute, strict regulation is in order. The government will not hesitate to impose production standards, consumption standards, even aesthetic standards. "Such action is condemned as inflexible—as putting business in a straitjacket. That should deter no one. A straitjacket is a reasonably accurate figure of speech for what is required."43 Galbraith goes even further. There must be a public planning authority to coordinate economic development:

---

*I am struck, every time I make this statement, how counterintuitive it is in our society to say that money does not contribute to production. But recall the arguments of Chapter 1.

> Government machinery must . . . be established to
> anticipate disparity and to ensure that growth in differ-
> ent parts of the economy is compatible. The latter on
> frequent occasion will require conservation—measures
> to reduce or eliminate the socially least urgent use. On
> other occasion it would require public steps to expand
> output. [44]

So we see that Galbraith has anticipated my criticisms of capitalist growth—the problems of externalities and lack of balance. But
are the remedies as adequate as worker control? Notice, the government remains largely reactive; basic initiative remains with private
investors. The people of a community or nation do not, through the
political process, take control of the basic direction of their economy.
Furthermore, since investment funds remain privately generated, the
basic conflict between powerful financial interests and a government
trying to assert the public good is in no way resolved. If anything it is
exacerbated: government allows private enterprise to make the basic
investment decisions, and yet the government is advised to treat
with greatest suspicion the interests of that sector. A worker control
economy is by no means so schizophrenic.

Count Five: Rate of Growth. Once again Galbraith recognizes
the problem. Growth (even more than profit maximization, he proclaims) has become a supreme goal of the mature corporation. [45]
Galbraith is not happy about this. The merits of this goal are rarely
argued: "As always it proceeds by massive assumption. What other
goal could be socially so urgent?"[46]

What is to be done? Two Galbraithian reforms are relevant.
One is the already examined call to resist the blandishments of advertisers. The other is the insistence, perhaps backed by law, that individuals be given more options regarding the length of their workweek
or work-year. Presumably, if people resist compulsive consumption
and opt for more leisure instead, then the growth rate will taper off.

In my judgment this "solution" does not do justice to the problem.
Work flexibility is certainly desirable, for its own sake and as a
counter to reckless growth. In a worker-managed enterprise, where
individuals can express and enforce their preferences, one would expect to see this flexibility, so long as it does not seriously impinge
on efficiency. But under capitalism work flexibility founders on a
dilemma. If it succeeds in reducing growth, if more and more workers
opt for leisure over consumption—well, we know the scenario: demand
drops, so does investor confidence and the economy dives. If it does
not succeed, then the system continues to grow—until it smashes into
the environmental and resource barriers that are already looming
large. This basic contradiction is not overcome in the Ideal Industrial State.

Nor is the growth rate democratically determined. That is a criticism I leveled against both laissez-faire and Fair Capitalism, and it holds here as well. Under worker control the rate of investment is a political decision. Not so in the Ideal Industrial State.

Count Six: Instability. As Keynesianism was born of unemployment, post-Keynesianism has sprung from inflation. Nothing is more characteristic of post-Keynesianism than its insistence that neoclassicism cannot comprehend nor offer a fruitful solution to the wage-price spiral. Nor are any of the post-Keynesian reforms I have so far discussed so at odds with the Keynesian-neoclassical wisdom as those in this area: an incomes policy and price controls. The Keynesian weapons are retained to combat unemployment, but these two pieces of supplementary artillery are to be trained on inflation.

Will they work? Let me point to some dilemmas. An incomes policy is first and foremost an attempt to keep labor demands in line with productivity increases.* But if wages are restricted, but not profits, then workers become understandably disgruntled. On the other hand, if profits <u>are</u> restricted, then the basic, driving mechanism of the economy is thrown out of gear. Profits, after all, serve as the primary source of investment funds, the determinant of investor confidence, and the indicator of investment opportunity.

So post-Keynesians shy away from profit control. Galbraith proposes price controls instead. The rationale, presumably, is that workers will accept wage restraints tied to productivity increases so long as prices are held stable, so long as they don't feel compelled to play catch-up with inflation. (Neoclassical economists recoil in horror from this prescription—because of the bureaucracy involved and also, surely, because of the violence it does to the market paradigm. But since their own prescriptions have been so remarkably unsuccessful in recent years, it seems inevitable that such controls will be attempted with increasing frequency in the future.)

Perhaps wage and price controls will work—for a time at least. But notice, they do not touch what I claim to be the ultimate root of capitalist instability: its fundamental dependence on growth. It is true,

---

*An "incomes policy" is essentially governmental wage-control with some supplements concerning other sources of income. A popular proposal has been "TIP," first proposed by H. Wallich and S. Weintraub, "A Taxed-Based Incomes Policy," Journal of Economic Issues 5 (June 1971): 1-19, whereby corporations that exceed certain guidelines incur a penalty tax. (For more on this proposal see Laurence Seidman, "TIP: Feasibility and Equity," Journal of Post-Keynesian Economics 1 [Summer 1979]: 24-37.)

if wage gains exceed productivity increases, then inflation will follow. But it is also true that if productivity gains are not forthcoming, then wage stagnation will heighten intra-societal antagonisms. In particular, class antagonisms are likely to intensify. Since worker gains are tied to productivity increases, and since productivity increases are dependent on new investment, workers are likely to become incensed about private wealth that flows into speculative, nonproductive channels. Government controls will be called for (especially in a state already controlling wages and prices)—the very controls that further erode the "animal spirits" of investors and exacerbate instability. It seems clear that a system that is not so growth dependent is vastly preferable.

Count Seven: Democracy. Galbraith would scarcely deny that in contemporary capitalist societies corporate interests dominate the government. In the United States, he says, the Republican Party does not even pretend to serve other interests, and the dominant wing of the Democratic Party, though less candid, behaves no differently. Moreover, the giant governmental bureaucracies that have emerged since the Second World War are symbiotically linked to the planning sector, thus insuring that corporate interests will be served, regardless of presidential rhetoric or ideology.[47]

Unless, that is, an aroused public "emancipates the state." How? Here again one's faith in Galbraith falters—for no structural reforms are proposed, at least none commensurate with the problem. Apart from urging an end to the congressional seniority system, he wagers all on "the Public Cognizance," a state of mind that "accepts the basic divergence between the goals pursued by the planning system and what serves the public need and interest."[48]

.   Now a socialist cannot deny the possibility—indeed the necessity—for a dramatic change of mass consciousness (not without being a very pessimistic socialist), but to rely on consciousness alone unaccompanied by fundamental structural changes to preserve a newly embodied ideal seems . . . well . . . implausible. In the Ideal Industrial State there will still be giant corporations, most of them privately owned. There will still be large disparities of wealth. The system will still be hostage to investor confidence. In short, there will still exist that privileged class that negates popular sovereignty. To count on "Public Cognizance" to guarantee democracy is surely wishful thinking.

Count Eight: Quality of Work. Perhaps the most striking lacuna in the post-Keynesian critique of contemporary society—which otherwise much resembles the socialist critique—concerns the time (eight hours a day, 40 hours a week, 48-50 weeks a year, 40-50 years) most people spend "on the job." The concern that is probably more central than any other to worker-control socialism is absent in Galbraith. Or rather, that which is expressed is the (valid) concern for more leisure options, but no thought is given to the problems of on-the-job work-alienation. The problem is not seen to be pressing.

> Outside of the industrial system, as in the cotton and vegetable fields, work can still be hard and tedious. But within the industrial system, though always with exceptions, work is unlikely to be painful and it may be pleasant. . . . Presiding over the console that regulates the movements of billets through a steel mill may be as pleasant as sojourning with a connubial fishwife.[49]

I don't think we need proceed further. Work in the Ideal Industrial State will be like work today. The last count of my indictment stands, as do the other seven. Worker control rests its case.

No—we've stopped too soon. For there remains an important counterargument to consider. Galbraith's acceptance of work as it is is part of a larger acceptance, one that can be construed as an attack against the very heart of the worker-control project. "Socialism," he has written, "has come to mean government by socialists who have learned that socialism, as anciently understood, is impractical."[50] Let me formulate the argument as follows. A modern industrial society is inconceivable without large, technically-complex corporations. Large, technically-complex corporations will inevitably be controlled by the "technostructure,"—that elite group of engineers, technicians, middle and upper managers, accountants, and lawyers who alone possess the expertise essential to coherent corporate decisionmaking. Hence it doesn't really matter what formal structure is imposed upon corporations. They will behave the same whether nominally controlled by stockholders, by the state, or by their employees. Or rather, they will only perform satisfactorily if the technocrats are granted the autonomy they demand. Excessive state or stockholder or worker interference will only create havoc.[51]

I will pass over the fact that Galbraith himself advocates a great many policies that impinge upon corporate autonomy. I think there is a contradiction here in his thinking—which cannot be avoided by simply stating that his strategy "excludes, by law, action that is inconsistent with the public interest but allows the firm the maximum freedom of decision as to how the conforming results are obtained."[52] But the more basic charge remains—that worker control (and perhaps even the Ideal Industrial State) is incompatible with a modern industrial society.

I don't think a wholly convincing response is possible. I am defending something that does not now exist and never has existed, when the only wholly convincing proof that something can exist is to

point to its existence. (Even among mathematicians, some refuse
to accept nonconstructive existence proofs.) Of course I can point to
specific examples of worker-managed firms, but I cannot point to a
modern industrial society structured as I have proposed. (I can point
to Yugoslavia, but it is neither fully industrialized nor correctly
structured with respect to investments.)

With this handicap in mind, let me proceed with a threefold response. First, it is not clear that the "technostructure" must necessarily control a large, complex corporation. That the technostructure
controls the modern <u>capitalist</u> corporation is itself a hotly contested
thesis.[53] If it does not, if capitalists (or stockholders) set general
priorities for contemporary firms, then workers would seem as capable of setting <u>their</u> priorities if given legal control. Even supposing
the technostructure to be in control of the corporate giants today, its
control is not absolute. Galbraith concedes that a company must turn
a "reasonable" profit in order to keep stockholders content (though
not, he insists, a maximal profit). Workers in a (nominally) worker-
managed enterprise must also be kept happy. They too can count, and
hence can detect mismanagement that results in financial loss. And
they are much better placed than stockholders to judge overall performance. They are in a position to rotate work, to conduct classes,
and so on, in short to familiarize themselves with the operation of
the enterprise. And they have far more <u>incentive</u> to do so. If a
stockholder becomes dissatisfied with "her" company, an effortless
remedy exists. She simply sells her stock. Needless to say, a
worker's relationship to her enterprise is far more intimate.

A second consideration in support of worker control: it is not
clear that enterprises need to be as large and complex as they are
now. Even now there are many, many businesses that are neither
large nor complex.* And much of the giganticism of the giants has involved diversification that has nothing to do with technical efficiency
(though much with their need to grow). Individual production units are
often rather small, a couple of thousand workers or less—much smaller, incidentally than their (not notably efficient) Soviet counterparts.†

---

*Though the largest 2000 corporations in the United States con-
tribute nearly half the wage bill of U.S. workers, there are 2 million
corporations, 11 million sole proprietorships and 1 million partner-
ships that file tax returns. (Seidman, "TIP," p. 24.)

†In machinery and metalworking, for example, the number of
employees per enterprise in the United States is 74, in the USSR,
2008. The figures for all industries (excluding power stations) are
48 and 565 respectively. (Alec Nove, <u>The Soviet Economic System</u>
[London: George Allen and Unwin, 1977], p. 84.)

It would appear that a much greater degree of decentralization is possible within the parameters of technical efficiency than exists today under corporate capitalism.

I am not saying that large corporations should be broken up and made more competitive. There is a substantial theoretical-empirical issue at stake here about which an advocate of worker control need not take an a priori stand. Neoclassicism inclines one to "trust-bust," but post-Keynesians may be right that it is more efficient for certain complex industries to coordinate their operations rather than compete. This fact—if it is a fact—does not detract from the case for worker control. Worker-managed firms might be permitted to make long-term agreements with other firms in their own or related industries. But of course when the market is superceded in this manner, the government is quite right (as the post-Keynesians correctly contend) to scrutinize incomes and prices, and to impose restraints when monopoly power threatens the public good. Whether this policy of permitting or even encouraging the subvention of the market or the alternative policy of maximizing competition is the more appropriate is a decision a worker-control administration would have to make, but neither is incompatible with the basic structure of worker control.

I've argued that a technostructure need not control a large, complex enterprise, and that, furthermore, enterprises as large as the ones we have today are not essential to an advanced industrial society. (Actually, I've not demonstrated these propositions so much as I've raised doubts about their negations.) Suppose I am wrong. Suppose an advanced industrial society requires Brobdingnagian corporations so complex that only technical elites can comprehend and direct them. If this should be the case, then I would not hesitate to make a third claim: if the human race wants a decent future, then it had better jettison "advanced industrial society" and opt for worker control. If some efficiency and some amenities must be sacrificed, then so be it. Needless to say, I'm not advocating a return to the Stone Age. Much technology is adaptable to production on a more modest scale. (Some writers, citing miniaturization, compact computers, multipurpose machine tools, solar technology and the like have argued that the most modern technology makes possible a decentralization of production that was unthinkable a few decades ago.[54]) But if it is our "way of life" that stands between us and a future without (with greatly reduced) mindless consumption, ecological spoliation, economic instability, and alienated work, between us and a truly democratic future, if the best that is compatible with our "way of life" is the Ideal Industrial State, then I don't see how a decent and rational human being can fail to make the obvious choice.

NOTES

1. See John Rawls, A Theory of Justice (Cambridge, Mass.: Belknap Press of Harvard Universtiy Press, 1971), pp. 46-53. Rawls is not as committed to the status quo as the grammar analogy suggests. He allows that a correct theory of justice, unlike a correct theory of grammar, might move us to reconsider and modify our "ordinary usage." (See p. 48.)

2. Cf. Brian Barry, The Liberal Theory of Justice (Oxford: Claredon Press, 1973) for an extended defense of this claim.

3. See Rawls, Theory of Justice, pp. 274-84. Rawls does not argue that only capitalist structures are just. This "ideological neutrality" is characteristic of modern liberalism, at least since the waning of the Cold War. Unlike classical liberals, modern liberals are usually content to argue that certain forms of capitalism can be just, without pressing the further claim that socialist forms can never be.

4. John Kenneth Galbraith, The Affluent Society (New York: New American Library, 1958); The New Industrial State (Boston: Houghton Mifflin, 1967).

5. V. S. Navasky, "Galbraith on Galbraith," The New York Times Book Review, June 25 1967, p. 3.

6. For a survey of Galbraith's work and its critical reception (through The New Industrial State), see Charles Hession, John Kenneth Galbraith and His Critics (New York: New American Library, 1972).

7. Paul Samuelson, Economics, 9th ed. (New York: McGraw-Hill, 1973). p. 849. Samuelson does not intend this remark to be a dismissal of Galbraith, for he continues, "His criticism cannot itself kill. But it acts like a virus, softening the way for more deadly critiques on the part of the New Left and its professional radical economists" (ibid.).

8. Cf. Alfred Eichner and J. A. Kregel, "An Essay on Post-Keynesian Theory: A New Paradigm in Economics," Journal of Economic Literature 13 (December 1975): 1293-1314, for details of this paradigm, including its origin. See also Alfred Eichner, ed., A Guide to Post-Keynesian Economics (White Plains, N.Y.: M. E. Sharpe, 1979). It is noteworthy that Galbraith, who was not even mentioned in the 1975 survey article, was listed as Chairman of the Honorary Board of Editors of the Journal of Post-Keynesian Economics when it was launched in 1978.

9. Rawls, Theory of Justice, pp. 73-78.

10. Ibid., pp. 233-4. Rawls, it should be noted, does not call this principle "autonomy." He reserves that term for the more Kantian sense: "acting autonomously is acting from principles that we would consent to as free and equal rational beings." (Ibid., p. 516.)

11. Cf. Galbraith, New Industrial State, pp. 74-84.
12. Rawls, Theory of Justice, p. 276.
13. Ibid., p. 278.
14. Ibid., p. 412.
15. Ibid., p. 278.
16. Ibid., p. 290.
17. Ibid., p. 408.
18. Galbraith, New Industrial State, p. 219.
19. Michael Kalecki, "Political Aspects of Full Employment," in A Critique of Economic Theory, ed. E. K. Hunt and Jesse Schwartz, (Baltimore: Penguin Books, 1972): 424-25.
20. Business Week (May 17, 1952). Quoted by Paul Baran, The Political Economy of Growth (New York: Monthly Review Press, Modern Reader Paperbacks, 1968), p. 102. Note: except for the brief reference to inflation, the interests expressed are exclusively those of capital.
21. Karl Marx, Capital (New York: Modern Library, 1906), p. 689.
22. Rawls, Theory of Justice, p. 276.
23. Ibid., pp. 284-98.
24. Milton Friedman, Capitalism and Freedom (Chicago: University of Chicago Press, 1962), p. 54. For more details, consult Milton Friedman, A Program for Monetary Stability (New York: Fordam University Press, 1959).
25. Milton Friedman, "The Role of Monetary Policy," American Economic Review 58 (March 1968): 1-17. James Tobin, a Keynesian liberal, responds that this "natural rate," which seems to be about 5-6 percent in the United States, would likely entail 20 percent excess productive capacity and an unemployed force, two-thirds of whom are layoffs—a far cry from Pareto-optimality. (James Tobin, "Inflation and Unemployment," American Economic Review 62 [March 1972]: 8.)
26. Joan Robinson, Economic Heresies: Some Old-Fashioned Questions in Economic Theory (New York: Basic Books, 1971), p. 87.
27. Ibid., p. 86. Notice, the Federal Reserve does not have complete control over the money supply. The money supply fluctuates on its own in response to business activity; the Federal Reserve reacts to these autonomous movements with countervailing movements of its own. Hence the difficulty of identifying causal connections.
28. Cf. Paul Samuelson, "Monetarism Objectively Evaluated," in Readings in Economics, 6th ed., ed. Paul Samuelson (New York: McGraw-Hill, 1970), pp. 145-54.
29. See, for example, Milton Friedman and Walter Heller, Monetary vs. Fiscal Policy: A Dialogue (New York: W. W. Norton, 1969).

30. See Samuelson, Economics, p. 498, for a standard version of the formal argument.

31. Galbraith, New Industrial State, p. 193.

32. John Kenneth Galbraith, Economics and the Public Purpose (Boston: Houghton Mifflin, 1973), pp. 279-85, 272.

33. Cf., for example, Galbraith, New Industrial State, Chapter IX.

34. See Galbraith, Public Purpose, Part Five, for the bulk of the reforms I identify as constituting the Galbraithian ideal. Cf. also New Industrial State, Chapter XX ff.

35. Galbraith, Public Purpose, p. 257.

36. Ibid., pp. 261, 263.

37. Ibid, p. 263.

38. Cf. The Writings of the Young Marx on Philosophy and Society, ed. Loyd Easton and Kurt Guddat (Garden City, N.Y.: Doubleday, Anchor Books, 1967), p. 281: "Suppose we had produced things as human beings. (1) In my production I would have objectified my individuality and its particularity, and in the course of my activity I would have enjoyed my individual life. . . . (2) In your satisfaction and your use of my product I would have had the direct and conscious satisfaction that my work satisfied a human need. . . . (3) I would have been the mediation between you and the species . . . I would have been affirmed in your thought as well as your love. (4) In my individual life I would have directly created your life; in my individual activity I would have immediately confirmed and realized my true human and social nature. . . . My labor would be a free manifestation of life and an enjoyment of life. . . . [But] under the presupposition of private property my individuality is externalized to the point where I hate this activity and where it is a torment for me."

39. Galbraith, New Industrial State, p. 293.

40. Galbraith, Public Purpose, p. 230.

41. Galbraith, New Industrial State, p. 200.

42. Galbraith, Public Purpose, pp. 271-72. A predictable socialist response to this proposal is to label it utopian: the power of capital is so entrenched that it will not be peacefully put to sleep. This may well be true—but it should be noted that hand-waving about "revolution" doesn't add much to the discussion. Any viable transition strategy must think concretely about "expropriation"—taking fully into account that in Western capitalist countries millions of workers own (small amounts of) stocks and bonds. (Since we are not discussing the transition problem, we need not pursue this issue here.)

43. Ibid., p. 290.

44. Ibid., p. 318.

45. Galbraith, New Industrial State, p. 171: "Once the safety of the technostructure is insured by a minimum level of earnings, there

is then a measure of choice as to goals. Nothing is so compelling as
the need to survive. However, there is little doubt as to how, over-
whelmingly, this choice is exercised: It is to achieve the greatest possible rate of corporate growth as measured by sales."

46. Ibid., p. 174.

47. Galbraith, Public Purpose, pp. 241-52.

48. Ibid., p. 241.

49. Galbraith, New Industrial State, pp. 364-65.

50. Ibid., p. 101.

51. Commenting on postcolonial India and other Third World
countries, Galbraith writes, "The effect of the denial of autonomy and
the ability of the technostructure to accomodate itself to changing
tasks has been visibly deficient operations. . . . The experience with
public enterprises, where autonomy is denied, thus accords fully—and
tragically—with expectation." Ibid., pp. 102-3.

52. Galbraith, Public Purpose, p. 290.

53. Cf. Bernard Gendron, Technology and the Human Condition
(New York: St. Martin's Press, 1977), pp. 191-207, for a representative socialist critique of this claim. See Robert Solow, "Son of Affluence," The Public Interest (Fall 1967): 100-8, for a Keynesian-liberal
response.

54. Cf. Murray Bookchin, Post-Scarcity Anarchism (Berkeley:
Ramparts Press, 1971), especially his essay "Toward a Liberatory
Technology," pp. 83-140. See also E. F. Schumacher, Small Is
Beautiful (New York: Harper and Row, 1973).

7

CONCLUDING REMARKS: HOW, WHICH, AND THEN WHAT?

My argument is done. I've concluded (whether validly or not the reader must judge) that worker-control socialism is a worthier ideal than any of the leading capitalist contenders. I've shown (tried to show) that worker-control socialism is structured so as to be more efficient than the capitalist alternatives, more rational in its growth, and better in accord with important noneconomic values. I've tried to address all the major questions germane to this specific issue.

There are a number of questions I haven't addressed—important questions, but questions peripheral to the specific focus of this study. Perhaps it would be worthwhile to reflect for a moment on several of these neglected items. No exhaustive analysis will be attempted, but let me make a few remarks.

THE TRANSITION TO SOCIALISM

The question that clamors most loudly for attention at this juncture is doubtless the transition question. Suppose it is true that worker control is a worthy future. How do we make it _our_ future? How do we get from here to there?

Plato was put this question regarding his ideal state. His famous reply: "Either philosophers become kings in their countries or those who are now called kings and rulers come to be sufficiently inspired with a genuine desire for wisdom."[1] Marx, wholly impatient with such "idealism," spoke instead of "tendencies working with iron necessity toward inevitable results."[2] But for us neither of these responses will do. The cataclysms of this century have undermined our faith in the inevitable triumph of a rational order, to say nothing of belief in philosopher-kings. Ours is an age of neither faith nor reason. Ours is an age of anxiety.

So no definite answer can be given as to how to get from here to there. The fact of the matter is, we may not get there. Still, a few observations might be made. As Marx and many others have pointed out, capitalist institutions—the market, a new concept of property, wage-labor—emerged within the feudal order; they gradually eroded that order until a series of political revolutions applied the coup de grace. It strikes me as not without interest that the two key institutions of worker-control socialism—worker self-management of enterprises and societal control of investment—are both embryonically present in most capitalist countries today. They are present and they are likely to grow stronger. The need to deal with worker alienation and lagging productivity has encouraged more and more firms to experiment with participation schemes. (Labor union pressure, at least in Europe, has also been a stimulus.) At the same time the growing domination of capitalist economies by a handful of corporate leviathans with multinational allegiances has provoked increasing calls for regulation: for restrictions on the placement and movement of factories, for requiring "environmental impact" statements concerning new products, facilities and technologies, for more "corporate responsibility."* A consciousness is emerging that workers have a right to participate in shaping the conditions of their work, and that society has a duty to oversee and regulate economic development. This is not, in my view, an insignificant or transitory phenomenon. This consciousness—and the events generating it—will likely intensify.

I am not suggesting that capitalism will "wither away." There is a current of socialist thought that tends to think in such terms.†

---

*Classical liberals, needless to say, are outraged by all this. Regarding the last element, consider Friedman: "Few trends could so thoroughly undermine the very foundations of our free society as the acceptance by corporate officials of a social responsibility other than to make as much money for their stockholders as possible." (Milton Friedman, Capitalism and Freedom [Chicago: University of Chicago Press, 1962], p. 133.)

†This current is traceable to Eduard Bernstein's crystallizing revision of Marx. (Cf. Eduard Bernstein, Evolutionary Socialism [New York, Schocken, 1961].) It is noteworthy that Bernstein was much impressed with the burgeoning consumer-cooperative movement of the time, but hostile to producer-cooperatives. About the latter, he writes, "[Large industrial undertakings] are absolutely unfit for the

Against this current I would urge three points. (1) Worker participation in management is not worker self-management and governmental regulation of investment is not societal control. Neither per se negates the privileged position of capital. Decisive power will remain with capital until it is effectively challenged by a political force cognizant of what it is doing; it will not silently melt away. (2) Genuine worker-managed enterprises are possible within a capitalist framework, and they might well be important as models—but they will not transform society. Such firms are not expansionary, so they will not gradually and quietly come to dominate the economy, not even if they are economically superior to their capitalist rivals.* (3) Wealth will remain enormously concentrated, even if worker-participation experiments proliferate and governmental regulation of investment intensifies. The productive apparatus of advanced capitalism (and the wealth it both represents and breeds) will remain in private hands—until it is quite consciously taken from those hands. Some will rage, but sooner or later "the knell of capitalist private property [must] sound. The expropriators [must be] expropriated."[3] This may occur peacefully or in the face of violent resistance. Expropriation may be accomplished with or without compensation, but it must be accomplished. Worker control remains an idle concept otherwise.

Of course worker control, expropriation, the challenging of capitalist power all remain idle concepts in the absence of an agent of change. About this I will say only that a sine qua non is a consciously socialist political party that represents the aspirations and commands the allegiance of a significant segment of the population, a party that is capable of becoming the party of the vast majority. That's a large order—but it's an order that must be served.

Obviously much more needs to be said about this extremely important question, but I have little more to offer. I have opinions about further details, but no magical solution to this problem, which has been so vexing to the Left in all advanced capitalist countries. "What is to be done?" remains an open question.

---

associated management of the employees themselves"—this against Marx, whom he quotes as saying, "We recommend workmen to embark on co-operative production rather than on co-operative stores. The latter touch only the surface of the economic system of today, the first strikes at its foundations." (Ibid., pp. 120, 111.)

*Recall our discussion, pp. 168-70.

VARIETIES OF SOCIALISM

Let me turn to another topic about which I have so far said little. The thesis of this work is that worker-control socialism is superior to capitalist alternatives. But what about other socialist alternatives? This question too is of interest and importance.

A fundamental feature of worker-control socialism is control of the workplace by those who work there. I have called this feature "worker self-management."* Commitments to liberty, democracy, participatory autonomy and the value of meaningful work all provide a basis for a commitment to worker self-management. If one calls "socialist" any economic system that prohibits private ownership of most of the means of production, it is plain that not all socialist societies are worker self-managed. Less obvious but more significant to the model-comparison analysis we have been doing, some forms of socialism are incompatible with worker self-management. Unless major countervailing considerations can be brought to bear, these forms of socialism should be judged inferior to worker control by anyone subscribing to the values I've discussed.

One form of socialism is incompatible with worker self-management virtually by definition. "Technocratic socialism" is an economic system without private ownership of the means of production in which production units are run by more or less autonomous technical elites within bounds set by the state. If stockholders were "put to sleep" in Galbraith's Ideal Industrial State, the result would be a technocratic socialism. Also technocratic is a recent proposal by Leland Stauber to institute socialism by simply transferring all corporate stock to local-government investment funds, to be managed by experts—who

---

*Terminological uniformity is not a feature of the literature on this subject. "Worker-controlled," "self-managed," "labor-managed," "labor-governed," "participatory" are all adjectives attached sometimes to "socialism" and sometimes to "economy" to designate an economic system with worker self-management. The corresponding nouns, "worker control," "self-management," "labor management," etc., are often used for the worker self-management feature itself. Throughout this work I've used "worker-control socialism" or just "worker control" to signify the specific model I've been defending. "Worker self-management" refers to that specific feature—control of individual enterprises by those who work there—that worker control shares (or might share) with other forms of socialism. (Recall the discussion on p. 49.)

would now serve the public interest instead of the interests of the wealthy few.[4] As is characteristic of a technocratic socialist, Stauber rejects

> the syndicalist idea of ownership and control by firms
> totally or primarily by their employees . . . on the
> grounds that it underestimates the relevance to economic
> performance of professional management, particularly in
> large, complex organizations, and can also obstruct or
> retard the closing of uneconomic plants and dismissals of
> excess labor.[5]

I have already discussed the thesis that technocratic control is indispensable to an advanced industrial society. As to the "obstructing or retarding the closing of uneconomic plants and dismissals of excess labor," that is a virtue of worker control, not a vice.* Until the technocratic socialists confront the empirical record of successful worker self-management, I don't think more need be said.

The Soviet system best represents a second form of socialism that is difficult to reconcile with worker self-management. It is the economic form once identified with socialism: central planning by the state. A governmental planning board assumes control of the entire economy; it specifies for each production unit quantitative and qualitative output quotas, the inputs to be used, the prices to be charged and the wages to be paid. All economic mystification dissolves, since human agents now consciously decide what gets produced, how, and to whom it is distributed.

Unfortunately this model, so conceptually clear, is subject to serious practical difficulties—due not (primarily) to the ill-will or class bias of the planners, but to the sheer immensity of the task at hand. "The essential point," says Nove,

> is that in most instances the centre does not know just
> what it is that needs doing, in disaggregate detail, while
> the management in its situation cannot know what it is
> that society needs unless the centre informs it. . . .
> The trouble lies in the near impossibility of drafting
> micro-economic instruments in such a way that even the
> most well-meaning manager will not be misled.[6]

---

*Recall pp. 79–80.

Consider a single example: the production of sheet steel. The planning center must specify a quota for each factory. In what units? Suppose tons are selected. Then a manager, who has no other information upon which to base his decision, will tend to produce thick sheets, since it is more "efficient" to satisfy the quota that way. On the other hand, if square meters are selected, he will tend to produce sheets as thin as possible. Of course consumer feedback will have some effect, but this is largely nonquantifiable, difficult to evaluate, and in any event an unwelcome obstacle, from the production unit's point of view, to its primary goal—speedy execution of the plan. (Nove cites a cartoon published in Krokodil, showing an enormous nail hanging in a large workshop: "The month's plan fulfilled," said the director, pointing to the nail. In tons, of course.)[7]

One must not lose one's perspective in the midst of the myriad examples of Soviet inefficiency (so happily recorded by neoclassical economists). For all its inefficiencies the Soviet economy works. In some respects it works better than Western capitalist economies: there is less unemployment, less nonrational sales persuasion, (probably) less inequality; the system is better designed to decide and control the kind and rate of growth it undertakes, and it is less prone to inflation-recession instability. Micro-efficiency, after all, is but one value by which to judge an economic system; in a relatively affluent society it would hardly seem the most important.

In fact my main objection to central planning is not its inefficiency (though the demoralizing effects of waste and irrationality should not be discounted entirely), but to its problematic relationship to noneconomic values. Central planning requires centralized authority, and that leads (at least under conditions of scarcity) to a dangerous concentration of power. The classical liberal concern for liberty is not misguided here. Nor is the concern (not shared by classical liberals) for participartory autonomy. To be sure, it is possible for a centrally-planned economy to grant formal control of enterprises to their workers instead of to appointed managers—but since the planning board sets production quotas, prices, inputs and wages, there is little real scope for worker decision. Even if some flexibility were granted in these areas, two important decision classes would almost certainly be ruled out: the choice of more leisure over more production and the choice of more "humane" but less "efficient" technology. But these choices—which serve to check compulsive consumption and work alienation—are important strengths of worker control. They are difficult to reconcile with central planning.

There is also the problem of discipline. Granted, the central planners could discipline the entire workforce of an enterprise for failure to meet its quota—but such an approach would surely provoke an antagonistic reaction. It is far more "efficient" (from the point of view of the central planners) to appoint a director and make her responsible. But if she is responsible for quota fulfillment, then she cannot be accountable to her workforce—and so an authoritarian structure must be imposed. This tendency toward authoritarianism seems to me almost irresistible.

If technocratic and centrally-planned socialism stand in conflict with worker self-management (and the value of participatory autonomy), no such conflict exists between self-management and a participatory "pure market socialism"—a laissez-faire economy in which workers, not stockholders, have full legal control of their enterprises. Discipline, for example, is no problem, since an impersonal market imposes discipline. Enterprises are constrained by the necessity of economic survival, but within this constraint they have a range of options concerning distribution of income, labor-leisure tradeoffs, goods to produce, and technologies to employ.

Unfortunately, a pure market socialism with worker self-management is economically unsound.* Its difficulties trace to two basic factors: first, the workforce of a labor-managed firm is disinclined to expand; second, investments are in no way coordinated or controlled. With pure market socialism we get anarchy of production, replete with unemployment that has no tendency to diminish, widespread and growing inequalities, consumption and production externalities, an unplanned growth, and inflationary and recessionary instabilities. (This "anarchy" is somewhat different from capitalist anarchy, since enterprises are less likely to be expansionary. This might count as an improvement, since competition would be less ruthless and consumption less compulsive, but on the other hand, with profits either consumed or invested in one's own firm, economic development is in no way directed to the general needs of the community. Not even the admittedly imperfect profitability criterion is employed, much less conscious social planning, with respect to society-wide investment opportunities.)

Against this background of alternatives, the essential strengths of worker-control socialism come sharply into view. By planning investment—but not the whole economy—the basic virtues of central planning are (approximately) achieved. By relying on the market to coordinate the daily activities of existing firms, the micro-efficiencies of the market are preserved, the economy is decentralized, and a

---

*This model bears strong resemblance to Yugoslavia in the late 1960s. (Cf. David Granick, Enterprise Guidance in Eastern Europe: A Comparison of Four Socialist Economies [Princeton, N.J.: Princeton University Press, 1975], pp. 467-9.

structure prevails that is fully compatible with worker self-management. Thus the strengths of both plan and market are maintained, and the weaknesses of each minimized. This, in my view, is a remarkable accomplishment.

It is not good enough for some socialists. A tradition rooted in the New Left rejects both central planning and the market, and all combinations of the two. Central planning, these theorists agree, has all the defects I've ascribed to it, but the market is also proscribed, on the grounds that

> it involves as motivations only the maximization of personal immediate consumption pleasure and profit (per worker). The market involves a continual possibility of competitive failure, and thus creates basic insecurities, which themselves elicit defensive behaviors counterproductive to societal well-being. . . . Markets simultaneously require competitive behavior and prohibit cooperation as irrational. For markets create a direct opposition of interests between those who produce a certain good and those who consume it. . . . As an economic agency, markets establish the opposite solidarity—they declare the war of each against all.[8]

But if neither the market, central planning nor some combination of the two is acceptable, what is the alternative? Albert and Hahnel don't flinch at the question. Democratic councils and iterative planning, they reply. Each workplace and each neighborhood is to be organized as a democratic council, responsible for the day-to-day activities of that unit, and for initiating and revising proposals concerning what it will give to society and what it will take. These proposals, via a "back-and-forth iterative procedure," will generate an economic plan.[9]

And how will this happen? Let me quote:

> Each council would have to estimate from past experience the kinds of efforts required by others to supply a list of proposed inputs, and the uses to which others would put a given list of proposed outputs. Then, learning the results of all units' first proposals, each council would get much new information to work with.[10]

Stop! Consider for a moment some numbers. There are more than 200 million persons in the United States. Place each in a neighborhood of say 2000, and a workplace of similar size. That gives us 100,000 neighborhood councils and 100,000 work councils, each of

which is to draw up a proposal to be read by every other council. (Even
if a council reads only the reports of those it affects or is affected by,
the numbers are staggering.) Consider also the construction of each
proposal. Each member of each neighborhood unit estimates the kinds
and quantities of goods he would like to consume during the next year.
This information is somehow collated, and, in addition, estimates are
made of the kinds of effort required to produce all these things. (How
much effort went into producing the book you are now reading? How
many books, and of what types would you like next year? How many
paper clips, 12-penny nails and cans of chicken soup? And what effort
goes into producing them?)

To call this "alternative" mind-boggling is an understatement.
To call it preposterous is not unfair. Such silliness need not be taken
seriously.

And yet . . . And yet there is something right about the critique
that prompted this proposal. So long as one's material well-being is
tied to the production of things that one must sell on an open market,
one is inhibited from experiencing one's activity as part of the collective, cooperative labor of society. One is tempted to deceive or take
advantage of others (especially one's customers and competitors).
The antagonistic relations generated by the market serve to promote
an efficient allocation of goods, but they also promote suspicion, insecurity, duplicity, and selfishness.

It has long been the socialist dream to abolish this contradiction
of capitalism, along with the many others. It has long been the dream
to eliminate money, economic competition and all the attendant "fet-
ishisms." Worker-control socialism does not. To a considerable
degree it softens the antagonisms associated with the market, but it
does not dissolve them. It is my belief (widely though not universally
shared on the Left) that the objective conditions of contemporary society, even allowing for the considerable change of consciousness that
can be presumed to accompany the advent of socialism, render the
abolition of the market unfeasible.* To replace it by centralized planning is undesirable; to replace it by "democratic councils and iterative
planning" is fantasy.

---

*Even such sharp critics of Eastern European "market social-
ism" as Paul Sweezy and Charles Bettelheim concede this point.
Bettelheim writes that "the contradiction between 'market' and 'plan'
will continue throughout the transition from capitalism to socialism. . . . The notion of a 'direct' and 'immediate' abolition of market
relations is as utopian and dangerous as the notion of the 'immediate

THE TRANSITION TO COMMUNISM

Though the market is a fundamental feature of worker-control socialism, it does not follow that the market should remain forever a feature of socialist society. Worker control (as I have defined it) is not the best of all possible worlds. It is not inconceivable that a worker-controlled society structured as I have proposed would evolve over time into something rather different, into something rather like the marketless, moneyless, even stateless, utopia, the "communist" terminus of the socialist project. Let me sketch a scenario.

Suppose worker control is established in an advanced industrial society. Suppose, after a period of time, the many adjustments of production and consumption that worker control will entail have been made. Suppose that consumption begins to stabilize, that the switch to ecologically sound technologies and recyclable products is well underway, that work is becoming less alienating, more satisfying. As the "economic problem" declines in importance, the society slows its growth and approaches a stationary state of relative affluence. We observe, first that as this happens the role of the investment boards decline, since its primary function is to plan and finance growth. Thus an important organ of government begins to "wither away."

Something else happens. It becomes feasible to supply more and more items of consumption free of charge. Consider a product whose supply is readily forthcoming at current prices and whose demand is stable and not likely to increase substantially if it is made a free good. (Salt is a favorite example, but in a society without poverty the list might be readily expanded to include other items of basic foodstuff, certain types of clothing, intra-city mass transportation, most kinds of health care, and so on.) Producers of such items could agree to supply them without charge, in return for a governmental guarantee of income maintenance (at a level pegged to other income levels in society). Producers have little to lose by such an

---

abolition' of the state and is similar in nature: it disregards the specific characteristics (i.e., the specific contradictions) of the period of transition which constitutes the building of socialism." Sweezy acknowledges that "market relationships (which of course imply money and prices) are inevitable under socialism," though he warns that "they constitute a standing danger to the system and unless structurally hemmed in and controlled will lead to degeneration and retrogression." (Paul Sweezy and Charles Bettelheim, On the Transition to Socialism [New York: Monthly Review Press, 1971], pp. 19-27.)

agreement, since prices and incomes in these industries can be assumed to have stabilized, and the other members of society have much to
gain: the security and freedom that comes from having guaranteed access to consumption. Of course the discipline of the market is lost.
Workers might slacken production, increase their leisure, etc.—but
then again they might not. If the agreement is perceived as fair, if
the work itself is nonalienating, then the self-respect of individual
workers and the collective self-discipline of the work group might well
prove adequate. If so, then the arrangement is highly desirable.

If such experiments work, then one would expect to see more and
more enterprises leaving the market, more and more incomes guaranteed by the state. But notice, since these incomes are paid from tax
revenues, people's spendable income diminishes—as well it should,
since fewer and fewer items need to be purchased. Money, competition, production for profit all begin to wither—even the state, to the
extent that the availability of satisfying work and the absence of economic insecurity dry up the need for police, judges and jails. The
classic communist vision—from each according to her ability, to each
according to her need—begins to glimmer on the horizon.[11]

Perhaps all this will come to pass. I hope so. I find it encouraging that there is a form of socialism feasible today that does not
contradict the aspirations that gave birth more than a century ago to
the socialist project—to a project that, despite the ravages of a
brutal environment, despite its own horrific blunders, refuses to die,
refuses to renounce its claim as the true future of our species.

Of course the question of "true communism," the final goal of
the socialist project, is not the concrete question we must confront
today. Would that it were so. Unfortunately we have other, more
urgent concerns.

NOTES

1. Plato, The Republic of Plato, trans. Francis MacDonald
Cornford (Oxford: Oxford University Press, 1945), p. 178. Plato
added pessimistically that neither eventuality seemed likely.

2. Karx Marx, Capital (New York: Modern Library, 1906),
p. 13.

3. Ibid., p. 837.

4. Leland Stauber, "A Proposal for a Democratic Market Economy," Journal of Comparative Economics 1 (1977): 235-58. These
experts are to be recruited from existing trust departments and investment counseling services of commercial banks and from local
stock brokerage firms. Ibid., p. 242.

5. Ibid., p. 239.

6. Alec Nove, The Soviet Economic System (London: George Allen and Unwin, 1977), p. 85. See the whole of Chapter 4, "Individual Management and Micro-economic Problems," for further details.

7. Ibid., p. 94.

8. Michael Albert and Robin Hahnel, Unorthodox Marxism (Boston: South End Press, 1978), pp. 262-63.

9. Ibid., pp. 257-58.

10. Ibid., pp. 269-70. Albert and Hahnel insist that this is not a utopian proposal for some distant time, but the kind of socialism they want now.

11. Cf. Karl Marx, Critique of the Gotha Program (Moscow: Progress, 1971), pp. 17-8; "In a higher phase of communist society, after the enslaving subordination of the individual to the division of labour, and therewith also the antithesis between mental and physical labour, have vanished; after labour has become not only a means of life but life's prime want; after the productive forces have also increased with the all-round development of the individual, and all the springs of cooperative wealth flow more abundantly—only then can the narrow horizon of bourgeois right be crossed in its entirety and society inscribe on its banner: From each according to his ability, to each according to his need:"

BIBLIOGRAPHY

Adizes, Ichak. _Industrial Democracy: Yugoslav Style_. New York: The Free Press, 1971.

Adizes, Ichak, and Elizabeth Mann Borgese, eds. _Self-Management: New Dimensions to Democracy_. Santa Barbara: ABC-Clio, 1975.

Albert, Michael, and Robin Hahnel. _Unorthodox Marxism_. Boston: South End Press, 1978.

Amin, Samir. _Unequal Development: An Essay on the Social Formations of Peripheral Capitalism_. New York: Monthly Review Press, 1970.

Argyris, Chris. _Integrating the Individual and the Organization_. New York: Wiley, 1964.

Aristotle. "Politics." In _The Basic Works of Aristotle_, edited by Richard McKeon, pp. 1126-1316. New York: Random House, 1941.

Aronson, Richard; Eli Schwartz; and Andrew Weintraub, eds. _The Economic Growth Controversy_. White Plains, N.Y.: International Arts and Sciences Press, 1973.

Aronowitz, Stanley. _False Promises: The Shaping of American Working Class Consciousness_. New York: McGraw-Hill, 1973.

Arrow, Kenneth. "A Difficulty in the Concept of Social Welfare." _Journal of Political Economy_ 58 (1950):328-41.

____. "The Limitation of the Profit Motive." _Challenge_ 22 (1979): 23-27.

____. _Social Choice and Individual Values_. New Haven: Yale University Press, 1951.

Arrow, Kenneth and Tibor Scitovsky, eds. _Readings in Welfare Economics_. Homewood, Illinois: Richard D. Irwin, 1969.

Backman, Jules. Advertising and Competition. New York: New York University Press, 1967.

Balzer, Richard. Clockwork: Life In and Outside an American Factory. Graden City, N.Y.: Doubleday, 1976.

Baran, Paul A. The Political Economy of Growth. New York: Monthly Review Press, Modern Reader Paperbacks, 1968.

Baran, Paul A., and Paul Sweezy. Monopoly Capital. New York: Monthly Review Press, Modern Reader Paperbacks, 1966.

Barnet, Richard, and Ronald Müller. Global Reach: The Power of the Multinational Corporations. New York: Simon and Schuster, 1974.

Barry, Brian. The Liberal Theory of Justice. Oxford: Clarendon Press, 1973.

Baumol, William. Economic Theory and Operations Analysis. 3rd ed. Englewood Cliffs, N.J.: Prentice-Hall, 1972.

Baumol, William, and Wallace Oates. The Theory of Environmental Policy: Externalities, Public Outlays and the Quality of Life. Englewood Cliffs, N.J.: Prentice-Hall, 1975.

Becker, Lawrence. Property Rights: Philosophical Foundations. Boston: Routledge and Kegan Paul, 1977.

Beckerman, Wilfred. In Defense of Economic Growth. London: Jonathan Cape, 1974.

Bell, Daniel, and Irving Kristol, eds. Capitalism Today. New York: Basic Books, 1970.

Bergson, Abram. Essays in Normative Economics. Cambridge, Mass.: Belknap Press of Harvard University Press, 1966.

____. "A Reformulation of Certain Aspects of Welfare Economics." Quarterly Journal of Economics 52 (1938):310-34.

Berlin, Isaiah. Two Concepts of Liberty. Oxford: Oxford University Press, 1958.

Bettelheim, Charles, and Paul Sweezy. On the Transition to Socialism. New York: Monthly Review Press, 1971.

223

Bićanić, Rudolf. Economic Policy in Socialist Yugoslavia. Cambridge: At the University Press, 1973.

Blowers, Andrew, and Grahame Thompson, eds. Inequalities, Conflict and Change. Milton Keynes, England: Open University Press, 1976.

Blumberg, Paul. Industrial Democracy: The Sociology of Participation. New York: Schocken, 1969.

Bookchin, Murray. Post-Scarcity Anarchism. Berkeley: Ramparts Press, 1971.

Boulding, Kenneth. "The Shadow of the Stationary State." In The No-Growth Society, edited by Olson and Landsberg, pp. 89-102.

Braverman, Harry. Labor and Monopoly Capital: The Degradation of Work in the Twentieth Century. New York: Monthly Review Press, 1974.

Brecht, Bertholt. Die Driegroschenoper. In Gesammelte Werke. Stüke I, pp. 393-497. Frankfurt: Suhrkamp Verlag, 1967.

Bronfenbrenner, Martin. Income Distribution Theory. Chicago: Aldine-Atherton, 1971.

Chamberlin, Edward H., ed. Monopoly and Competition. London: Macmillan, 1954.

Chaney, Fredrick B., and Kenneth S. Teal. "Participative Management—A Practical Experience." Personnel 49 (1972): 8-19.

Clark, John Bates. The Distribution of Wealth. New York: Kelley and Millman, 1956.

Cohen, G. A. "Robert Nozick and Wilt Chamberlain: How Patterns Preserve Liberty." Erkentniss 11 (1977):5-23.

Comanor, William S., and Thomas A. Wilson. Advertising and Market Power. Cambridge, Mass.: Harvard University Press, 1974.

Cornwall, John. "Post-Keynesian Theory: Macrodynamics." Challenge 21 (1978):11-17.

Dahl, Robert A., and Charles E. Lindblom. Politics, Economics and Welfare. New York: Harper and Brothers, 1953.

Daly, Herman E., ed. Toward a Steady-State Economy. San Francisco: W. H. Freeman, 1973.

Debreau, Gerard. Theory of Value: An Axiomatic Analysis of Economic Equilibrium. New Haven: Yale University Press, 1959.

Diamond, James J., ed. Issues in Fiscal and Monetary Policy: The Eclectic Economist Views the Controversy. Chicago: DePaul University, 1971.

Dobb, Maurice. An Essay on Economic Growth and Planning. London: Routledge and Kegan Paul, 1960.

____. Papers on Capitalism, Development and Planning. New York: International Publishers, 1967.

____. Studies in the Development of Capitalism. London: Routledge and Kegan Paul, 1963.

____. Welfare Economics and the Economics of Socialism. Cambridge: At the University Press, 1969.

Domar, Evesy. "The Soviet Collective Farm as a Producer Cooperative." American Economic Review 56 (1966): 734-57.

Domhoff, G. William. Who Rules America? Englewood Cliffs, N.J.: Prentice-Hall, 1967.

Drucker, Peter. "Pension-Fund 'Socialism'." The Public Interest (Winter 1976): 3-46.

____. The Practice of Management. New York: Harper and Brothers, 1954.

____. The Unseen Revolution: How Pension Fund Socialism Came to America. New York: Harper and Row, 1976.

Dunstan, Reginald, and Michael Ivens, eds. The Case for Capitalism. London: Michael Joseph, 1967.

Dworkin, Gerald, Gordon Bermant and Peter Brown, eds. Markets and Morals. Washington: Hemisphere Publishing, 1977.

Dworkin, Ronald. "Liberalism." In Public and Private Morality, edited by Hampshire, pp. 113-143.

Easton, Loyd, and Kurt Guddat, eds. Writings of the Young Marx on Philosophy and Society. Garden City, N.Y.: Doubleday, Anchor Books, 1967.

Eckstein, Alexander. China's Economic Revolution. Cambridge: Cambridge University Press, 1977.

Edwards, Richard. Contested Terrain: The Transformation of Work in the Twentieth Century. New York: Basic Books, 1979.

Edwards, Richard, Michael Reich and Thomas Weisskopf, eds. The Capitalist System: A Radical Analysis of American Society 2nd ed. Englewood Cliffs, N.J.: Prentice-Hall, 1978.

Eichner, Alfred. "Post-Keynesian Theory: An Introduction." Challenge 21 (1978):4-10.

Eichner, Alfred, and J. A. Kregel. "An Essay on Post-Keynesian Theory: A New Paradigm in Economics." Journal of Economic Literature 13 (1975):1293-1314.

Eichner, Alfred, ed. A Guide to Post-Keynesian Economics. White Plains, N.Y.: M. E. Sharpe, 1979.

Elliott, John E. Comparative Economic Systems. Englewood Cliffs, N.J.: Prentice-Hall, 1973.

Emmanuel, Arghiri. Unequal Exchange: A Study of the Imperialism of Trade. New York: Monthly Review Press, 1972.

Ewen, Stuart. Captains of Consciousness: Advertising and the Social Roots of the Consumer Culture. New York: McGraw-Hill, 1976.

Fairfield, Roy P., ed. Humanizing the Workplace. Buffalo, N.Y.: Prometheus Books, 1974.

Farkas, Richard. Yugoslav Economic Development and Political Change: The Relationship between Economic Managers and Policy-Making Elites. New York: Praeger, 1975.

Feinberg, Joel. Social Philosophy. Englewood Cliffs, N.J.: Prentice-Hall, 1973.

Ferguson, C. E. The Neoclassical Theory of Production and Distribution. Cambridge: At the University Press, 1969.

Ferguson, James M. Advertising and Competition: Theory, Measurement and Fact. Cambridge, Mass.: Ballinger, 1973.

Fitzgerald, Thomas. "Why Motivation Theory Doesn't Work." Harvard Business Review 49 (1971):37-44.

Forrester, J. W. World Dynamics. Cambridge, Mass.: Wright-Allen Press, 1971.

Friedman, Milton. Capitalism and Freedom. Chicago: University of Chicago Press, 1962.

____. Essays in Positive Economics. Chicago: University of Chicago Press, 1953.

____. A Program for Monetary Stability. New York: Fordham University Press, 1959.

____. "The Role of Monetary Policy." American Economic Review 58 (1968):1-17.

Friedman, Milton, and Walter Heller. Monetary vs. Fiscal Policy: A Dialogue. New York: W. W. Norton, 1969.

Fromm, Erich. The Sane Society. New York: Holt, Rinehart and Winston, 1955.

Galbraith, John Kenneth. The Affluent Society. New York: New American Library, 1958.

____. Economics and the Public Purpose. Boston: Houghton Mifflin, 1973.

____. The New Industrial State. Boston: Houghton Mifflin, 1967.

____. "Power and the Useful Economist: Presidential Address to the 85th Meeting of the American Economic Association." American Economic Review 63 (1973):1-11.

____. "Review of a Review." The Public Interest (Fall 1967): 109-17.

_____. The Theory of Price Control. Cambridge, Mass.: Harvard University Press, 1952.

Gambs, John. John Kenneth Galbraith. Boston: Twayne Publishers, 1975.

Garson, David, ed. Worker Self-Management in Industry: The West European Experience. New York: Praeger, 1977.

Gendron, Bernard. Technology and the Human Condition. New York: St. Martin's Press, 1977.

Goode, W. J., and I. Fowler. "Incentive Factors in a Low Morale Plant." American Sociological Review 14 (1949): 618-24.

Granick, David. Enterprise Guidance in Eastern Europe: A Comparison of Four Socialist Economies. Princeton, N.J.: Princeton University Press, 1975.

Gregory, Paul R., and Robert C. Stuart. Soviet Economic Structure and Performance. New York: Harper and Row, 1974.

Guerin, Daniel. Fascism and Big Business. New York: Monad Press, 1973.

Gurley, John. China's Economy and the Maoist Strategy. New York: Monthly Review Press, 1976.

Hahn, F. H., and R. C. O. Mathews. "The Theory of Economic Growth: A Survey." Economic Journal 74 (1964): 779-902.

Hampshire, Stuart, ed. Public and Private Morality. Cambridge: Cambridge University Press, 1978.

Hansen, Alvin. Full Recovery or Stagnation? New York: W. W. Norton, 1938.

_____. A Guide to Keynes. New York: McGraw-Hill, 1953.

Harcourt, G. C. "The Cambridge Controversies: Old Ways and New Horizons or—Dead End?" Oxford Economic Papers 28 (1976): 25-65.

_____. Some Cambridge Controversies in the Theory of Capital. Cambridge: At the University Press, 1972.

Harrington, Michael. _The Other America: Poverty in the United States_. New York: Macmillan, 1962.

_____. _Socialism_. New York: Saturday Review Press, 1972.

_____. _The Twilight of Capitalism_. New York: Simon and Schuster, 1976.

Harrod, Roy. "An Essay in Dynamic Theory." _Economic Journal_ 49 (1939): 14-33.

_____. "The Possibility of Economic Satiety." In _Problems of United States Economic Development_. Vol. 1. New York: Committee for Economic Development, 1958.

Hayek, Friedrich A. _The Constitution of Liberty_. London: Routledge and Kegan Paul, 1960.

_____. _Individualism and Economic Order_. Chicago: University of Chicago Press, 1948.

_____. _The Road to Serfdom_. Chicago: University of Chicago Press, 1944.

_____. _A Tiger by the Tail: The Keynesian Legacy of Inflation_. Tonbridge, Kent: Institute of Economic Affairs, 1972.

_____, ed. _Collectivist Economic Planning_. New York: Augustus M. Kelley, 1935.

Heilbroner, Robert. _Between Capitalism and Socialism: Essays in Political Economy_. New York: Random House, 1970.

_____. "The Clouded Crystal Ball." _American Economic Review_ 64 (1974): 121-24.

Hession, Charles H. _John Kenneth Galbraith and His Critics_. New York: New American Library, 1972.

Hirsch, Fred. _Social Limits to Growth_. Cambridge, Mass.: Harvard University Press, 1976.

Hirschman, A. O. _The Passions and the Interests: Political Arguments for Capitalism before its Triumph_. Princeton, N.J.: Princeton University Press, 1977.

Hollis, Martin. Models of Man: Philosophical Thoughts on Social Action. Cambridge: Cambridge University Press, 1977.

Hollis, Martin, and Edward Nell. Rational Economic Man: A Philosophical Critique of Neoclassical Economics. Cambridge: Cambridge University Press, 1975.

Horowitz, David, ed. Marx and Modern Economics. London: MacGibbon and Kee, 1968.

Horvat, Bronko. The Yugoslav Economic System: The First Labor-Managed Economy in the Making. White Plains, N.Y.: International Arts and Sciences Press, 1976.

Hunnius, Gerry; G. David Garson; and John Case, eds. Workers' Control: A Reader on Labor and Social Change. New York: Vintage Books, 1973.

Hunt, E. K., and Jesse G. Schwartz, eds. A Critique of Economic Theory. Baltimore: Penguin Books, 1972.

Huntington, Samuel. "The Democratic Distemper." The Public Interest (Fall 1975): 9-38.

Jenkins, David. Job Power: Blue and White Collar Democracy. Garden City, N.Y.: Doubleday, 1973.

Johnson, Elizabeth. "John Maynard Keynes: Scientist or Politician? In After Keynes, edited by Joan Robinson, pp. 11-25. New York: Barnes and Noble, 1973.

Johnson, Harry G. The Theory of Income Distribution. London: Gray-Mills, 1973.

Kahn, Alfred. "The Tyranny of Small Decisions: Market Failures, Imperfections and the Limits of Economics." Kyklos 19 (1966): 23-47.

Kalecki, Michael. "Political Aspects of Full Employment." In A Critique of Economic Theory, edited by Hunt and Schwartz, pp. 420-30.

_____. Selected Essays in the Economic Growth of the Socialist and the Mixed Economy. Cambridge: At the University Press, 1972.

Kant, Immanuel. Foundations of the Metaphysics of Morals. Translated, with an introduction, by Lewis White Beck. Indianapolis: Bobbs-Merrill, Library of Liberal Arts, 1959.

Kapp, K. William. The Social Costs of Private Enterprise. Cambridge, Mass.: Harvard University Press, 1950.

Key, William. Media Sexploitation. Englewood Cliffs, N.J.: Prentice-Hall, 1976.

____. Subliminal Seduction. Englewood Cliffs, N.J.: Prentice-Hall, 1973.

Keynes, John Maynard. The Economic Consequences of the Peace. New York: Harper Torchbooks, 1971.

____. Essays in Persuasion. New York: W. W. Norton, 1963.

____. The General Theory of Employment, Interest and Money. New York: Harcourt, Brace and World, 1936.

Klein, John. Money and the Economy. 3rd ed. New York: Harcourt Brace Jovanovich, 1974.

Knight, Frank H. Freedom or Reform. New York: Harper and Brothers, 1947.

____. Risk, Uncertainty and Profit. New York: Houghton Mifflin, 1921.

Kolko, Gabriel. Wealth and Power in America. New York: Praeger, 1962.

Kravis, Irving, Alan Heston, and Robert Summers. "Real GDP Per Capita For More Than One Hundred Countries." Economic Journal 88 (1978): 215-42.

Kregel, J. A. "Post-Keynesian Theory: Income Distribution." Challenge 21 (1978): 37-43.

____. The Reconstruction of Political Economy: An Introduction to Post-Keynesian Economics. New York: John Wiley and Sons, 1973.

Kuhn, Thomas. The Structure of Scientific Revolutions. Chicago: University of Chicago Press, 1962.

Kuznets, Simon. Economic Growth and Structure. New York: W. W. Norton, 1965.

____. Modern Economic Growth. New Haven: Yale University Press, 1966.

____. Toward a Theory of Economic Growth. New York: W. W. Norton, 1968.

Lane, David. The Socialist Industrial State: Toward a Political Sociology of State Socialism. Boulder: Westview Press, 1976.

Lange, Oscar, and Fred M. Taylor. On the Economic Theory of Socialism. Edited by Benjamin Lippincott. Minneapolis: University of Minnesota Press, 1938.

Laslett, P., and W. C. Runciman, eds. Philosophy, Politics and Society. 2nd Series. London: Blackwell, 1962.

Leeman, Wayne E., ed. Capitalism, Market Socialism and Central Planning. Boston: Houghton Mifflin, 1963.

Lekachman, Robert. Economists At Bay: Why the Experts Will Never Solve Your Problems. New York: McGraw-Hill, 1976.

Leontief, Wassily. "Observations on Some Worldwide Economic Issues of the Coming Years." Challenge 21 (1978):22-30.

____, et al. The Future of the World Economy: A United Nations Study. Oxford: Oxford University Press, 1977.

Lerner, Abba P. The Economics of Control. New York: Macmillan, 1944.

Lindblom, Charles. Politics and Markets. New York: Basic Books, 1978.

Linder, Staffan. The Harried Leisure Class. New York: Columbia University Press, 1970.

Lipset, Seymour Martin, and Earl Raab. The Politics of Unreason: Right-Wing Extremism in America 1790-1977. 2nd ed. Chicago: University of Chicago Press, 1977.

Louis, Arthur M. "America's Centimillionaires." Fortune, May 1968, pp. 152-57.

_____. "In Search of the Elusive Big Rich." Fortune, February 12, 1971, pp. 92-104.

_____. "The New Rich of the Seventies." Fortune, September 1973, pp. 170ff.

Lundberg, Ferdinand. The Rich and the Super-Rich. New York: Bantam Books, 1968.

MacEwan, Arthur, and Thomas Weisskopf, eds. Perspectives on the Economic Problem: A Book of Readings in Political Economy. Englewood Cliffs, N.J.: Prentice-Hall, 1973.

Mandel, Ernest. Late Capitalism. London: New Left Books, 1975.

_____. Marxist Economic Theory. 2 Vols. New York: Monthly Review Press, 1968.

Marcuse, Herbert. An Essay on Liberation. Boston: Beacon Press, 1969.

_____. One-Dimensional Man. Boston: Beacon Press, 1964.

Marris, Robin. "Galbraith, Solow and the Truth About Corporations." The Public Interest (Spring 1968):37-46.

Marshall, Alfred. Principles of Economics. 8th ed. New York: Macmillan, 1948.

Marx, Karl. Capital. New York: Modern Library, 1906.

_____. Critique of the Gotha Programme. Moscow: Progress, 1971.

_____. Wages, Price and Profit. Moscow: Progress, 1947.

_____, and Frederick Engels. The Communist Manifesto. New York: International Publishers, 1948.

_____, and Frederick Engels. The German Ideology: Part One with Selections from Parts Two and Three and Supplementary Texts. Edited by C. J. Arthur. New York: International Publishers, 1970.

Maslow, Abraham H. Motivation and Personality. New York: Harper and Row, 1954.

Meade, James E. Efficiency, Equality and the Ownership of Property. Cambridge, Mass.: Harvard University Press, 1965.

Meadows, Donella; Dennis Meadows; Jørgen Randers; and William Behrens. The Limits to Growth. New York: New American Library, 1972.

Meek, Ronald. Economics and Ideology and Other Essays. London: Chapman and Hall, 1967.

Miliband, Ralph. The State in Capitalist Society. New York: Basic Books, 1969.

Mill, John Stuart. Considerations on Representative Government. New York: Bobbs-Merrill, Library of Liberal Arts, 1958.

____. On Liberty. Edited by Elizabeth Rapaport. Indianapolis: Hackett, 1978.

____. Principles of Political Economy. In Collected Works of John Stuart Mill. Vol. 3. Toronto: University of Toronto Press, 1965.

____. The Six Great Humanistic Essays of John Stuart Mill. New York: Washington Square Press, 1963.

____. Socialism. Chicago: Belforde, Clarke and Company, 1879.

Mills, C. Wright. The Power Elite. New York: Oxford University Press, 1956.

von Mises, Ludwig. The Anti-Capitalist Mentality. South Holland, Ill.: Libertarian Press, 1972.

____. "Economic Calculation in the Socialist Commonwealth." In Collectivist Economic Planning, edited by Hayek, pp. 87-131.

Mishan, E. J. The Economic Growth Debate: An Assessment. London: George Allen and Unwin, 1977.

Monsen, Jr., R. Joseph. Modern American Capitalism: Ideologies and Issues. Boston: Houghton Mifflin, 1963.

Morishima, Michio. Marx's Economics: A Dual Theory of Value and Growth. Cambridge: Cambridge University Press, 1973.

Nagel, Thomas. "Libertarianism Without Foundations." Yale Law Journal 85 (1975): 136-49.

Navasky, V. S. "Galbraith on Galbraith." The New York Times Book Review, June 25, 1967, pp. 2ff.

Nichols, Theo, and Huw Beynon. Living with Capitalism: Class Relations in the Modern Factory. London: Routledge and Kegan Paul, 1977.

Nordhaus, William, and James Tobin. "Is Growth Obsolete?" In Economic Growth, Fiftieth Anniversity Colloquium V, pp. 1-81. New York: National Bureau of Economic Research, 1972.

Nove, Alec. An Economic History of the USSR. Baltimore: Penguin Books, 1969.

_____. Political Economy and Soviet Socialism. London: George Allen and Unwin, 1979.

_____. The Soviet Economic System. London: George Allen and Unwin, 1977.

_____, and D. M. Nuti. Socialist Economics. Baltimore: Penguin Books, 1972.

Nozick, Robert. Anarchy, State and Utopia. New York: Basic Books, 1974.

Olson, Mancur, and Hans Landsberg. The No-Growth Society. New York: W. W. Norton, 1973.

Packard, Vance. The Hidden Persuaders. New York: Pocket Books, 1958.

_____. The Waste Makers. New York: D. McKay, 1960.

Palm, Göran, The Flight from Work. Cambridge: Cambridge University Press, 1977.

Pareto, Vilfredo. Cours d'economique politique. Vol. 2. Lausanne: Rouge, 1897.

Pateman, Carole. Participation and Democratic Theory. Cambridge: Cambridge University Press, 1970.

Pejovich, Svetozar. The Market-Planned Economy of Yugoslavia. Minneapolis: University of Minnesota Press, 1966.

Pen, Jan. Income Distribution: Facts, Theories, Policies. New York: Praeger, 1971.

Phelps, Edmund S. "Growth and Government Intervention." In Growth Economics, edited by Sen, pp. 496-533.

____. ed. Economic Justice: Selected Readings. Baltimore: Penguin Education, 1973.

Phelps Brown, E. H. Pay and Profit. New York: Augustus M. Kelley, 1968.

Pigou, A. C. The Economics of Welfare. 2nd ed. London: Macmillan, 1924.

____. Socialism Versus Capitalism. London: Macmillan, 1937.

Plato, The Republic of Plato. Translated by Francis MacDonald Cornford. Oxford: Oxford University Press, 1941.

Polanyi, Karl. The Great Transformation. Boston: Beacon Press, 1970.

Proudhon, P. J. What Is Property? New York: Dover, 1970.

Quinton, Anthony. Utilitarian Ethics. New York: St. Martin's Press, 1973.

Rainwater, Lee. What Money Buys. New York: Basic Books, 1974.

Rawls, John. A Theory of Justice. Cambridge, Mass.: Belknap Press of Harvard University Press, 1971.

Reeves, Rosser. Reality in Advertising. New York: Knopf, 1961.

Rescher, Nicholas. Distributive Justice. Indianapolis: Bobbs-Merrill, 1966.

Resheter, Jr., John. A Concise History of the Communist Party of the Soviet Union. New York: Praeger, 1960.

Robbins, Lionel. An Essay on the Nature and Significance of Economic Science. New York: Macmillan, 1932.

Robinson, Joan. The Accumulation of Capital. London: Macmillan, 1956.

____. "The Age of Growth." Challenge 19 (1976):4-9.

____. "Capital Theory Up to Date." Canadian Journal of Economics 3 (1970):307-17.

____. Collected Economic Papers. Vol. 1. New York: Augustus M. Kelley, 1951; Vol. 2. Oxford: Basil Blackwell, 1964; Vol. 3. Oxford: Basil Blackwell, 1965; Vol. 4. New York: Humanities Press, 1973.

____. Economic Heresies: Some Old-Fashioned Questions in Economic Theory. New York: Basic Books, 1971.

____. Economic Philosophy. Chicago: Aldine, 1962.

____. The Economics of Imperfect Competition. London: Macmillan, 1933.

____. An Essay on Marxian Economics. London: Macmillan, 1942.

____. Freedom and Necessity: An Introduction to the Study of Society. New York: Pantheon Books, 1970.

____. "The Production Function and the Theory of Capital." Review of Economic Studies 21 (1953):81-100.

____, and John Eatwell. An Introduction to Modern Economics. London: McGraw-Hill, 1973.

____, ed. After Keynes. Oxford: Basil Blackwell, 1973.

Rousseau, Jean-Jacques. The Social Contract. Translated by Maurice Cranston. Baltimore: Penguin Books, 1968.

Rowstow, W. W. Getting From Here to There: America's Future in the World Economy. New York: McGraw-Hill, 1978.

____. The Stages of Economic Growth: A Non-Communist Manifesto. Cambridge: At the University Press, 1960.

Ryan, Cheyney. "Yours, Mine and Ours: Property Rights and Individual Liberty." Ethics 87 (1977):126-41.

Samuelson, Paul. Economics. 9th ed. New York: McGraw-Hill, 1973.

____. Foundations of Economic Analysis. New York: Antheneum, 1965.

____, ed. Readings in Economics. 6th ed. New York: McGraw-Hill, 1970.

Sarti, Roland. Fascism and the Industrial Leadership in Italy, 1919-1940. Berkeley: University of California Press, 1971.

Scanlon, Thomas. "Nozick on Rights, Liberty and Property." Philosophy and Public Affairs 6 (1976):3-23.

Schumacher, E. F. Good Work. New York: Harper and Row, 1979.

____. Small is Beautiful. New York: Harper and Row, 1973.

Schumpeter, Joseph. Capitalism, Socialism and Democracy. New York: Harper Torchbooks, 1962.

Scitovsky, Tibor. The Joyless Economy. Oxford: Oxford University Press, 1976.

____. Papers on Welfare and Growth. Stanford: Stanford University Press, 1964.

____. "Two Concepts of External Economies." Journal of Political Economy 62 (1954):143-51.

____. Welfare and Competition. Rev. ed. Homewood, Ill.: Richard D. Irwin, 1971.

Seidman, Laurence. "TIP: Feasibility and Equity." Journal of Post-Keynesian Economics 1 (1979):24-37.

Sen, Amartya K. Collective Choice and Social Welfare. San Francisco: Holden-Day, 1970.

____. On Economic Inequality. Oxford: Clarendon Press, 1973.

____. "On Optimizing the Rate of Savings." Economic Journal 71 (1961):479-95.

_____, ed. Growth Economics: Selected Readings. Baltimore:
Penguin Education, 1970.

Sennett, Richard. "The Boss's New Clothes." New York Review of
Books, February 22, 1979, pp. 42-46.

Sharpe, Myron E. John Kenneth Galbraith and the Lower Economics.
White Plains, N.Y.: International Arts and Sciences Press, 1973.

Shaw, Gerge Bernard. The Intelligent Woman's Guide to Socialism,
Capitalism, Sovietism and Fascism. London: Constable, 1928.

Sheppard, Harold L., and Neil Q. Herrick. Where Have All the
Robots Gone? Worker Dissatisfaction in the 70's. New York:
Macmillan, 1972.

Shonefield, Andrew. Modern Capitalism: the Changing Balance of
Public and Private Power. New York: Oxford University Press,
1965.

Šic, Ota. Plan and Market Under Socialism. White Plains, N.Y.:
International Arts and Sciences Press, 1967.

_____. The Third Way: Marxist-Leninist Theory and the Modern
Industrial Society. White Plains, N.Y.: International Arts and
Sciences Press, 1976.

Simon, Julian. "Interpersonal Comparisons Can Be Made—And Used
for Redistribution Decisions." Kyklos 27 (1974): 63-98.

_____. Issues in the Economics of Advertising. Urbana, Ill.:
University of Illinois Press, 1970.

Simons, Henry. Economic Policy for a Free Society. Chicago:
University of Chicago Press, 1948.

Smith, Adam. An Inquiry Into the Nature and Causes of the Wealth
of Nations. New York: Modern Library, 1937.

Smith, James D., and Stephen D. Franklin. "The Concentration of
Personal Wealth, 1922-1969." American Economic Review 64
(1974): 162-67.

Smith, Hedrick. "How the Soviet Elite Lives." Atlantic Monthly,
December 1975, pp. 39-51.

Smith, Richard A. "The Fifty-Million Dollar Man." Fortune, May 1957, pp. 176ff.

Solow, Robert. Growth Theory: An Exposition. Oxford: Oxford University Press, 1970.

_____. "Is the End of the World at Hand?" Challenge 16 (1973): 39-50.

_____. "Science and Ideology." In Capitalism Today, edited by Bell and Kristol, pp. 94-107.

_____. "Son of Affluence." The Public Interest (Fall 1967): 100-08.

_____. "The Truth Further Refined: A Comment on Marris." The Public Interest (Spring 1968): 47-52.

Sraffa, Piero. Production of Commodities By Means of Commodities. Cambridge: At the University Press, 1960.

Staines, Graham. "Is Worker Dissatisfaction Rising?" Challenge 22 (1979): 38-45.

Stauber, Leland. "A Proposal for a Democratic Market Economy." Journal of Comparative Economics 1 (1977): 235-58.

Steinfels, Peter. The Neoconservatives: The Men Who Are Changing America. New York: Simon and Schuster, 1979.

Stretton, Hugh. Capitalism, Socialism and the Environment. Cambridge: Cambridge University Press, 1976.

Sward, Keith. The Legend of Henry Ford. New York: Rhinehart, 1948.

Sweezy, Paul. Modern Capitalism and Other Essays. New York: Monthly Review Press, 1972.

_____. The Theory of Capitalist Development. New York: Monthly Review Press, 1942.

_____, and Charles Bettelheim. On the Transition to Socialism. New York: Monthly Review Press, 1971.

Talmon, J. L. The Origins of Totalitarian Democracy. London: Secker and Warburg, 1952.

Tawney, R. H. _Equality_. London: Unwin Books, 1964.

Taylor, Frederick Winslow. _Scientific Management_. New York: Harper and Brothers, 1947.

Terkel, Studs. _Working_. New York: Avon Books, 1975.

Tobin, James. "Inflation and Unemployment." _American Economic Review_ 62 (1972):1-18.

Turner, Jr., Henry. "Big Business and the Rise of Hitler." _American Historical Review_ 75 (1969):56-70.

Vanek, Jan. _The Economics of Workers' Management: A Yugoslav Case Study_. London: George Allen and Unwin, 1972.

Vanek, Jaroslav. _The General Theory of Labor-Managed Market Economies_. Ithaca: Cornell University Press, 1970.

_____. _The Labor-Managed Economy_. Ithaca: Cornell University Press, 1977.

_____. _The Participatory Economy_. Ithaca: Cornell University Press, 1971.

_____, ed. _Self-Management: Economic Liberation of Man_. Baltimore: Penguin Education, 1975.

Vroom, Victor and Edward Deci. _Management and Motivation_. Harmondsworth: Penguin Books, 1970.

Wachtel, Howard M. _Workers' Management and Workers' Wages in Yugoslavia: The Theory and Practice of Participatory Socialism_. Ithaca: Cornell University Press, 1973.

Wallich, H., and S. Weintraub. "A Taxed-Based Incomes Policy." _Journal of Economic Issues_ 5 (1971):1-19.

Ward, Benjamin. "Market Syndicalism." _American Economic Review_ 48 (1958):566-89.

_____. _The Socialist Economy: A Study of Organizational Alternatives_. New York: Random House, 1967.

Werth, Alexander. _Russia at War 1941-1945_. New York: E. P. Dutton, 1964.

Wheelwright, E. L., and Bruce McFarlane. The Chinese Road to Socialism: Economics of the Cultural Revolution. New York: Monthly Review Press, 1970.

Wilczynski, J. The Economics of Socialism. 3rd ed. London: George Allen and Unwin, 1977.

____. Socialist Economic Development and Reforms: From Extensive to Intensive Growth under Central Planning in the USSR, Eastern Europe and Yugoslavia. New York: Praeger, 1972.

Wild, Rolf H. Management by Compulsion. Boston: Houghton Mifflin, 1978.

Wiles, Peter. Distribution East and West. Amsterdam: North-Holland, 1974.

Wilken, Folkert. The Liberation of Work. New York: Roy, 1968.

Williams, Bernard. "The Idea of Equality." In Philosophy, Politics and Society, edited by Laslett and Runciman, pp. 110-31.

Wilson, H. B. Democracy in the Work Place. Montreal: Black Rose Books, 1974.

Witte, Bernd. "Benjamin and Lukacs: Historical Notes on the Relationship Between Their Political and Aesthetic Theories." New German Critique (Spring 1975): 3-26.

Wolff, Robert Paul. In Defense of Anarchism. New York: Harper and Row, 1970.

____. Understanding Rawls: A Reconstruction and Critique of 'A Theory of Justice'. Princeton: Princeton University Press, 1977.

Work In America: Report of a Special Task Force to the Secretary of Health, Education and Welfare. Cambridge, Mass.: MIT Press, 1973.

INDEX

abstinence, 24 (see also sacrifice)

advertising, 83-86, 89 (see also sales effort)

Albert, Michael, 217-18

alienation, 159, 202, 215 (see also dehumanization of workers)

Aristotle, 53

Aristotelian Principle, 141-42, 164

Arrow, Kenneth, 109n

autonomy (see participatory autonomy)

Baran, Paul, 81, 130

Barone, Enrico, 70-71

Benjamin, Walter, 143n

Bergson, Abram, 64n

Bernstein, Eduard, 211n

Bettelheim, Charles, 218n

Blumberg, Paul, 164

Boulding, Kenneth, 120-21

Brecht, Bertolt, 58

bureaucracy, 105, 109, 156-57, 201, 202

capital, nature of, 1, 6n, 17-18, 18-19, 21, 24-25; opportunity cost of, 93; providing, not a productive activity, 11, 13, 17-19; tax on, under worker control, 52-53, 112n, 114

capitalism, arguments against, 176; concerning democracy, 153-56, 183, 202; concerning inequality, 93-95, 183, 198-99; concerning instability, 124-31, 189-91, 201-2; concerning kind of growth, 106-12, 187-88, 199-200; concerning rate of growth, 114, 115-16, 119-24, 188-89, 200; concerning the sales effort, 83-87, 184-85, 197-98; concerning unemployment, 76-80, 185-87, 197; concerning work, 158, 163-67, 184, 202-3

capitalism, nature of, 4, 38; relative to innovation and growth, 14, 47, 105, 118

capitalism, origin of, 28, 29-30

capitalism, justifications for: comparative versus noncomparative, 3-4, 36-37; contribution, 5-9, 14-17; democracy, 150-51; efficiency, 45-47, 67-70; growth, 47, 103, 104-5, 113, 189; historical sketch, 1-3; liberty, 44, 138; Nozick's entitlement theory, 27-29, 30-31; Rescher's canon of claims, 12; sacrifice, 21-23

centralized planning, 50-51, 147-48, 214-16

Chicago School economics, 40, 78n

Chile, 78n

China, 137-38

Clark, John Bates, 5-12 passim

class conflict, 125, 127, 129, 132, 186-87, 189, 201-2 (see also privileged class)

classical liberal ideal (see laissez-faire)

classical liberalism, 39, 40; and corporate responsibility, 211n; and the critique of socialism, 70-71, 142-48; and democracy, 103, 150-51; and equality, 40, 61-63, 96-98; and laissez-faire, 39, 43,

243

67, 107, 131, 189-90; and
liberty, 44, 138; and participatory autonomy, 140
choice, collective versus individual, 108-9, 118n
communism, 219-20
competition, under Fair Capitalism, 182; and the Ideal Industrial State, 195-96; under
laissez-faire, 44, 68; perfect,
8, 41-42, 46, 65, 77, 193;
under worker control, 118,
205, 219-20
consciousness, 202, 211
conservative, 38-39 (see also
classical liberalism, neoconservative)
consumer sovereignty, 81-82
contribution: buying stocks and
loaning money as, 199; entrepreneurial definition of, 14;
as an ethical canon, 5, 9, 12-
13; of an instrument of production, 5-7; as the justification of capitalist distribution, 5-20, 27n; neoclassical
definition of, 7
corporations, 193, 196, 198-99,
203-5, 204n, 211n

Dahl, Robert, 153
dehumanization of workers, 158-
60, 163, 167, 168 (see also
alienation; labor, deskilling of)
demand, aggregate, 77, 125, 130-
31, 181, 189, 191; stimulation
of, 83 (see also supply and
demand)
democracy, defined, 153; equalizing tendencies of, 95, 150;
and Fair Capitalism, 183-84;
and the Ideal Industrial State,
202; and laissez-faire, 114-
16, 152-56; possibility of,
150-56, 157-58; as a value,

103, 116, 138-40, 150, 181; and
worker control, 49-50, 51-52,
79, 106, 110, 114-19, 151-53,
156-57
democratic centralism, 147-48
depreciation reserves, 50, 54,
54n, 110, 110n
development economists, 17
distribution of income, under capitalism, 5-8, 22; laissez-faire
and worker control compared
with respect to, 90-98; under
worker control, 51-52, 73-74,
152-53 (see also inequality)
Dobb, Maurice, 104, 111
Drucker, Peter, 166

economic efficiency, and centralized planning, 50-51, 214-15;
concept of, 45-46, 58-59, 63;
and laissez-faire, 44-45, 45-
47, 64-65, 66-70, 78, 86, 88;
and material incentives, 91-93;
property income not necessary
for, 93-94; of worker control,
70-74
Eichner, Alfred, 42n
employment (see full employment,
unemployment)
Employment Agency, 73
Engels, Frederick, 37, 104, 147
entitlement theory, 27-32
entrepreneur, 11n, 18, 20, 21, 23,
45; socialist, 55, 105
equality, 61-63, 63n, 141; classical
liberalism and, 40, 61-63, 96-
98; and envy, 97; Galbraith and,
180-81; modern liberalism and,
41, 61; Rawls and, 61, 180-81;
more likely under worker control, 95 (see also distribution
of income, inequality)
ethical theory, 12, 36, 58-60
Euler's Theorem, 7-8
expropriation, 199, 212

externalities, 104, 106-8, 182, 187

Fair Capitalism, 41, 182-83; and democracy, 183; and inequality, 183; and instability, 189-91; and kind of growth, 187-88; and rate of growth, 188-89; and the sales effort, 184-85; and unemployment, 185-87; versus worker control, 183-91; and workplace autonomy, 184
fiscal policy, 80n, 190-91
Ford, Henry, 162
freedom (see liberty)
free goods, 219
free market, 4, 39, 68, 95 (see also capitalism, nature of; capitalism, origins of; competition, perfect; laissez-faire; market)
Friedman, Milton, on capitalism and democracy, 151; and capitalist distribution, 5, 93; as a classical liberal, 39-40; and consumer sovereignty, 82; on corporate duty, 211n; as a Keynesian, 178n; on monetary policy, 190; on monopolies, 67n; and the natural rate of unemployment, 76n, 190; Samuelson on, 41; on socialism, 142, 146-47
full employment, 77-78, 182, 197, (see also unemployment)

Galbraith, John Kenneth, 16, 42-43, 82, 111-12, 178-81, 192-203 passim, 213
government, and classical liberalism, 39, 155; in Fair Capitalism, 182, 187, 189; in the Ideal Industrial State, 195-96, 199-200; and modern liberalism, 40, 40n, 177;

under worker control, 49, 52-55, 80, 87, 143, 219-20 (see also governmental control of investment)
governmental control of investment, 52-55, 73-74, 80, 143-44, 152, 211-12
Great Depression, 40, 47, 75, 124
growth, arguments that capitalism optimizes, 47-48, 103-6, 113; balanced, 110-12, 114; and capitalist instability, 124-31; on the desirability of rapid, 119-23; determination of the rate of, 114-16; and externality difficulties, 106-8; and Fair Capitalism, 187-91; and the Ideal Industrial State, 183-85; rate of, in the U. S., 122, 122n, and worker control, 106, 112, 114, 118, 131-32, 141 (see also investment)

Hahnel, Robin, 217
Hansen, Alvin, 130
Harrod, Roy, 122-23, 124
happiness, 60-61, 141
Hayek, Friedrich A., and capitalist distribution, 5; as a classical liberal, 39-40; on democracy, 103, 119, 138, 150-51; and equality, 62, 96, 97, 113, 155; on Keynesian theory, 75-76, 76n; on monopolies, 67n; on the need for rapid growth, 119-20; on socialism, 2, 143
Heilbroner, Robert, 127
Hirsch, Fred, 122
Hopkins, Claude, 86
Horvat, Branko, 80n

ideal models, 38 (see also Fair Capitalism, Ideal Industrial State, laissez-faire, worker control)
Ideal Industrial State, 195-96; and democracy, 201-2; and inequality, 198-99; and instability,

200-2; and kind of growth, 199-200; and rate of growth, 200; and the sales effort, 197-98; and unemployment, 197; and quality of work, 202-3; versus worker control, 196-203
incentives, 68-69, 91-93, 106, 116
income (see distribution of income)
incomes policy, 201, 201n
inequality, arguments for, stated and analyzed, 96-98; under Fair Capitalism, 183; in the Ideal Industrial State, 195, 198-99; laissez-faire and worker control compared with respect to, 93; and private property, 93-95, 155; statistics on, 93n, 94n, 96; under worker control when growth slows, 191-92 (see also equality)
inflation, 80-81, 191, 200-2
inheritance taxes, 15, 198
initiative, 105-6, 132
innovation, 15, 19, 103, 105-6, 128-30
instability, capitalist, 124-31, 155, 189-91, 200-2; democracy and, 139-40, 151-53, 154-55; worker control and, 131-32, 191-92
interest, 20-21, 23, 53, 53n
investment, funds for, 18, 26-27, 52-53, 105-6, 112n, 183, 200; political versus market determination of, 108-10; rate of, 114-15, 117-19, 188-89; and stability, 130-31, 132
investment banks, 53-54, 73, 105, 109-10
investment boards, 53-54, 109-10, 152, 188, 219
investment strike, 132, 155
investor confidence, 125, 130,

184, 191
Isolation Paradox, 108, 120

job security provisions, 51-52, 79, 146
Johnson, Harry, 12
Journal of Post-Keynesian Economics, 42n
justice, theories of, 12, 27-28, 177-78

Kalecki, Michael, 179, 186-87
Kant, Immanuel, 139
Keynesian-liberal ideal (see Fair Capitalism)
Keynesian liberalism, 39, 40-41, 177, 178, 185-86; and the Ideal Industrial State, 195-96; Rawls as representative of, 41, 178 (see also Fair Capitalism, modern liberalism)
Keynesian monetary and fiscal policies, 189-91
Keynes, John Maynard, 2, 40, 40n; on capital, 19; and capitalist instability, 124-25; on the "double bluff" structure of capitalism, 115; on entrepreneurs and financiers, 91; and post-Keynesianism, 180; radio exhortation of, 186n, on saving and investing, 26, 76, 78n; on unemployment, 75-76
Kregel, J. A., 42n
Kroc, Ray, 94n
Kuhn, Thomas, 179n
Kuznets, Simon, 24

labor, allocation of, 69-70, 74; as a central element of well-being, 197; deskilling of, 161-62, 165-67; 170 (see also alienation, dehumanization of workers); meaningful, 160, 164, 184; as the sole source of value, 1-2, 8, 19, 21-22; —leisure tradeoff,

88-89, 189, 196
labor power as a commodity, 4,
51, 52, 149, 158, 170
labor theory of value, 1-2
labor unions, 75, 76n, 78, 154n,
169n, 196
laissez-faire, 43-45, 67; and
classical liberalism, 39, 43,
67, 107, 131, 189-90; conflict resolution under, 149,
151-52; and democracy, 114-
16, 153-55; and efficiency,
44-45, 45-47, 64-65, 66-70,
78, 86, 88; eight count indictment against, 176; and inequality, 93-95, 154-55; and
initiative, 105-6; and instability, 124-31; and kind of
growth, 107-13; and liberty,
44, 149; and rate of growth, 114-
23; and the sales effort, 81,
84-86; and unemployment,
75-78; and work, 163-70
leisure, 58, 88-89, 117, 120,
121, 189, 196
Lenin, Vladimir I., 147n
Lerner, Abba, 63n
liberal, 38-39 (see also classical
liberalism, Keynesian liberalism, modern liberalism, post-
Keynesian liberalism)
liberty, 2, 44, 138, 142-49, 215
Lindblom, Charles, 149-54
passim
Linder, Staffan, 87n
liquidity preference, 130, 132
Ludwig, Daniel Keith, 94n
Lukes, Steven, 63n

Marcuse, Herbert, 37n
market, abolition of, 218-19,
219n; difficulties with, 68, 83,
90, 118n, 112, 218; money-,
23; and post-Keynesian liberalism, 43, 193-94; under worker control, 50-52, 205, 219-
20 (see also competition, free

market, price mechanism,
supply and demand)
Marshall, Alfred, 21-25 passim,
36
Marx, Karl, attitude of, toward
Utopian speculation, 37; Benjamin on, 143n; on capitalist
abstinence, 24; on the "classical tale" of capitalist accumulation, 29-30; on the contribution of an instrument of production, 5-6; on the dynamism of
capitalism, 14, 47, 118; on the
Industrial Reserve Army, 187;
and the "laws of motion" of
capitalism, 124, 210; on leaving
the "free market" and entering
the factory, 158-59; on the
nature of capital, 1, 17; on
socialism, 194n, 211; on
worker cooperatives, 211n
meaningful work (see labor, meaningful)
millionaires, 94
Mill, John Stuart, 74n, 125n, 139
minimum wage laws, 78, 195, 197
Mises, Ludwig von, 2n, 70-71
Mishan, E. J., 122
modern liberalism, 41, 42, 177,
180-81; and Fair Capitalism,
182; and post-Keynesianism, 42-
43, 194-95 (see also Keynesian
liberalism, post-Keynesian
liberalism)
monetarism, 131, 189-91
money, 17-19, 23, 94, 155, 189-
90, 199, 220
monopoly, as a cause of unemployment, 75; and economic efficiency, 46-47, 66, 192-93; post-
Keynesian attitude toward, 192-
93; under worker control, 73-
74, 205

neoclassical economics, 2-3;
assumptions of, 9, 77, 80-81,

247

107; efficiency theorem of, 46-47, 64-66; and full employment, 76-77; and income distribution, 5-7, 12; and Keynesian liberalism, 39, 177; and the labor-leisure tradeoff, 88; and laissez-faire, 44-46; misleading tendencies of, 12-13, 22, 93, 158, 162-3, 169-70. 199; and post-Keynesianism, 41-42, 192-94, 200-1; Rawls and, 41, 178; and the sacrifice argument, 23-24

neoconservative, 39n

neo-neoclassicism, 2

Nixon, Richard, 178n

Nove, Alec, 214-15

Nozick, Robert, 3-4, 27-32; on choice of conditions of work, 160; as a classical liberal, 40; and "contribution," 5, 24; on equality, 61, 62-63, 97; on forbidding "capitalist acts," 144; on investor altruism, 164; and the "law of conservation of envy," 121; and participatory autonomy, 140-41; on setting up worker-self-managed firms within capitalism, 168-69; on union funds, 169n

paradigm shifts, 179n

Pareto optimality, 45-46, 59, 64, 66, 71n, 78, 90n, 182

participatory autonomy, 139-41, 161, 164, 170, 181, 215-16

party, 147-48, 156, 212

Pasic, Najdan, 148n

Pension Fund Act of 1974, 169n

perfect competition (see competition, perfect)

perpetual reward, 16-17, 55

Phelps, E. S., 103-4

planning, 199-200 (see also centralized planning, govern-mental control of investment)

Plato, 150, 210

polyarchy, 153

population growth, 127

post-Keynesian liberal ideal (see Ideal Industrial State)

post-Keynesianism, 2-3, 25n, 41-42, 179-80, 196n, 200-1; Galbraith and, 179-80; and modern liberalism, 41-43, 194-95; and socialism, 42, 205 (see also Ideal Industrial State, post-Keynesian liberalism)

post-Keynesian liberalism, 39, 41-42, 43, 179-80, 181, 195 (see also Ideal Industrial State, post-Keynesianism)

postponement of gratification, 21-22, 22-26 (see also sacrifice)

price controls, 51, 196, 201-2

price mechanism, 67-68 (see also market)

private ownership of the means of production, 4, 37, 50, 70, 149; income from, 5, 93-95, 183, 199 (see also reward for owner-ship)

private sector-public sector, 111-12

priveleged class, 153-57, 202

production function, 6-7

productive activity, 9-11, 13, 17-19, 26-27, 93-94

productivity, 76, 129-30, 191

profit, 21, 69, 71-72, 167; as an unreliable criterion for investment, 107, 110-11, 113; under worker control, 51, 71-72, 170

Proudhon, P. J., 149

public sector (see private sector-public sector)

rationality, and consumer behavior, 86-87, 87n; goodness as, for Rawls, 185

Rawls, John, 3, 41, 43, 141,

178-92 passim, 197
recession, 125, 126, 129, 130, 132, 189 (see also instability)
redistribution of wealth, 28, 41, 182
Rescher, Nicholas, 12
resource shortages, 122, 129, 132
reward for ownership, as reward for contribution, 5-20; as reward for prior activity, 14-20; as reward for waiting, 21-25
Robinson, Joan, 2, 180, 190
Rousseau, Jean-Jacques, 139, 140
Russia (see Soviet Union)
Russian Revolution, 2

sacrifice, 21-24, 120
sales effort, under capitalism, 84-86, 88, 131, 184-85, 197-98; and rational persuasion, 85-87, 87n; under worker control, 87-89, 185, 198 (see also consumer sovereignty)
Samuelson, Paul, 20, 41, 179
saving, concept of, analyzed, 26-27, 188; and investment, 23, 26-27, 76, 78n, 105, 183; and "justice between generations," 188; by the wealthy, 24
Say's Law, 78n
Schumpeter, Joseph, 14, 20, 116, 139
Scientific Management, 165-66
Scitovsky, Tibor, 64-65, 66n, 91, 111
Sen, Amartya K., 108, 120
Sennett, Richard, 167
Shaw, George Bernard, 145
Simon, Julian, 83n
Smith, Adam, 7, 38-39, 43-44, 120-21, 193
socialism, centrally planned,

147-48, 214-16; definitions of, 49, 194, 194n, 213; economic impossibility of, 2, 70-71; and liberty, 2, 37, 142-49; non-market council, 217-18; participatory pure market, 216; and post-Keynesianism, 42; as punishment for our sins (Nozick), 28; technocratic, 194-95, 213-14; and worker self-management, 213 (see also worker-control socialism)
Solow, Robert, 82, 84-85, 121, 122, 123n
Soviet Union, 48, 50, 71, 94-95, 94n, 95n, 137-38, 147n, 204n, 214-15
Sraffa, Piero, 180
stability (see instability)
Stalin, Joseph, 48, 116, 123
Stauber, Leland, 213-14
state capitalism, 194n
stationary economy, 120-21, 125-27, 131-32, 219
Stretton, Hugh, 144n
supply and demand, 44-45
Sweezy, Paul, 81, 130, 218n

taxation: under modern liberal systems, 182-83, 189, 190-91, 195, 198, 201n; as theft, 28; under worker control, 52-53, 112n, 114, 117, 152-53
Taylor, Frederick Winslow, 165-66
technology, assumed fixed, 6-7, 11, 14, 63, 103; changing, 15, 103, 104, 105; and economic instability, 128-30; effective utilization of, 68-69; and the possibility of worker control, 203-5; and work, 163, 165-67
"technostructure," 157, 181, 203-5
Terkel, Studs, 159
TIP, 201n

transition, from capitalism to socialism, 192n, 210-12; from socialism to communism, 219-20

"tyranny of small decisions," 108-10, 188

unemployment: and class conflict, 186-87; in the Ideal Industrial State, 197; and Keynesianism, 75, 76, 185-86; and laissez-faire, 74-79; "natural rate of," 76n, 190; under worker control, 73, 79-80, 186-87

United States, advertising expenditures in, 83n; campaign contributions in, 154n, contemporary class struggle in, 125; corporations in, 204n; council socialism in, 217-18; growth rate of, 122n; income and wealth in, 93n, 94, 96, 116n; investment and depreciation statistics for, 54; and the USSR compared, 94n, 137, 204n; working conditions in, 159

Ure, Andrew, 165

usury, 53n

utilitarian, 3, 45, 61, 63n, 90, 92, 116

utopian speculation, 37-38, 192

values, 36, 58-63, 103, 120, 138-42, 180-81

Vanek, Jaroslav, 54n, 71-72n, 72, 73n

von Mises (see Mises, Ludwig von)

wage and price controls (see incomes policy, price control)

Ward, Benjamin, 72

welfare economics, 64, 64n

Wiles, Peter, 94n

Williams, Bernard, 63n

work (see labor)

worker-control socialism, 43, 48-55, 213n; alleged incompatibility with modern industrial society, 203-5; and bureaucracy, 105, 156-57; compared with the Keynesian-liberal ideal, 183-92; compared with the post-Keynesian-liberal ideal, 196-203; and democracy, 49-50, 51, 79, 106, 110, 114-19, 151-53, 156-57; elements of, within capitalism, 211-12; expropriation necessary for, 212; and growth, 106-7, 113, 114, 118-19, 131-32, 191-92; inequalities under, 93-95, 152-53, 191-92; and initiative, 105-6, 132; and instability, 131-32, 191-92; and investment, 52-55, 80, 105, 108-10, 110n, 112, 114, 117-18, 132, 156; labor-leisure options under, 88-89, 117; liberty within, 142-49; monetary incentives under, 55, 92; nonexpansionary nature of firms under, 72-74, 89; and the sales effort, 87-89, 185, 198; strength of, vis a vis other socialisms, 216-17; and unemployment, 73, 79-80, 187; workplace organization under, 50, 170-71

worker participation, 167-68, 184, 211-12

worker self-management, 49-50, 168-70, 211-12, 213-16

workplace organization, 50, 158-71, 184

Yugoslavian socialism, 48-49, 52, 70, 73n, 80n, 110n, 137-38, 145, 148, 147n, 203, 216n

ABOUT THE AUTHOR

DAVID SCHWEICKART is Assistant Professor of Philosophy at Loyola University of Chicago. In 1969 he was Assistant Professor of Mathematics at the University of Kentucky, Lexington, Kentucky. From 1970-75 he taught mathematics and philosophy at the Ohio State University.

Dr. Schweickart has published numerous articles in philosophy. His articles have appeared in The Philosophical Forum, Social Theory and Practice and Radical Philosophers' Newsjournal.

Dr. Schweickart holds a B.S. from the University of Dayton, a Ph.D. in mathematics from the University of Virginia, and a Ph.D. in philosophy from the Ohio State University.